T0340312

The meaning of market process

Foundations of the market economy series
Edited by Mario J. Rizzo, *New York University* and Lawrence H. White, *University of Georgia*

A central theme of this series is the importance of understanding and assessing the market economy from a perspective broader than the static economics of perfect competition and Pareto optimality. Such a perspective sees markets as casual processes generated by the preferences, expectations and beliefs of economic agents. The creative acts of entrepreneurship that uncover new information about preferences, prices and technology are central to these processes with respect to their ability to promote the discovery and use of knowledge in society.

The market economy consists of a set of institutions that facilitate voluntary co-operation and exchange among individuals. These institutions include the legal and ethical framework as well as more narrowly 'economic' patterns of social interaction. Thus the law, legal institutions and cultural or ethical norms, as well as ordinary business practices and monetary phenomena, fall within the analytical domain of the economist.

The meaning of market process

Essays in the development of modern Austrian economics

Israel M. Kirzner

Routledge
Taylor & Francis Group

LONDON AND NEW YORK

First published 1992
by Routledge
2 Park Square, Milton Park, Abingdon, Oxon OX14 4RN
605 Third Avenue, New York, NY 10017

Routledge is an imprint of the Taylor & Francis Group, an informa business

First published in paperback 1996

Typeset in Baskerville by
Pat and Anne Murphy, Highcliffe-on-Sea, Dorset

British Library Cataloguing in Publication Data
A catalogue record for this book is available from the
British Library

Library of Congress Cataloguing in Publication Data
Kirzner, Israel M.
    The meaning of market process: essays in the development
of modern Austrian economics/Israel M. Kirzner.
        p.   cm.
    Includes bibliographical references and index.
    1. Austrian school of economists.
    2. Economics – History – 20th century.   I. Title.
HB98.K56   1991   91–9515
330.15'7–dc20   CIP

This book has been sponsored in part by the Austrian
Economics Program at New York University.

ISBN 13: 978-0-415-13738-6 (pbk)
ISBN 13: 978-0-415-06866-6 (hbk)

B'EZRAS HASHEM

Contents

Preface

This collection of essays is offered as a contribution both to the modern history of economic doctrines and to the contemporary revival of interest in the Austrian School of economics. Because mainstream economic thinking during most of this century has veered away from the line of enquiry begun by the founders of the Austrian School, the contemporary rediscovery of the insights of this school has inspired the re-examination of the early doctrinal insights pioneered in the Austrian tradition and their survival, in the 'underworld' of twentieth-century economic ideas, until their re-emergence in our own time. Not at all coincidentally, these *dogmengeschichtliche* explorations have led to a deepened understanding of the nature of the Austrian market process, and of the role of subjectivist insights in the explication of that process. This deepened understanding has informed our reaffirmation of the basic, century-old Austrian perspective upon the market process, seeing it as a systematic, co-ordinative sequence of plan revisions. This reaffirmation has been called for by attempts, made in certain radically subjectivist contributions, to declare Austrian subjectivism to be thoroughly and fundamentally inconsistent with appreciation for market-equilibrating tendencies. The author firmly believes these attempts, though made in the course of valuable efforts to further the Austrian approach, nonetheless to be profoundly unfortunate and mistaken. In fact, he would insist, consistent deepening of Austrian understanding must lead us, not to deny the central thrust of mainstream economics (i.e. its understanding of market outcomes as tending to reflect relative consumer preferences in the light of resource constraints), but to argue that these conclusions of mainstream economics can be coherently defended *only* by introducing the subjectivist insights of the Austrian tradition. The author hopes that these essays may contribute to this way of seeing things.

Much of the work leading to these essays was made possible by the generosity of the Sarah Scaife Foundation and of the John M. Olin Foundation. To both of these foundations (and to James Piereson and, especially, to Richard M. Larry) the author is profoundly grateful. A number of these essays have been discussed, over a period of years, in the weekly Austrian Economics Colloquium at New York University. The author deeply appreciates the stimulation and assistance afforded by members of the colloquium, and would mention particularly the late Ludwig M. Lachmann, Mario J. Rizzo, Lawrence H. White, Peter J. Boettke, Stephan Boehm, Sanford Ikeda and Esteban Thomsen. Of course, none of these bears any responsibility for the shortcomings in these papers.

Israel M. Kirzner

Acknowledgements

The publisher and author gratefully acknowledge permission to publish the following essays (which first appeared in the books and journals cited below):

'The meaning of market process', originally published in A. Bosch, P. Kalikowski and R. Veit (eds) *General Equilibrium or Market Process, Neoclassical and Austrian Theories of Economics*, Tubingen: J.C.B. Mohr, 1990.

'The Austrian school of economics', reprinted from *The New Palgrave: Dictionary of Economics*, edited by John Eatwell, Murray Milgate and Peter Newman, 4 Volumes, published by The Macmillan Press (London), Stockton Press (New York) and Maruzen Company Ltd (Tokyo) 1987. Reprinted with permission from the publishers.

'Carl Menger and the subjectivist tradition in economics', first published in the German language as 'Carl Menger und die subjektivistische Tradition in der Ökonomie' in: 'Carl Mengers wegweisendes Werk' in: Engels/Hax/Hayek/Recktenwald (ed.), 'Klassiker der Nationalökonomie', Düsseldorf: Verlag Wirtschaft und Finanzen GmbH, 1990.

'Menger, classical liberalism and the Austrian School of economics', originally published in the journal *History of Political Economy*.

'The economic calculation debate: lessons for Austrians', originally published in *The Review of Austrian Economics* (1988: vol. 2).

'Ludwig von Mises and Friedrich von Hayek: the modern extension of Austrian subjectivism', originally published in N. Leser (ed.) *Die Wiener Schule der Nationalökonomie* (Böhlau Verlag GmbH).

'Prices, the communication of knowledge and the discovery process', originally published in K.R. Leube and A.H. Zlabinger (eds) *The Political Economy of Freedom: Essays in Honor of F.A. Hayek* (Philosophia Verlag, 1984).

'Economic planning and the knowledge problem', originally published in *Cato Journal*, 4 (2) (1984).

'Knowledge problems and their solutions: some relevant distinctions', originally published in the journal *Cultural Dynamics* (1990).

'Welfare economics: a modern Austrian perspective', originally published in W. Block and L. Rockwell (eds) *Man, Economy and Liberty: Essays in honor of Murray N. Rothbard* (Ludwig von Mises Institute, 1988).

'Self-interest and the new bashing of economics: a fresh opportunity in the perennial debate?', originally appeared in vol. 4, nos. 1–2 (Winter–Spring 1990) of *Critical Review*, P.O. Box 14528, Chicago, IL 60614.

'Discovery, private property and the theory of justice in capitalist society', reprinted from *Journal des Economistes et des Etudes Humaines*, Vol. 1, No. 3, octobre 1990, pp. 209–24, by permission of Institut Européen des Etudes Humaines.

Part I

The market process approach

Chapter 1

Market process theory: in defence of the Austrian middle ground

The chapters in this book have all, in one way or another, to do with the Austrian view of the market as a systematic process of mutual discovery by market participants. An overview of this Austrian understanding of the market, and of the task of economic theorizing in explicating this process, is provided in Chapter 2. The present introductory chapter has the purposes of reaffirming the thesis that this Austrian approach occupies the middle ground between two more 'extreme' positions in contemporary economic thinking, and of defending the viability of this middle ground against some recent criticisms raised by proponents of a radical subjectivism. Identification of the Austrian approach with the middle ground is not merely a matter of doctrinal classification; it will turn out that this identification (and especially a defence of this position against current criticisms) can contribute significantly to an appreciation of what market process theory can offer towards economic understanding. It is because of this contribution that this chapter can perhaps usefully serve to introduce the present volume. I shall call the thesis that the market process approach occupies the middle ground the Garrison thesis.[1]

THE GARRISON THESIS

In a comment on a paper contributed by Professor Loasby to a conference volume a number of years ago, Roger Garrison first introduced the important insight that Austrian economics occupies a position intermediate between two more extreme perspectives in contemporary economics (Garrison 1982). On the one hand we have the mainstream neoclassical perspective, based on the assumption that equilibrium positions are strongly relevant to explanations of real world markets. On the other hand we have the perspective of those (including post-Keynesians) who are profoundly sceptical concerning both the meaningfulness and the real world relevance of the equilibrium models of mainstream theory. It turns out, Professor Garrison showed us, that on a number of important issues the Austrians differ from *both* of the (divergent) positions taken by these approaches. Let us take notice of two of these issues; they will be particularly useful for our subsequent discussions.

Knowledge and market co-ordination

Mainstream economics, Garrison pointed out, has gravitated to one polar position on knowledge. 'Perfect knowledge – or perfect knowledge camouflaged beneath an assortment of frequency distributions – has been the primary domain of standard theory for several decades now' (Garrison 1982: 132). (We may add that, in multiperiod models of general equilibrium incorporating intertemporal exchange, this perfect knowledge assumption has been extended, in principle, to knowledge of all future time.) Much of the criticism, from post-Keynesians, Shackle and others, of mainstream economics has taken its point of departure to be the radical uncertainty which shrouds the future. This uncertainty is seen as so impenetrable as to render absurdly irrelevant all those neoclassical theories built up from individual optimizing decisions, assumed to be made between well-defined alternative future possibilities. As Shackle (1972: 465) put it, the 'gaps of knowledge' which arise from an uncertain future 'stultify rationality' (see also pp. 229f.). Knowledge is not, of course, *completely* absent but, the critics would maintain, there is no way, within a theory of markets, that existing 'open-ended' (Shackle 1972: 230) ignorance can be systematically eliminated. (Search is no solution because the 'worth of new knowledge cannot begin to be assessed until we have it. By then it is too late to decide how much to spend on breaching the walls to encourage its arrival' (pp. 272f.)). Thus the brute circumstance of ignorance concerning the future actions of other people makes it impossible for markets to induce consistency among individual decisions (Lachmann 1986a: 56f.).

It is here that the Austrian theory of market process takes a position concerning knowledge and possible market equilibration which avoids both these extremes. On the one hand the perfect knowledge assumption makes it pointless to ask how the market process can induce co-ordination among decisions; such co-ordination is already implied in the perfect knowledge assumption. On the other hand the assumption of invincible ignorance places the possibility of a systematic market process of systematic co-ordination entirely beyond reach. For Austrians, however, mutual knowledge is indeed full of gaps at any given time, yet the market process is understood to provide a systemic set of forces, set in motion by entrepreneurial alertness, which tend to reduce the extent of mutual ignorance. Knowledge is not perfect; but neither is ignorance necessarily invincible. Equilibrium is indeed never attained, yet the market does exhibit powerful tendencies towards it. Market co-ordination is not to be smuggled into economics by assumption; but neither is it to be peremptorily ruled out simply by referring to the uncertainty of the future.

Volatility of data and the viability of economic science

Mainstream economics, Garrison further pointed out, often appears to occupy a polar position which recognizes no variability in the underlying data at all. At this extreme, 'preferences, resource availabilities, and technology, do not change at all. Here, apart from the path dependency issue, the equilibrating tendency is not in doubt. This pole of the spectrum has been the popular stomping ground for neoclassical theorists . . .' (Garrison 1982: 133). On the other hand there is the possible extreme position which sees economic data as being 'more volatile than we care to imagine. In these circumstances we can predict not only that the question of an equilibrating tendency would be answered in the negative, but also that economic science . . . would itself be nonexistent' (p. 133). Between these two perceptions of the changing world is that which has nourished the Austrian tradition (and, surely, informed the thinking of most economists). This perception is that the world is indeed constantly changing in unpredictable ways. People die, babies are born, tastes change spontaneously. Resource availabilities change over time; technological knowledge may evolve autonomously. But, it would be insisted, the rapidity and unpredictability of these changes is not, in general, so extreme as to frustrate the emergence of powerful and pervasive economic regularities. It is because these changes are frequent enough to ensure perennial disequilibrium that we need to understand the nature of equilibrating forces. It is because of the possibility, at least, of a benign limit to the volatility of these changes that these equilibrating forces do, at least sometimes, manifest themselves as unmistakable economic regularities. The scope of and possibility for a relevant economic science depends, as Garrison noted, on recognizing not only the variability of economic data but also the extent to which the co-ordinating properties of markets may be able to make themselves felt in spite of this variability.

ENTREPRENEURSHIP AND THE AUSTRIAN MIDDLE GROUND

In a paper several years ago (Kirzner 1985a: ch. 1 and fn. 9), which explicitly drew its inspiration from the Garrison thesis, the present writer applied the thesis to locating an Austrian view of the entrepreneur within the spectrum of relevant viewpoints to be found within the profession. Two opposing 'extreme' views concerning entrepreneurship were identified.

One view of the entrepreneur sees him as responding frictionlessly, and with full co-ordination, to market conditions, with pure profit the corresponding reward which these market conditions require and make possible. An excellent example of this view is that provided by T.W. Schultz (1975), for whom the entrepreneur is seen as responsively and smoothly providing a needed service to the market, that of reallocating resources under conditions of disequilibrium. Because this service is valuable there is a demand curve for it. And, because the ability to deal with disequilibria is scarce, there is a supply curve with respect to this service. Thus the entrepreneurial service of dealing with disequilibria commands a market price, as implied by the intersection of the relevant supply and demand curves. It is clear that this Schultzian view sees the market as, in the relevant sense, *always* fully co-ordinated: the market is always generating the correct volume of services needed to correct incorrect decisions. This extreme view, it must seem, has managed to squeeze entrepreneurship – even though it is defined as the ability of dealing with disequilibrium – back into the neoclassical equilibrium box.

The second 'extreme' view of the entrepreneur sees his activity in an almost precisely opposite way. This view is best exemplified by the perspective developed in the profound and prolific work of G.L.S. Shackle. For Shackle entrepreneurship simply cannot be fitted into the framework of equilibrium theory made up of strictly rational decisions (Shackle 1972: 92, 134). More seriously, for Shackle the human choice, in *all* its manifestations, involves (in exactly the same way as entrepreneurship itself does) an 'originative and imaginative art' (p. 364), in no sense an automatic response to given circumstances. Thus, for Shackle, recognition of the ubiquity of the entrepreneurial element carries with it extremely damaging implications for the entire body of neoclassical theory. So, far from being able to assimilate a problematic entrepreneurship to an equilibrium theory of unchallenged validity, Shackle finds insoluble problems with equilibrium theory precisely because of its total incompatibility with the entrepreneurial element in human choice.

Between these two extreme views, one seeing entrepreneurship as consistent with equilibrium economics, the second seeing entrepreneurship as utterly destroying the relevance of equilibrium economics, this writer proposed to locate a third ('Austrian') view of entrepreneurship. This third view, developed from Misesian insights by the writer in several earlier works, finds entrepreneurship incompatible with the equilibrium state, but compatible with, and indeed essential for, the notion of the equilibration process.

Pursuing this third view, it was argued, can enable us to salvage elements of important validity from each of the more extreme views. We can, with Shackle, retain our appreciation for the 'originative' (i.e. the entrepreneurial) aspect of human choice. Yet we need not surrender the insight concerning the co-ordinative role of the entrepreneur which was emphasized by Schultz. The third view of the entrepreneur, that recognizing the propensity of the entrepreneur alertly to discover failures in existing patterns of co-ordination among market decisions, permits us to see how systematic ('equilibrating') market tendencies can be traced back to creative, originative, entrepreneurial alertness.

THE DOUBLE-EXPOSURE OF THE MIDDLE GROUND

It is in the nature of a centrist position to provoke criticism from each of the polar perspectives which it has eschewed. Such centrist positions must then be defended from two quite different sides. Two quite different types of attack may have to be rebutted, calling for simultaneous arguments pointing, it might at first sight appear, in almost diametrically opposed directions. This has indeed been the situation in which Austrian economics has, quite naturally, found itself.

Austrian economists must defend themselves against mainstream neoclassical economists unhappy with the vagueness, the indeterminateness and the imprecision which they see as inseparable from an approach prepared to recognize perennial disequilibrium. At the same time Austrians are placed on the defensive by critics of mainstream neoclassical economics, who are unhappy with the postulation, by the Austrians, of possibly powerful equilibrating tendencies.

Until recently Austrians found it necessary to devote much of their attention to defending themselves against mainstream neoclassical critical concerns. This was rather to be expected. It was, after all, their divergence from that mainstream that was the most obvious feature of the Austrian position. Recently, however, the centrist position of the Austrians has drawn criticism from a different direction, a criticism rooted not in mainstream equilibrium convictions but in the most uncompromising rejection of those convictions. This line of radical subjectivist criticism has assailed the Austrian middle ground position not for its recognition of open-ended uncertainty, of the creativity of individual choice, of the pervasiveness of disequilibrium market conditions, but for what the subjectivist critics have seen as the incompleteness of that recognition.

In particular, this line of criticism has challenged the very possibility of a middle ground position in the arena occupied by mainstream neoclassical theorists and their most radical opponents. If we are prepared to reject the set of constricting assumptions which characterize the equilibrium models of mainstream theory, consistency requires, this line of criticism insists, that we accept the utter irrelevance of these models for economic understanding. If Austrians reject an economics which in effect recognizes only the equilibrium state, they must reject, as well, the notion of equilibration altogether. There can be no halfway house. The middle ground which Austrians seek to occupy does not enjoy the strengths of the two polar positions from which they seek to escape. It suffers, rather, from the inconsistencies arising from the attempt to have the best of two utterly irreconcilable worlds.

The purpose of this chapter is to reaffirm the viability of the Austrian middle ground by addressing, in particular, the line of subjectivist criticism offered by those insisting upon the most complete rejection of the neoclassical paradigm. Such a defence of the Austrian middle ground assumes a special significance in the light of the historical attitude of the Austrian tradition towards the social function of the market.

MARKET CO-ORDINATION AND THE AUSTRIAN TRADITION

The early theoretical contributions of the Austrian economists brought them into sharp conflict with the historicism of the German School. At issue was the validity and relevance of a body of theory proclaiming the existence of important economic regularities. The postulation of economic regularities has implied, throughout the history of economics, certain consequences for the evaluation of the market economy. In the absence of such recognized regularities, a market economy may be perceived as a social system the apparent inadequacies of which invite deliberate corrective measures on the part of a benevolent state. A pattern of income distribution which seems offensive to an intuitive sense of justice can be corrected by appropriate redistributive policies. Market prices which appear, to the eyes of the policy makers or their constituents, to be too high or too low can be corrected by appropriate legislation. It was always the objections raised by the economic theorists which seemed to challenge the effectiveness of such proposed social policies. The existence of economic regularities implied severe limits to the corrective powers of the state. In fact, in the light of these regularities, the apparent inadequacies of the market often turn out to be not inadequacies at all, but unavoidable costs necessary for social co-ordination. Price controls, far from improving conditions for the consumer or for the farmer or whomever, are shown by economic theory to generate disastrous man-made shortages or gluts. Redistributive taxation policies are shown to generate undesired and undesirable disincentive or incentive effects.[2] The tendency of economic theory to suggest a more sensitive appreciation for the social-efficiency properties of a market system has been so powerful and pervasive over the history of economics as to make economic theory the obvious obstacle to (and enemy of) would-be radical economic reformers (Stigler 1959: 522–32; Zweig 1970: 25). The early Austrian theorists indeed came, not surprisingly, to be identified with a generally classical liberal policy stance (see for example Streissler 1988: 192–204; see also this volume, Chapter 5).

For Carl Menger and his followers the market economy tends to allocate resources and assign incomes according to the valuations of consumers. As Menger (1981: 173) put it, 'the *price* of a good is a consequence of its *value* to economizing men, and the magnitude of its price is always determined by the magnitude of its value'. Those who object to market outcomes simply do not appreciate the faithfulness and consistency with which markets transmit valuations. 'It may well appear deplorable to a lover of mankind that possession of capital or a piece of land often provides the owner a higher income for a given period of time than the income received by a laborer for the most strenuous activity during the same period. Yet the cause of this is not immoral, but simply that the satisfaction of more important human needs depends upon the services of the given amount of capital or piece of land than upon the services of the laborer' (p. 174). Clearly all this results from a theoretical perspective which sees consumer valuations as being quite faithfully translated into market decisions concerning resource allocation and resource prices.

What we wish, indeed, to emphasize is not so much the conservatism, or classical liberalism, of the early Austrian tradition with regard to economic policy,[3] as the extent to which that tradition shared in understanding the powerful and systematic character of market forces. What happens in markets is not haphazard, but the consequence of inescapable economic regularities, expressing themselves in obviously relevant tendencies. Given the institutional framework of the market economy, given an available array of scarce resources, the preferences of consumers must, almost inexorably it appears, result in a particular configuration of methods of production, resource allocation and market prices. It was with respect to this perspective that Austrian economics differed most drastically from that of the German Historical School and of other dissenters from economic theory. And, of course, this perspective was shared not only by the Austrians but by all the turn-of-the-century schools of economic thought. As neoclassical economics advanced in prestige and influence during the first decades of this century, the contrary teachings of the Historical School faded from the centre stage of professional atention. It was the shared appreciation for the power of systematic market forces which was the feature common to the various schools of economic theory. The victory of the theoretical approach over the historicist approach was a victory for the recognition of the co-ordinative properties of the market. In achieving this victory the Austrian economists were prominent. In the now famous inter-war debate concerning the possibility of economic calculation under socialism, it was the Austrian Mises who provocatively asserted that there was nothing, in any programme for centralized economic planning, to serve as a substitute for the calculative and co-ordinative capacities of the market process. And it has been the mid-century extension, by Mises and by Hayek,[4] of the Austrian understanding of the entrepreneurial-competitive market process which has supported the most consistent and profound appreciation for the benign consequences of market co-ordination.[5] It is against this background of consistent understanding, within the Austrian tradition, of the systematic co-ordinative properties of the market that we must take note of the thrust of the new line of subjectivist criticism, directed against the Austrian middle ground, that we shall be addressing in this chapter.[6]

THE ATTACK ON MARKET CO-ORDINATION: PARADOX IN THE HISTORY OF IDEAS?

Although, as noted, the early-twentieth-century developments in economic thought found the Austrians in alliance with the other theoretical schools in neoclassical economics, this alliance began rapidly to unravel towards mid-century. Whereas Mises, in 1932, was able to declare any difference between the various schools to be more a matter of style than of substance, within a few years he was to be emphasizing with some acerbity the substantive differences between the Austrians and the neoclassical mainstream (Chapter 6, pp. 110f., and Mises 1960). The decisive elements in the Austrian approach which rendered it incompatible with the ascendant Walrasian version of neoclassical theory were elements which grew out of a more lively sense for the subjectivism of the Austrian tradition. Mises stressed the autonomy of individual choice, the uncertainty of the environment within which choices are made, the entrepreneurial character of market decisions, and the overriding importance of human purposefulness. Hayek stressed the role of knowledge and discovery as facilitated during the process of dynamic competition. For Mises and Hayek these subjectivist insights in no way compromised the traditional centrality, within Austrian economics, of systematic market co-ordination and consumer sovereignty. On the contrary, they argued, that it is only by incorporating these subjectivist insights that we can adequately understand the spontaneous, co-ordinative properties of the market process. We can now perceive the paradoxical character of the new line of subjectivist criticism of the modern Austrian approach, which we are considering in this chapter.

What the critics are calling for is acknowledgement by Austrians that their subjectivist insights – insights enthusiastically applauded by the critics – must inevitably lead to the rejection of precisely those conclusions concerning markets which have been central to the Austrian tradition since its very beginnings.[7] The subjectivist basis for Austrian unhappiness with the mainstream equilibrium paradigm must, according to the critics, inexorably impel Austrians not only to reject the dominance of that paradigm, but also to reject the very notion of market co-ordination. To be consistent in regard to their subjectivism, Austrians must surrender their traditional appreciation for the contributions of the market. Any hope to stand on a stable middle ground, on which their subjectivism and their appreciation for market subjectivity might coexist, is declared illusory and self-contradictory. Consistent pursuit of Austrian subjectivism must compel the abandonment of Austrian recognition of the social co-ordinative properties of the free market economy. Let us turn to consider the major arguments offered in this new line of criticism.

SUBJECTIVISM AND EQUILIBRATION: FRIENDS OR FOES?

A good deal of the criticism has been directed at this writer's attempt to restate the Mises–Hayek extension of Austrian theory in terms of an explicitly entrepreneur-driven market process of equilibration (see especially Kirzner 1973 and later work). What renders the market process a systematic process of co-ordination is the circumstance that each gap in market co-ordination expresses itself as a pure profit opportunity. It is the existence of these profit opportunities which attracts the attention of alert entrepreneurs. A gap in co-ordination is itself the expression of sheer mutual ignorance on the part of potential market participants. The profit-grasping actions of entrepreneurs dispel the ignorance which was responsible for the profit opportunities, and thus generate a tendency towards co-ordination among market decisions. In this way economic theory is able to understand how market prices, market allocation of resources and market distribution of incomes can be understood as the outcomes of a systematic equilibrating tendency – a tendency indeed never completed but, at the same time, never completely suspended. Market phenomena are not to be seen as nothing more than the immediate expression of spontaneously changing preferences and expectations, but as the outcome of a process which, while certainly not completely determined, is nonetheless systematically set in motion by the relevant underlying realities.

In this understanding of the market process, Austrian subjectivist insights play a significant role. It is this role which sets the Austrian theory decisively apart from mainstream neoclassical attempts to understand the market. In the latter attempts many of the subjectivist insights came to be suppressed. In particular, the notions of entrepreneurial creativity and discovery, entrepreneurial alertness to opportunities generated by sheer ignorance, the potential for entrepreneurial injection of surprise, were notions which simply could not be fitted into the neoclassical models. In order to demonstrate a determinate nexus linking market phenomena to the underlying realities, it was necessary for these models to postulate a market mechanism capable of inexorably translating these realities into equilibrium conditions, undisturbed by entrepreneurial surprises and by the vagaries that might be introduced by open-ended uncertainty. For the Austrian view, on the other hand, entrepreneurship emerged not as the foe, but as the indispensable friend, of the notion of equilibration. It is this claim that entrepreneurship can be seen as the very source of the equilibrating tendency that has drawn fire from the critics who wish to deny the viability of the Austrian middle ground. Brian Loasby has been a gently persistent critic in this regard.[8]

Loasby (1982: 122) expresses profound scepticism concerning the ability of entrepreneurs to generate market co-ordination: 'What assurance can we have that entrepreneurial perceptions will not be so seriously in error as to lead them in quite the wrong direction. . .?' Loasby emphasizes the distinction between entrepreneurial alertness to existing conditions that have somehow escaped attention and entrepreneurial imagination with regard to future possibilities (pp. 116, 119; see also Loasby 1989: 161). With regard to the latter, in particular, Loasby challenges the claim that entrepreneurs can be relied upon to make correct decisions. Their own decisions may in fact frustrate each other's forecasts, and, moreover, there is simply no systematic set of forces to guide entrepreneurs towards making correct, co-ordinative decisions with regard to the unknowable future. 'But while one might be prepared to grant, with some misgivings, that present opportunities are facts, the anticipation of future coordination failures . . . must surely open up the possibility that the entrepreneur will generate, rather than correct, error' (Loasby 1989: 161). Exactly as (at least according to some philosophers of science) we cannot prove that scientific processes must produce true knowledge, so also 'Kirzner's endeavours to demonstrate that the market process must work well cannot succeed . . .' (p. 163). Loasby stresses not only the possibility of entepreneurial mistakes in the face of an uncertain future, but also the possibility that entrepreneurs discover profit opportunities through deliberately misleading the consumer (Loasby 1982: 121) or through speculatively purchasing assets 'in order to sell them a little later at a higher price to someone who hopes to resell them at a higher price still' (p. 127). Although Loasby recognizes that such scepticism concerning the co-ordinative properties of the market need not supply immediate justification for government action (p. 121), his conclusion nonetheless is that 'it is inherently impossible to use Austrian methods to prove that planning cannot work' (Loasby 1989: 166). The very recognition by Austrians of the circumstances of and importance of 'subjective assessments and incompletable knowledge' (p. 166) must, it seems, prevent economists from ascribing any peculiar co-ordinative virtues to unregulated markets. The very open-endedness of the entrepreneurial economy precludes, it appears, any support, from a subjectivist understanding of that economy, for the notion of a systematic tendency towards market equilibration and co-ordination.

SUBJECTIVISM AND THE MEANING OF SOCIAL EFFICIENCY

The relationship between market co-ordination and the attainment of social efficiency has never been a simple one. The history of welfare economics is the history of changing concepts of social economic optimality, as well as of changing evaluations of the success of the market economy in its attainment (see also Chapter 11). But any claims for achievement of social optimality for the market have certainly depended on parallel claims for the systematic achievement by the market of definite outcomes. If market outcomes are wholly indeterminate, nothing systematic can begin to be claimed with regard to the welfare properties of the market economy. Austrian economists, as noted earlier, have generally given a high rating to the degree to which market outcomes correspond to the allocation of resources implied by consumer preferences. Challenges to the validity of claims for equilibrating tendencies thus imply, of course, challenges to Austrians' assertions of market efficiency.[9] The radical subjectivist insights (on the basis of which challenges to the theory of equilibration have been advanced) thus deny viability to the supposed Austrian middle ground not only in regard to positive economics but also in regard to its welfare (and policy) implications.

What emerges from the recent line of subjectivist criticism of Austrian economics considered in this chapter, however, is not merely the rejection of traditional Austrian welfare claims on behalf of the market, but in fact the rejection, in principle, of the very notion of social efficiency on *any* terms and on *any* definition of social efficiency. No matter how it is formulated, it turns out, the notion of social efficiency must be pronounced meaningless, on strictly subjectivist grounds. This rather surprising development deserves some further attention.

Let us immediately distinguish sharply between this subjectivist-inspired critique of the meaningfulness of conventional welfare criteria and that contained in Hayek's celebrated thesis concerning the welfare implications of dispersed knowledge (see Chapter 11). Hayek pointed out the fallacy in approaches to the evaluation of the social usefulness of the market which erroneously assume the relevance, in principle, of complete, centralized knowledge concerning the underlying realities. In a world of dispersed information, Hayek argued, it is idle to measure social efficiency against the irrelevant yardstick of complete information (available, in principle, to, say, a central planning authority) (Hayek 1949b). The subjectivist-inspired critique of the social efficiency notion which we wish to consider here is quite different. It does not rest on the circumstance of incomplete information concerning the underlying realities. It rests, rather, upon the claim that the very notion of 'underlying objective realities', in terms of which to evaluate social efficiency, is fundamentally inconsistent with a full subjectivist recognition of uncertainty. Hayek had no difficulty with the notion, in principle, of a social optimum mapped out by the underlying data of preferences and scarcities. He merely declared this optimum not to be the relevant criterion for social policy, since the knowledge needed for the formulation of such an optimum is never given or available to a single mind; the relevant problem facing society is never the deployment of such knowledge concerning the attainable optimum, but rather the mobilization of the bits of information dispersed throughout the economy. But what the subjectivist critics here being discussed wish to question is the very idea of realities in terms of which a social optimum might possibly be defined. Professor Jan Kregel has been explicit in questioning the meaningfulness of the idea of underlying objective realities. He feels that Austrian economists have embraced an inadequate subjectivism (compared with that which characterizes post-Keynesian economics) in not realizing the questionability of these 'objective facts'.

This questionability, Kregel explains, arises because the future 'objective facts' are themselves partly determined by the entrepreneurial actions being taken today (on the basis of expectations concerning these supposedly 'objective facts' of the future). Kregel (1986: 160) discusses the impact of this point upon the possibility of equilibration: 'There can be no tendency to equilibrium based on a relation between expectations and the objective data of what the consumer will demand and the price he will pay which describes the conditions of equilibrium because the incomes available to consumers will be determined ultimately by the very decisions taken by entrepreneurs on the basis of these expectations. . . . Expectations themselves determine the objective facts of the conditions of equilibrium. . . .'[10] Although Kregel does not pursue his line of reasoning towards a critique of standard concepts of welfare criteria, the implications are fairly clear. To the extent that entrepreneurial activity itself *creates* the future which entrepreneurs wish to anticipate, it seems idle to judge the social optimality of such activity against the yardstick of that objective future. Such an efficiency judgement would make sense only if one could postulate a set of objective future facts (independent of current actions) to which these current actions are seeking to adjust.[11] We shall have reason to return to this radical implication of Professor Kregel's contention later in this chapter.

In a recent unpublished paper James Buchanan and Viktor Vanberg have touched on this issue in a similar vein. The very notion of remediable inefficiency, they argue, rests on the neoclassical view that knowledge of the future is imperfect not because of the intrinsic unknowability of the future but because of ignorance that could, in principle, have been avoided (Buchanan and Vanberg 1990: 11). Full subjectivism, however, requires us to understand the future as undetermined and intrinsically unknowable. From such a subjectivist perspective, the idea of erroneous decision making must appear highly artificial, if not completely incoherent. Buchanan and Vanberg quote with approval (p. 12) the observation by Shackle (1983: 33) to the effect that 'unknowledge' of the future is not 'a deficiency, a falling-short, a failure of search and study'.

The point made by Buchanan and Vanberg recalls the observation insisted upon by Professor Buchanan himself a number of years ago. 'In economics,' he remarked, 'even among many of those who remain strong advocates of market and market-like organization, the "efficiency" that such market arrangements produce is independently conceptualized. Market arrangements then become "means", which may or may not be relatively best. Until and unless this teleological element is fully exorcised from basic economic theory, economists are likely to remain confused and their discourse confusing' (Buchanan 1982). This reference to the 'teleological' element, which Buchanan describes as misleading economists to conceptualize an abstract notion of efficiency, apart from the actual progress in which it emerges, calls for a separate section. It represents a special example of the radical subjectivist criticism of modern Austrian economics which is being considered in this chapter.

ON TELEOLOGICAL AND NON-TELEOLOGICAL PERSPECTIVES

Buchanan and Vanberg (1990) develop the distinction between what they call the 'teleological' and the 'non-teleological' perspectives as follows. In the teleological view 'the efficacy of market adjustment is measured . . . in terms of the relative achievement of some pre-defined, pre-existing standard of value' (p. 18). Clearly it is the teleological view which depends upon the conceptualization of 'objective facts' (the very notion of which was challenged, we saw, by Kregel), independent of entrepreneurial activity, in terms of which the effectiveness of such activity can be judged. Against this teleological perspective Buchanan and Vanberg argue for 'a radical subjectivist understanding of the market' (p. 19) which recognizes the fallacy of visualizing 'some well-defined objective that exists independently from the participants' own creative choices' (p. 18). For the non-teleological view 'the whole general equilibrium concept is questionable when applied to a constantly changing social world which has no predetermined "telos", neither in the pompous sense of a Marxian philosophy of history, nor in the more pedestrian sense of a conceptually definable "equilibrium" towards which the process of socio-economic change could be predicted to gravitate' (p. 13).

What is significant, for the present chapter, is the assertion by the authors that there is, in their view, 'no systematically sustainable "middle-ground" between a teleological and a non-teleological perspective' (p. 19). One cannot, they claim, simultaneously profess to recognize both the originative, creative character of human choice and any sense in which such a choice can be described as 'discovery of error'. This writer's attempt to develop a theory of systematic entrepreneurial equilibrating tendencies that is rooted in creative entrepreneurial alertness is pronounced to fail because the 'subliminal teleology' (p. 23) implicit in notions of equilibration is thoroughly inconsistent with true creativity. Our defence, in this paper, of the Austrian middle ground will require us to address this criticism. We shall, indeed, argue that creativity and the correction of 'error' need not be mutually exclusive categories.

One aspect of the position taken by Buchanan and Vanberg which is sufficiently arresting to demand separate notice is their conviction that a full critique of socialism is impossible within a teleological framework. Both neoclassical and Austrian critiques of central planning, they assert, have failed to identify the core fallacy in the idea of central planning. That fallacy consists in the belief that, given omniscience and benevolence, it would be entirely feasible, in principle, for a central planner to attain the social optimum. This belief is fallacious because 'even the planner so idealized cannot create that which is not there and will not be there save through the exercise of the creative choices of individuals, who themselves have no idea in advance concerning the ideas that their own imaginations will yield' (Buchanan and Vanberg 1990: 33). Socialism cannot conceivably become equivalent to 'the market as a creative process that exploits man's imaginative potential'. What is noteworthy here is that the subjectivist considerations on the basis of which Buchanan and Vanberg denied (just as Kregel denied) the objectivity of those 'future facts', in terms of which the effectiveness of markets might be judged, have apparently led them to welfare conclusions quite different from those reached in the preceding section.

In the preceding section we noted that the obvious implication of Kregel's critical insights concerning the 'objective facts' of the future is that the very notion of social efficiency (supposedly in terms of the effectiveness with which current activities are adjusted to the requirements imposed by the future facts) loses its meaning. Unless those future facts can be conceived independently of these current activities, we suggested, a subjectivist critic of welfare economics may well challenge the very possibility of any efficiency appraisal (with regard to those future facts). Claims by economists that the market economy is an efficient social institution turn out, we noted, to disintegrate in the light of the questionability of those 'underlying realities' necessary to confer meaning upon the notion of social efficiency. Now we have the apparently surprising assertion by Buchanan and Vanberg that challenging the meaningfulness of the 'underlying future realities' leads, not to the renunciation of all claims of comparative superiority for the market (relative to socialism), but to the discernment of the core weakness of the socialist idea.

While a detailed critique of this apparently surprising conclusion is only peripherally germane to the central concerns of this chapter, it will be useful briefly to ponder the paradoxes which it seems to raise. On the one hand we are told that the non-teleological, radically subjectivist perspective calls into question any objective standards against which to measure market efficacy; on the other hand we are somehow given to understand that the market economy possesses important merits as a social system – merits denied by definition to socialism – precisely because it promotes the creative imagination of its individual participants. Yet we are given no reason why we are entitled to feel confident that the imaginative creativity of individual market participants is likely to lead to individual (let alone social) well-being, rather than to social (or even individual) disaster. Unless creativity is to be valued for its own sake – regardless of what is created, and regardless of the possibility of different creativities colliding with and stultifying one another – one is left wondering how (in the absence of any meaningful objective facts which might serve to formulate criteria for evaluation) one is able, as economist, to rank a system which fosters creativity more highly than one which does not.

THE SUBJECTIVIST CRITICISM OF THE AUSTRIAN MIDDLE GROUND: A SUMMARY

The radical subjectivist criticisms of the Austrian middle ground position that we have proposed to defend seem to boil down to several key contentions.

Entrepreneurial error

Austrian claims for an equilibrating tendency rest on the assumption that entrepreneurs will tend to discover and grasp pure profit opportunities, thus correcting the market ignorance present in disequilibrium. The critics contend that entrepreneurs may make mistakes (and, especially in regard to the uncertain future, can hardly avoid making mistakes). There can be no assurance that entrepreneurs will systematically tend to reduce market ignorance; the exact opposite may be true.

Underlying realities and the notion of equilibrium

Austrian claims for an equilibrating tendency appear to rest on the notion of a relevant equilibrium configuration, considered to be implicit in the 'underlying realities' which constitute the given framework for economic analysis. It is this equilibrium configuration which acts (so the critics appear to understand the middle ground Austrians to be asserting) as a kind of magnet shaping the course of subsequent events. The critics challenge the meaningfulness of such 'underlying realities'. As soon as we admit the dynamics of time into our analysis, we must recognize that the relevant realities of the future (in terms of which any intertemporal idea of equilibrium must be enunciated) are themselves not 'realities' at all (in the sense of having an independent existence to which human activities must somehow be adjusted) but are created by the very activities the consistency of which is under examination.

In general, it appears to be argued, the picture of social history which emerges from a radical subjectivist viewpoint is one entirely inconsistent with Austrian middle ground economics. For radical subjectivism, history is a continual series of Shacklean 'new beginnings'; the uncertainty of the future, subject as it is to unceasing injections of sheer surprises, makes it absurd for us to envisage systematic market processes of equilibration. To do so must be judged absurd both because ceaseless injections of surprise must continually abort any incipient equilibrating tendencies and, further, because awareness of the inevitability of such ceaseless injections of surprise must paralyse any entrepreneurial illusions of somehow correctly anticipating the future (or, as noted, even of *defining* that future, as an independent set of facts to be taken into account). The limited subjectivism which sets the Austrian middle ground apart from the neoclassical mainstream is, in this view, so moderate and diluted as to blind middle ground Austrians with regard to the fundamental incoherence of their position. Far from being able to enjoy the best of both worlds, middle ground Austrians have placed themselves in a position shot through with inner inconsistencies.

Let us attempt to clarify the middle ground position of modern Austrian economists in a way that can address these criticisms and show them to be far less formidable than might at first sight appear. It may be useful, first, to dispel some misunderstandings concerning the possibility for (and meaning of) *error* in the Austrian middle ground theory of equilibration.

AUSTRIAN MIDDLE GROUND AND ENTREPRENEURIAL ERROR

Sometimes radical subjectivist critics seem to ascribe to middle ground Austrians the notion that alert entrepreneurs are exempt from the possibility of making errors; they somehow have the capacity of seeing future events correctly. This is certainly *not* the case; or, at the very least, not without careful qualification. First, the Austrian theory of the entrepreneurial equilibration process relies, as Loasby (1982: 117; 1989: 160–1) has perceptively noted, on some entrepreneurs being more alert than others (and it is the relative unalertness of the latter which is responsible for the errors which create the opportunities and the incentives for profit). Second, the postulation of a tendency for profit opportunities to generate equilibration has not been put forward as an inexorable, determinate sequence. The emphasis upon the incentive to win profits has not been intended to deny the possibility of entrepreneurial losses. To show how entrepreneurial alertness can account for apparently systematic market adjustments is not, as we shall emphasize again and again, to predict sure-fire equilibration under all circumstances.

Sometimes radical subjectivist critics ascribe to middle ground Austrians a position which associates entrepreneurial error with a certain culpability or guilt. Because an error is seen as, in principle, avoidable, it seems to follow that a failure correctly to forecast the future must be blamed on carelessness, or something. And therefore, because radical subjectivists emphasize the intrinsic unknowability of the future, they are strongly inclined to deny the meaningfulness of the term 'error' in regard to the future. 'There can only be "error" if the future *can* be known. But, if the future is acknowledged to be created by choices that are yet to be made, how can it be known?' (Buchanan and Vanberg 1990: 27). It must be emphasized that, in the Austrian middle ground, lack of 'alertness' with regard to the future need not be blameworthy in any literal sense. An 'error' with regard to the future need involve no carelessness and no negligence. Certainly the future, especially in the light of the uncertainties injected by the creativity of future choices, is difficult (if perhaps not quite entirely impossible) to be correctly guessed at in advance.

In fact it may be contended, from the Austrian middle ground perspective, that the radical subjectivist critics have themselves perhaps *over*estimated the objectivity (the 'knowability') of present facts compared with future facts. Critics who are unhappy with Austrian notions of error in regard to the future are apparently uncritical of the idea of error in regard to existing facts. Existing facts are existing facts; an error in regard to any such fact is seen as a truly avoidable error. Future facts are intrinsically unknowable; ignorance of future facts is unavoidable and thus considered as no error at all. But existing facts are different. Greater diligence in search would have revealed the full truth concerning existing facts. So runs the radical subjectivist insistence on the sharp difference introduced by the recognition of futurity with all its uncertainty. But, from the middle ground Austrian perspective, ignorance of an existing fact need involve no more blame, no more 'avoidability', than ignorance of a future 'fact'. What is involved, in regard to ignorance of the future, is what this writer has called 'sheer' or 'utter' ignorance (i.e. one is ignorant of the fact that there is a specific fact which one does not know). Such 'sheer ignorance' is, of course, fully possible also in regard to existing facts. One may be completely ignorant of the opportunity to learn about an important fact. Such ignorance – even in regard to existing facts – is not avoidable (in the sense that greater diligence in search could have yielded more complete information) and may be deemed not to involve any carelessness at all. One cannot blame one who is utterly ignorant in this way; one cannot upbraid him for not looking more carefully, for not searching more carefully; after all, he was totally unaware of where to begin searching, of the very opportunity of searching, of the very need to search altogether. If we describe him as having acted 'in error', we mean, simply, that he *might* have known the existing facts had he been 'more alert'.[12] There seems to be no fundamental difference between the capacity to notice an existing fact (concerning which one had previously been in a state of sheer ignorance) and the capacity to 'notice' or to sense a future event which one might possibly have taken into account in formulating one's present plans. In the light of subsequent discovery of an existing fact (concerning which one had been utterly ignorant at a time of action) one may retrospectively pronounce oneself to have acted 'in error'; it seems entirely consistent for one to pronounce a similar judgement upon one's action which turns out later to have been taken under a mistaken anticipation of the future. If there is a difference between the 'alertness' capable of sensing future events and the alertness needed to notice present facts (concerning the very existence of which one has been up to this time utterly ignorant), it must be a matter of degree, not of kind. The 'error' involved in overlooking a present fact seems to be no more heinous an oversight than failure to see the shape of future events correctly. And the failure so correctly to see the future must appear, in many cases at least, to be no less an example of error than failure to see what is already a knowable fact in the present.

It will be helpful for us to explore a little further the radical subjectivist position in regard to the utter unknowability of the future, a future in regard to which, it is contended, it is impossible to err.

A WORLD WITHOUT ERROR?

A little thought should convince us that the radical subjectivist denial of the possibility of true error in regard to the unknowable future must lead to quite bizarre implications, implications with which the radical subjectivists must themselves surely feel uncomfortable. We are told that the future is not a rolled-up tapestry waiting to be unfurled, but a void 'waiting' to be filled by the creative, originative, unpredictable free choices of human beings (see for example Shackle 1986: 281ff). 'The essence of the radical subjectivist position is that the future is not simply "unknown", but is "non-existent" or "indeterminate at the point of decision" ' (Wiseman 1990: 160). So much it is possible for middle ground Austrians to accept with warm concurrence. It is when radical subjectivists conclude directly, from this circumstance of the as-yet-non-existent future, that no future-oriented action can be described as erroneous that the warmth of this concurrence begins to evaporate with alarmed rapidity. We have already seen how this conclusion has been arrived at: if the future does not exist, it is inherently unknowable; if it is unknowable, no action taken can be denounced as having failed to avoid an avoidable disaster; the most disastrous action taken, then, cannot be denounced as an error. Ignorance of the future, Wiseman argues, should not be seen 'as leading to "inefficient" behaviour' but 'as an inescapable characteristic of the human condition'. To see things differently is to imply 'that there is some stock of knowledge about the future which agents "ought" to have, and some consequent set of decisions that they therefore "ought" to take, and that it is these that identify an "efficient outcome" (Wiseman 1990: 155).

It is at this point that one pauses to take in, with some amazement, what seems to be stated here in the most matter-of-fact tones. The usual, layman's, perceptions of human decisions is that some of them are taken wisely, judiciously, successfully. These are the decisions which, in retrospect, one recognizes as having been crucial to the achievement of some desirable outcome. Other decisions, the usual perception has it, turn out to have been unsuccessful; in retrospect, at least, they are seen to have been mistakes. The issue here is not moral culpability in any simple sense, but recognition, at least from the *ex post* perspective, that the latter decisions were not well attuned to the way subsequent events in fact turned out. Here we have the nub of our apparent disagreement with the radical subjectivists: is it or is it not meaningful to describe a decision as having been appropriate, in the light of subsequent events, or as having been inappropriate? We must press the question a little further. Is it or is it not meaningful for a decision maker to *try* to shape his decision so that it will be able to be pronounced to have been the right decision? Are we really to say that, because, at some philosophical level, the future does not exist, that because it is not 'waiting' to be known (since it has yet to be created), it is therefore meaningless for a human being *to seek* to be successful in his future-oriented decisions? The point at issue turns out to be even more troublesome when we consider the idea of economic policy.

Are we really to say that, since no genuine error is conceivable in regard to the future, we are forbidden to distinguish between wise and unwise economic policies? Must we say that while, subjectively speaking, individual and public decision makers may *believe* themselves to be striving to peer ahead in order to make the correct choices, this must, from a more perceptive philosophical perspective, be set down as nothing more than an illusion? Are we really to say that the indeterminacy of the future entails that, since there *is* as yet no future, it is idle even *to attempt* to adjust one's actions to avoid disaster in that future? Does the *in*determinacy of the future lead to precisely that sense of utter helplessness (and hence to the same numbing sense of never having to worry about making a mistake) that must follow from the view of the future as *fully* determined in every respect (regardless of what individuals may believe themselves to be trying to achieve or to avoid)? Must a world the future of which is shrouded in the uncertainties generated by the creativity of human action degenerate into a world in which genuine action is ruled out by the impossibility of error? Surely these are implications which must trouble all subjectivists, of whatever degree of radicalness. George Shackle's life's work on the understanding of how men choose between courses of action *each* of which is associated, in their *imaginations*, with myriads upon myriads of competing hypothesized futures assures us that even the master subjectivist of our time has had no truck with the apparently seductive idea that choice should be recognized as nothing but a chimera, a self-delusion. If the uncertainty of the future has made it impossible to discriminate between more or less advisable courses of action, then choice *has* been reduced to emptiness. 'When the decision-maker is free to suppose that any act can have any consequence without restriction, there is no basis of choice of act. The boundedness of uncertainty is essential to the possibility of decision' (Shackle 1970: 224). The very idea of 'bounded uncertainty' must mean that the prospective chooser feels entitled to conclude, in spite of the uncertainties he faces, that one course of action appears more likely to be successful than another.

CHOOSING FOR A NON-EXISTENT FUTURE

If we are to salvage the very notion of choice from the impasse threatened by a world without errors, we must clearly insist on several simple but fundamental truths. Without daring to tread in philosophical waters which threaten unwitting economists with mine-fields about which they may be suffering 'sheer ignorance', it is necessary for us to pin down several matters of everyday experience. Because we can *imagine* the future, even a non-existent, unknowable future,[13] we do choose, endeavouring to shape the future flow of events in such a fashion that the free, originating future choices of others can redound to our benefit. We do seek, that is, to tailor our choices to take account of those future events – imagined events – which do not now exist in any sense whatever. And, when the time comes for us to look back upon our earlier exercises in imagination we do, whatever the radicalness of our subjectivism, judge the extent to which our imaginations were helpful. From the *ex post* perspective we do judge our actions as having been the correct ones to have made, or not. We may not judge an 'incorrect' action to have been an unwise one, a blameworthy one, in the light of the picture of the world we had at the moment of decision. We may in fact be con-vinced that, even after our bitter experience, we would now repeat the earlier action (the one now deemed to have been incorrect) were we to find outselves once again in circumstances similar (and with similar pictures of the world) to those in which the earlier decision was made. Yet we will still rue our earlier inability to have somehow conjured up a more prescient picture of the world. The endeavour to make the 'right decision', to formulate the 'right economic policy' (or, for that matter, the 'right foreign policy'), is one which has definite meaning. The non-existent, indeterminate future does not forbid men from imaginatively anticipating what creative acts will fill the future void. And, most significantly, it does not forbid them, with hindsight, from ranking those imaginative anticipations in order of their correctness. All of our *ex ante* endeavours to make the right choice are endeavours to be able, in the future, to stand up to such retrospective judgements successfully. We are *not* satisfied, in making our choices, merely to choose in a way which will not, in the future, be judged to have been rash or overcautious, unwise, and thus *blameworthy* – we seek to choose in a way which will turn out to have been the correct, the successful, choice.

SCOPE FOR SUPERIOR ENTREPRENEURIAL PRESCIENCE

The future does not now exist, but we endeavour to grasp that future somehow in our imaginations. Some of us are more successful at this endeavour than others are. The mistakes, the errors, made by the latter, turn out to constitute the profit opportunities grasped by the more successful. In fact, it is the opportunity for profit so constituted which sparks the entrepreneurial imagination of the more prescient, the more 'alert', among human beings.[14] (It is certainly not any equilibrium configuration which operates – as magnet or 'telos' – to stimulate entrepreneurial prescience, but rather entrepreneurial errors, in the form of profit opportunities, which attracts anticipatory discovery.) Once we acknowledge the meaningfulness of endeavouring to imagine the future more correctly, we can hardly refuse to recognize the quality of 'alertness' (or of more correctly fertile imagination, or of greater prescience – call it what one will) in human beings. We must, that is, recognize something like 'entrepreneurial ability', understood as the capacity independently to size up a situation and more correctly reach an imagined picture of the relevant (as yet indeterminate) future. All of us share in this ability to some extent – or we would surely have learned long ago not to bother to make choices at all in a world so full of surprises as to frustrate all our attempts at controlling our lives. But some have higher degrees of this ability – some in some lines of endeavour, others in other lines of endeavour. Economists, psychologists and other social scientists have not developed, as yet, very helpful or extensive theoretical or empirical materials from which to be able to say much about the sources and determinants (if any) of such ability. But to deny its existence is to deny the most obvious of everyday facts of experience.

Moreover, once we recognize scope for entrepreneurial prescience, we cannot avoid acknowledging that it is the 'underlying realities' which inspire such prescience, and which thus shape entrepreneurial actions. It is true, of course, that what directly inspire and shape entrepreneurial actions are *imaginations* (of future realities) rather than these realities themselves. But what the alertness of the entrepreneur strives to notice and correctly to imagine are (what will turn out to be) future realities, and it is the *prospective gain offered by these realities* which 'switches on' entrepreneurial alertness. It follows therefore that what will turn out to be the future realities are indeed crucially involved in shaping entrepreneurial prescience and thus entrepreneurial actions. It is for these reasons that we shall be arguing that the equilibration process set in motion by entrepreneurial profit-oriented activity is inspired by the underlying realities, after all.

THE PUZZLE OF PRESCIENCE

Yet it must be immediately acknowledged that we have not yet fully grappled with the key problem raised by the radical subjectivists. We envisage entrepreneurs – and, as is well known from the work of Mises and of Shackle, we are *all* entrepreneurs – endeavouring to imagine the future. Yet that imagined future must depend upon their own decisions. The future-to-be-imagined is not the future course of events which would ensue (with all the creativity and novelty of the actions that will make up those events) in the absence of any action by the entrepreneur. The future-to-be-imagined is a future that will include the consequences of the entrepreneur's own present and future actions. The entrepreneur is not seeking to imagine correctly a course of events upon which his own actions will impinge, but the course of events that will, in part, be set in motion by his own actions (which must now be decided upon). It is true that this does not at all prevent us from recognizing, as we have been insisting, that the entrepreneur is endeavouring to express his ability correctly to imagine the future. But it does require us to acknowledge that the future 'realities' (i.e. what may eventually turn out to be the realities-to-be-created) which the entrepreneur is endeavouring correctly to imagine are such as to involve some logical knots and conundrums. The entrepreneur is not so much choosing a course of action that shall be *appropriate to the 'realities'* as he is choosing among alternative imaginable realities that his prospective action may be initiating. It must be freely acknowledged that the prescience called for, within this scenario, must appear rather different from the simple prescience discussed in the context of a future thought to be substantially determined independently of whatever the prescient person himself may decide to do. The sense in which the entrepreneur's actions are seen to be 'responding' to the 'realities' is certainly a modified one. Nonetheless, we wish to insist, scope for entrepreneurial alertness and escape from error, and the incentives needed to spark such alertness and escape, can be perceived within this more carefully understood framework in substantially unchanged fashion. Actions taken for the future are taken with the endeavour more correctly to imagine (and profit from) the future.

What may seem, however, to be more troublesome is the question we saw to have been raised by Professor Kregel. In a world in which entrepreneurial prescience takes the form just explained, in a world in which the market process consists of untold series of such interacting entrepreneurial decisions, just how meaningful is it to describe that market process as somehow approximating a trajectory marked out by the 'underlying realities' of preferences and resource availabilities? It is one thing to reinterpret, as we have attempted to do in the preceding paragraph, the realities which the decision maker seeks correctly to imagine, so as to recognize their dependence on the entrepreneur's own about-to-be-decided course of action. It is quite another to assert that the resulting series of entrepreneurial decisions and their market consequences are to be seen as constrained, through some 'economic law' of equilibration, to the trajectory marked out by the configuration of (present and future) consumer preferences and scarce available resource services (present and future). Surely Kregel is correct in denying any possible 'tendency to equilibrium based on a relation between expectations and the objective data . . .' (1986: 160)? How can we salvage the central notion of economic theory, that of the market tending to bring about co-ordination of market decisions in a manner which, in the light of the objective needs and constraints, avoids waste and inefficiency? To understand this it is necessary to step back and review the simplest notions of co-ordination in an imagined, stylized context in which we shall largely abstract from the uncertainties introduced by the dynamics of the market process.

THE MEANING OF CO-ORDINATION: THE SIMPLE CONTEXT

Consider a market in which there is a strong, unsatisfied demand for shoes, in spite of the presence of available necessary resources (now being used in other industries of lesser value to consumers). Clearly there is an opportunity for entrepreneurship here. The resources needed to produce shoes could be assembled at a total outlay that would be more than offset by the considerable revenues to be obtained by selling shoes to eager consumers.

Imagine now that a number of entrepreneurs have misjudged the needs of consumers and have erroneously concluded that shoes were not likely to be profitable, but that the production of bicycles *would* be highly profitable. Pursuing their mistaken assessments they have set up factories to produce bicycles, drawing away resources from other (in fact more urgently needed) potential lines of production (such as shoes). Certainly these factories constitute misallocated resources. Suppose now, with these factories in place, their owners encounter a shortage of steel needed for the bicycles. Fortunately an entrepreneur is able to locate a suitable source of steel and to deliver the steel, at a profit, to the bicycle manufacturers. How shall we evaluate this last entrepreneuriual step? Should we say that it is a mistake (since the steel *should* perhaps have been used to help build shoe factories, where an expansion should have been occurring)? Should we say that, in discovering the profitable opportunity offered by the steel shortage in bicycle manufacturing, the steel entrepreneur is failing to respond to the *true*, objective realities (i.e. the strong unsatisfied demand for shoes, in the context of available resources now being wasted on less urgently needed lines of production)? Or should we not rather recognize that, *given the already-committed entrepreneurial errors* of building the bicycle factories, bygones must be seen as no more than bygones – that the relevant realities have now changed? Right now, it *is* an act of co-ordination to bring together the eager bicycle manufacturers looking for steel with the willing sellers of steel. In other words, a mistake that has been made (i.e. a mistake which resulted in entrepreneurial moves *at odds with* the true underlying realities) may itself change the relevant realities in such a way as to construct valid profitable new opportunities for acts of entrepreneurial co-ordination in situations which, from the perspective of the *originally* relevant set of realities, must be pronounced to be unfortunate. All this is straightforward and well understood. We shall be able to apply the simple lesson it teaches to the multiperiod market process in which next year's future 'realities' will be created by this year's future, unpredictable, creative acts. It was in that context that we were forced to question the relevance (as a 'magnet' marking out the trajectory to be taken by the market's process of equilibration) of the key objective realities, preferences and resource constraints. Let us pause to notice some features of our simple shoes and bicycles case.

The entrepreneurship which sees profit in the transfer of steel to the bicycle industry is of course responding to *present* realities. It is no longer in fact the case that the most useful place for this steel is in the shoe industry. Given the capital invested – rightly or wrongly – in the bicycle factories, given the failure to have built shoe factories, the most useful place *now* for the steel is in fact the bicycle industry. The *original* realities (in terms of which the shoe factories 'ought' to have been built instead of the bicycle factories) have no relevance *now*, and have, indeed, correctly now failed to influence the allocation of resources. However, it would be incorrect to say that the original realities never did operate, in this scenario, to offer appropriate entrepreneurial incentives. The circumstance that entrepreneurs erred and failed to respond to those incentives should not lead us to say that the only realities which operated to influence entrepreneurial action were those which resulted from the irrevocable mistakes made in building the bicycle factories. The original realities (in which the true strength of consumer shoe demand was greater than that for bicycles) did offer relevant incentives; entrepreneurs simply failed to respond to these incentives – they were not sufficiently alert to recognize the true state of affairs. But whenever and wherever realities exist in the economy, they exercise their influence in offering appropriate profit incentives. Where these incentives, for reasons of insufficient entrepreneurial alertness, are not responded to, the actions taken by entrepreneurs, erroneous as they have been, nonetheless create a new reality which may now and will now exercise its own incentive power to attract the alertness of entrepreneurs to what is *now* called for in terms of social efficiency. Relevant realities always do exercise appropriate influence: as we know from the circumstance of possible entrepreneurial error, such influence may not be sufficient decisively to ensure efficient outcomes. Where they do not, the actual ('mistaken') outcomes achieved now assume their rightful role as the *currently* relevant realities in regard to the identification of the social optimal configurations.

The fact that, in its trajectory as marked out by the initial realities, the market slipped into error does indeed evoke a fresh relevant trajctory. As one period follows another, actual history is thus far from a faithful fulfilment of any one relevant trajectory. But it is always the case, nonetheless, that appropriate entrepreneurial incentives do, at any given moment, offer themselves in regard to the path relevant to the realities *of that moment*. We can now apply these straightforward insights to the more subtle and complex case where the course of equilibration implicit in an initial set of multiperiod realities is complicated by the circumstance that these multiperiod realities are themselves reflections of creative, unpredictable choices that will inevitably be made during the course of the market process – equilibrating or otherwise. We shall be making considerable use of the lessons we have learned in this section concerning the differences between (as well as the common features of) what we have called the 'original realities' and the 'new' realities which have been created by entrepreneurial mistakes.

THE MEANING OF CO-ORDINATION: THE DYNAMIC CONTEXT

The usual understanding of what is meant by market co-ordination emphasizes the capacity of the market process to guide entrepreneurial decisions towards a pattern of resource allocation consistent with the realities of consumer preferences and resource scarcities. Subjectivists, radical or otherwise, have pointed out that since entrepreneurial decisions are future oriented the relevant preferences and scarcities must, at least in part, be those perceived to pertain to future dates. Thus the 'realities' which supposedly shape entrepreneurial decisions must do so in the form of *expected* preferences and *expected* scarcities. Since, however, today's expectations of future preferences and scarcities must acknowledge that these future preferences and scarcities will themselves be shaped by series of prospective creative, unpredictable decisions on the part of many entrepreneurs, it is difficult, we have seen the radical subjectivist argument to run, to see how today's entrepreneurial decisions can be systematically related to (and appropriately adjusted to) the future arrays of preferences and scarcities (as they will in fact turn out to be). It would seem, surely, that it is more accurate to describe the future realities as having been shaped by today's entrepreneurial decisions than to declare the latter to be geared efficiently to take account of the former. Our discussion in the preceding section can help clear things up. It remains, we shall argue, entirely valid to perceive the market process as tending to co-ordinate decisions in a manner which takes systematic account of the priorities dictated by consumer preferences and resource scarcities. The middle ground Austrian recognition of the equilibrative and co-ordinative properties of the entrepreneur-driven and entrepreneur-inspired market process is not, in any essential way, disturbed by our acknowledgement of the indeterminacy of the future at each moment of decision.

Consider an entrepreneur A making a production decision at date t_1 that seeks to anticipate market demand (say, for shoes) at some future date t_{10}. The entrepreneur compares the present value of anticipated shoe revenues at t_{10} with the present relevant t_1 outlays. In so doing he is asking himself whether the revenues to be expected at t_{10} are such as to render the present outlays needed at t_1 erroneously low (i.e. whether the market has failed correctly to assess the true high value of the relevant resources, were they to be directed at t_{10} shoe consumers in the way considered by our entrepreneur). The t_{10} reality that he is assessing is one that will, at least at t_{10}, be an objective one. At t_1 it is an imagined reality. But, as we have emphasized previously, it is the imagined *reality* of t_{10} which inspires and shapes the entrepreneur's decision at t_1.

Suppose now that the entrepreneur A at date t_1 reasons as follows. 'The t_{10} demand for shoes that I am wondering about is not something that expresses some future fact of external nature. In part that revenue will depend on what happens to population, to life styles, between now and t_{10}. Perhaps at time t_3 some entrepreneur will introduce a new fashion (say, bicycle travel) that will turn out drastically to affect t_{10} shoe demand.' We may distinguish between the anticipated demand for shoes at t_{10} in the absence of bicycles, and the demand to be anticipated at t_{10} in the event that bicycles are introduced at t_3. (For simplicity we shall assume that these are the only alternative scenarios to be taken into account.) Only one of these two states of t_{10} demand will actually be the reality at t_{10}. Either bicycles will or they will not be introduced at t_3. But *both* possibilities exercise their effect upon present decision making. Our entrepreneur A must at t_1 plan his present activities on some perception of what the demand at t_{10} will in fact be. Both conceivable t_{10} 'realities' will enter his calculations at t_1. Of course A also knows that the very start of a shoe industry at t_1 may generate changes in consumer patterns of behaviour, so that the demand to be expected at t_{10} may not be the same as it might be were A *not* to start the shoe industry at t_1.

Nonetheless, in assessing the profitability of beginning now at t_1 A is asking a single question: supposing I begin to build a shoe factory at t_1 in order to sell shoes at t_{10}, will shoe revenues at t_{10} be such as to show that the value of inputs at t_1 has been erroneously low?

Just as in the simple case of the preceding section all relevant realities exercised an appropriate incentive influence upon the entrepreneurial nose for profits, so too in the more dynamic context all relevant imaginable realities exercise their comparable influence. In the preceding section different realities were relevant at different times (when the bicycle factory was built this altered the relevant realities); in the present section (on the dynamic problem) different imaginable realities may simultaneously exercise their influence upon the entrepreneurial nose for profit. But all of them enter, appropriately, into entrepreneurial consideration, to the extent that the entrepreneur is alert enough to take them into account.[15]

In the case of the preceding section the separate realities that, at different times, operate to create entrepreneurial incentives were (a) an 'original' reality and (b) a subsequent reality created by a 'mistaken' entrepreneurial decision. In the present discussion, too, the arrays of imagined alternative 'realities' which operate upon the entrepreneur's future-oriented profit antennae include imagined realities that might be created by 'mistaken' (future) decisions. But we must not misinterpret this circumstance.

It is true that the entrepreneur at time t_1, in assessing prospects at t_{10}, takes into account the possibility that those t_{10} prospects may turn out to be the results of erroneous entrepreneurial acts, say at time t_4. But this does not mean that the imagined t_{10} realities which operate on the entrepreneur's incentives at t_1 are *not* the 'true' t_{10} realities (i.e. those which *would* be relevant at t_{10} were no entrepreneurial mistakes to have been made earlier that might result in a different set of t_{10} realities). First, the entrepreneur at t_1 does have an incentive to take into account the possibility that mistakes between t_1 and t_{10} will *not* distort the situation at t_{10}. More important, entrepreneurial decisions at t_4 (and at *every* date) have every incentive *not* to be based on error. Thus at all times each and every entrepreneur is operating under the incentives set up by the 'true' underlying future realities, *as well as* by the possible 'mistake-induced' realities that may turn out to be relevant. Every entrepreneurial mistake creates a prospective intertemporal gap which offers the incentive correctly to anticipate the truth – with that truth reflecting both 'original' elements and elements introduced by earlier mistakes (with the latter elements being fully relevant to the genuine co-ordination needs introduced by those very mistakes).

WHAT MARKET EQUILIBRATION TENDENCIES MEAN

It may seem to critics that our attempt to grapple with radical subjectivist insights has forced us to recognize an equilibration process far more attenuated, far less reliable and meaningful, than that postulated traditionally by middle ground Austrian economists. What we have here acknowledged, it may be held, is that the manner in which 'underlying objective realities' exercise their influence upon entrepreneurial production decisions is far less direct and far less reliable than traditional Austrian statements would perhaps suggest. After all, we have recognized that entrepreneurial anticipations have to take into account future conditions, not as they might have been independently of the market process itself, but as they may turn out to be as a result of all the surprises and creativities of which the market process consists. Not only may that process include mistakes galore, that process and those mistakes may so 'alter' future conditions as to require present entrepreneurs to anticipate a future that may in fact be quite different from what it might have been in the absence of such a process.

We must certainly be grateful to our radical subjectivist colleagues for compelling us to spell out how the notion of a systematic equilibrating process is to be integrated with our subjectivist understanding of the creativity of choice and the radical uncertainty of the future. Yet, at the same time, it seems fair to insist upon several key points. What middle ground Austrians wish to assert (and it is this traditionally Austrian assertion which provides the common ground which Mises saw in 1932 as being shared by the Austrians and by other schools of economic theory) is that events that occur during the market process are subject to powerful constraining and shaping influences. These influences tend to reflect the relative urgencies of different consumer preferences, and the relative scarcities of different productive resources. Austrians, certainly, have never been under the illusion that the powerful constraining and shaping influence of the market is ever so complete as to ensure attainment, even fleeting attainment, of the equilibrium state. What Austrians have emphasized is the existence of important processes of equilibration. It is of course true that such processes exercise a dynamic of their own, continually modifying the subsequent realities which in turn must serve to set in motion still further segments of equilibrating processes. It is true that human history is far from being a sequence of overlapping sure-fire equilibrating trajectories each unerringly set in motion by relevant objective realities (that can be identified as such apart from these processes themselves). All this is true. Middle ground Austrians have not been in the habit of treating the general equilibrium configuration of market variables as a 'magnet' or 'telos' with the capacity inexorably to draw actual market phenomena towards them. But, at the same time, they have resisted the temptation to treat market phenomena as only accidentally consistent with underlying objective phenomena. The truth surely is that the sequence of market events can be understood only if we recognize each segment of market history as expressing, at least in part, the systematic co-ordinative properties of the entrepreneurial process. The degree of importance to be attached to this understanding of market history depends, it must be emphasized, on empirical circumstances. It depends upon the volatility of change in the independent realities; it depends upon the degree of entrepreneurial error, both existing and to be anticipated. The importance of this understanding may thus vary from market to market, from one period in history to another. Although theory insists on the formal validity of the market co-ordinating process under all relevant circumstances, it does not claim that the tendencies which make up the process operate with uniform power at all times and in all contexts. It is easy to imagine circumstances where the power of the co-ordinative market process is completely swamped by the volatility of change and by the high incidence of entrepreneurial error. No doubt there have been moments in capitalist history where this has been the case.

But economic science has always proceeded from the important empirical circumstance of economic order. As elementary textbooks have reminded us at least since Bastiat, great cities manage, without a great deal of centralized control, to attract daily provisions in a tolerably orderly way. The market obviously works. That the market works is perhaps the most significant lesson of modern history. Experiences in the past several decades have pressed this lesson into the consciousness of men on both sides of the Iron Curtain. The problem which has always worried theorists is how, without deliberate co-ordination, can markets *possibly* work. Economic theory has provided the explanation in terms of a theory of market co-ordination. Austrians, we maintain, have deepened our understanding of that theory by introducing explicit insights concerning entrepreneurial discovery and dynamic competition. These insights reflect the subjectivism of the Austrian tradition. It is only through appreciation for subjectivist insights concerning knowledge and discovery that we can make sense of the dynamic market forces which bring decisions into greater and greater co-ordination. There is a danger, however, that undue emphasis on the more exotic possible implications of subjectivism may, paradoxically, make it almost plausible to *reject* the central lesson of economic reasoning, the understanding of and appreciation for the market co-ordinating process. This would be profoundly regrettable.

It is easy enough to show how error may frustrate efficiency and co-ordination. It is easy enough to show how, once we introduce a multiperiod future during which a continually creative market process may be at work, it must seem almost fantastic to expect entrepreneurs correctly to anticipate the future. What is not so easy is to explain how, in spite of the untold opportunities for error and surprise, the market regularly appears to organize coherent long-range processes of production in profitable ways.

What the theory of the entrepreneur-driven process of market co-ordination provides is a framework within which to understand how current production decisions can possibly achieve the extraordinary degree of spontaneous co-ordination which casual experience convinces us that they do. The theory identifies the windows through which discovery of relevant opportunities can illuminate and inform the lattice-work of market decision making. No one needs to be told that these windows may be blurred and obscured, that entrepreneurs may fail to perceive what might be seen through these windows. But once we understand that these windows exist, we can in principle understand how, in spite of the uncertainty of the future, in spite of the cloud of unavoidable ignorance which obscures these windows, opportunities for profit can attract and inspire market actions which turn out to reduce market ignorance and misallocation.

Moreover, once we understand how it is through windows of entrepreneurial opportunity that the light of potential discovery inspires market efficiency, we can understand the Mises–Hayek demonstration of the fallacy of seeking social efficiency *without* the market. We can understand how, by walling up all such windows of entrepreneurial opportunity, central planning dooms itself to operating in a world of sheer ignorance concerning vital, ample and available pieces of information dispersed throughout the economy.

We cannot, as Austrians, follow mainstream neoclassical theory and simply assert perennial equilibrium. Yet we cannot, again as Austrians, follow subjectivist sceptics in denying co-ordinative properties to the market. We find ourselves, therefore, occupying the Garrisonian middle ground, finding deep understanding of systematic market processes in precisely those subjectivist insights which, if deployed without sufficient care, may tempt one to reject the idea of market co-ordination altogether.

Chapter 2

The meaning of market process

There is a double meaning attached to the word 'meaning' in the title of this chapter.[1] The title indicates that, as one objective, we have to distinguish two separate meanings that have been intended by the notion of market process (and, in doing so, to make it very clear which of these meanings is preferred by the writer). As a second objective, we shall attempt to answer the question: 'What does the market process mean for human liberty?'; in other words, we shall try to assess the significance of the market process view for an understanding of the free society.

These two tasks that we have set ourselves are by no means entirely separate. As we shall see, one's assessment of the likely economic achievements of a free society depends rather heavily on the way in which one sees the market and, in particular, on the character of the market process that one is prepared to recognize. It may be helpful, in assisting the reader to make his way through the pages ahead, to briefly state the writer's own position in advance. This position can be expressed in the form of a series of assertions: (a) under a system in which private property rights are respected, a free society is one in which economic endeavour flows predominantly through the market; (b) the market is in a continual state of flux and is never in or near a state of equilibrium; (c) this continual flux comprises *two* distinct layers of changing phenomena; (d) one of these two layers of changing phenomena is made up of *exogenous* changes, changes in preferences, population, resource availabilities and technical possibilities; (e) the second layer of change is endogenous – changes systematically induced as market forces move constantly to equilibrate the constellations of forces operating at any given moment; (f) the latter layer of change, consisting of systematic equilibrating tendencies (which never do manage to become fully completed before being disrupted by new exogenous changes) is responsible for the degree of allocative efficiency and of growth potential that market economies display; (g) it is to the latter layer of equilibrative change that the term 'market process' properly refers; (h) for market processes to work, the essential requirement is freedom for competitive entrepreneurial *entry*; (i) thus complete economic freedom of the individual is necessary if the market economy is to do its work; (j) moreover, the point to be emphasized is not merely that a society of free individuals can (counter-intuitively) achieve a measure of co-ordination, but that – even more counter-intuitively – *only* a society of free individuals is able to harness the forces of entrepreneurial competition to make and disseminate those discoveries upon which allocative efficiency and growth depend; (k) this leads directly to the Misesian proposition that only in a market society is it possible to solve the problem of economic calculation; a socialist society, were it to be isolated from contact with market economies, must tend towards inefficiency and economic failure.

As indicated these assertions are *not* universally accepted, even among the small subset of economists who profess a market process view. But in order to develop the position we have here outlined, and to consider the alternative meaning to the idea of market process, we must first briefly contrast the market process view (no matter which variant of it we wish to adopt) with the dominant approach in modern microeconomics – the equilibrium theory of the market.

THE EQUILIBRIUM VIEW OF THE MARKET

For most of the twentieth-century history of microeconomics, economists have, with rare exceptions, understood market phenomena in terms of equilibrium models. In other words, economists have seen the explanations to be provided for market data – prices, methods of production, sizes of industries – as able to be found in the values for these variables that would be consistent with market equilibrium. Take the simplest (and most widely used) example of microeconomic analysis, the perfectly competitive market for a single commodity. In applying this analysis to the market price for any given product, economists start out by assuming that this price is in fact that price at which quantity supplied equals quantity demanded. Underlying this approach is the apparent conviction that equilibrating forces are so powerful that it is an acceptable first approximation to the truth to assume that markets have already, at any given time, attained the neighbourhood of equilibrium. Observed changes in market data must, in this approach, be explained as reflecting corresponding changes in the underlying data. Observed discrepancies between the data of a market and the values to be expected on the basis of an adopted equilibrium model are taken to suggest, not any inadequacy in the assumption of attained equilibrium, but rather the possible relevance of some other, possibly more complicated equilibrium model.[2]

This is not the place to develop a complete critique of this dominant equilibrium approach to microeconomics. Nonetheless we mention one of the key objections that have been raised against it. This key objection is that, by concentrating exclusively on states of equilibrium, theory offers no explanation of the equilibrating process itself. As stated earlier, the unstated premise of the equilibrium approach is that equilibration processes are powerful and rapid – but this seems to assume away the task of explaining the nature of such processes. Economists dissatisfied with the dominant approach have become more and more aware of the formidable challenge to economic science which the phenomenon of equilibration poses.[3] As economists have become sensitive to problems of knowledge and learning, and of how these relate to the possibility of equilibration, these economists have become more and more sceptical of approaches which simply assume that equilibration occurs – and occurs instantaneously.

It must be acknowledged that the dominant approach has not entirely failed to address some of these difficulties. But it seems fair to assert that it has addressed these difficulties not by modifying its adherence to the complete equilibrium assumption, but by incorporating new variables into its equilibrium models – in fact, by *extending* the scope asserted for the equilibrium principle. For example, increased awareness of some of the problems raised for equilibrium economics by the phenomenon of ignorance has led economists to include the cost of ignorance-removal (i.e. the cost of learning) into their models. Thus, as it turns out, attention to problems of ignorance has not only not weakened the grip of the equilibrium assumption; quite the contrary, it has *extended* the scope of this assumption. Economists need no longer assume that some necessary process of equilibration has, somehow, rapidly been completed before we begin our work; they may claim that, at each and every instant in time, taking all relevant transactions costs (including the costs of learning) into appropriate account, each market situation *must* necessarily *always* be in equilibrium.[4] To assume otherwise would be to assume that some market participants have failed to take advantage of opportunities for mutual gain through exchange – even when the necessary costs of overcoming ignorance are so low as to render such failure inefficient. For the dominant approach, to admit such possibilities is to admit the unthinkable – irrational behaviour.

To sum up, the dominant position in economics has tended to keep equilibrium models at the very centre of market theory; it has done so by translating every apparent discrepancy (between the theory and reality) into a more complicated equilibrium theory based on the necessary costs of ignorance-removal.

THE MARKET PROCESS THEORISTS

Market process theorists of all varieties share in common a profound dissatisfaction with the way equilibrium economics looks at the world. Whereas, as we have seen, the latter see market phenomena, at each moment in time, as accurately expressing the balance of forces relevant to the underlying data of that moment, market process theorists see things quite differently. The constellations of prices, product qualities, methods of production and incomes observed at any given instant are not at all taken to be the relevant equilibrium values. (Some process theorists question the very meaningfulness of the notion of 'equilibrium values'.) Rather these variables are seen, at any given moment, to be subject to changes which market forces are likely to generate – even if we insulate, for analytical purposes, from the impact exercised by exogenous changes in the underlying variables.

Nor are these changes which endogenous market forces are likely to generate seen as mechanically determined by the relative strengths and speeds of these forces. Market process theorists do not conceive of these forces as operating in deterministic fashion. They see them, rather, as understandable only in subtle terms to which dominant microeconomic analysis is singularly irrelevant. For example, equilibrium theorists would approach a phenomenon of a price difference (for what are indeed different samples of the very same commodity) in different parts of the same market by focusing on the costs of learning about the availability of other prices. Once these costs are plugged in, the assumption is that at all times the different parts of the market are in equilibrium with each other. If we find a tendency for such price differentials to disappear, standard economics would explain the rate of disappearance as rigidly reflecting the underlying changes in the costs of learning (about remaining price differentials). Market process theorists, on the other hand, would view the process during which price differentials gradually disappear in much less deterministic terms. As we shall elaborate in more detail later, they would focus on the possibility of learning occurring not through deliberately absorbing the perceived costs of learning but through the phenomena of surprise and discovery. These phenomena, central to market process theory, are simply not reducible to the kinds of problems with which equilibrium economics, based solidly and exclusively on the analysis of rational decision making in a world free of surprises, is equipped to deal.

At this stage we are perhaps ready to identify the alternative versions of market process theory. Let us couch our discussion in terms of (a) the *underlying variables* (UVs), identified conventionally as preferences, resource availabilities and technological possibilities, and (b) the *induced variables* (IVs), consisting of the prices, methods of production and quantities and qualities of outputs which the market at any given time generates under the impact of the UVs. As we have seen, equilibrium economics postulates that at each and every instant the actual market values of the IVs are those equilibrium values predetermined by the relevant values of the UVs. Any apparent discrepancy is explained away by postulating that some relevant UV has somehow been overlooked (as, for example, the costs of overcoming ignorance had been overlooked in earlier equilibrium models). Market process theorists, however, claim that the movements of IVs in the market are *not* fully determined by the values of the UVs. The former retain a degree of freedom with respect to the latter. We may now identify the alternative variants of market process theory we have referred to.

One variant identifies market process as the actual sequence of values of the IVs over time (Lachmann 1986a). Now this sequence, clearly, reflects the *joint* effect of several possible sets of forces for change: (a) the changes in the UVs during this period of time can be understood, even in the market process view, as of course having a continual impact on the sequence of IV values; (b) quite apart from changes in the UVs we can see how any adjustment processes (equilibrating or otherwise) through which given UV values tend gradually to become reflected in IV values can be expected to contribute to the sequence of changing IV values during the period under discussion. By focusing on the joint effect of these sets of forces for change, this first possibility for defining 'the market process' thus refuses to accord any real analytical significance to the distinction between these two sets of forces (a) and (b). In Professor Lachmann's terminology the first set of forces are described as disequilibrating changes, the second as equilibrating changes; but the two sets are held to be so intertwined as to defy separate analytical treatment. This is reinforced by the circumstance that, in Professor Lachmann's view, the inevitable presence of disequilibrating changes radically undermines the determinacy of any equilibrating changes that might, in their absence, have been imagined. This is so, in his view, because the presence of the disequilibrating changes renders it impossible for market participants to identify with clarity the steps that need to be taken to achieve equilibrium.

The second variant of market process theory, and the one which this writer believes should be emphasized, defines the market process exclusively in terms of the second of the two sets of forces for change identified in the preceding paragraph. The concept of market process, on this understanding of it, is an analytical one. We distinguish, among the forces causing changes in the IVs, a distinct set of forces unleashed, at each moment, by the *absence* of equilibrium. The changes induced by these forces constitute the market process. These changes would continue to occur, constituting the market process in its purest analytical form, even if, as of a given date, all changes in the UVs were suspended. If we wish to analyse the market process it is therefore most useful to conduct mental experiments against the imagined background of unchanging UVs. In full reality, of course, the market process never does proceed in pure form. Rather, what we encounter over time is a mass of changes in IVs that reflect, in addition, the continual changes in the UVs. Thus these changes in IVs express not just *the* market process, but the total impact of innumerable separate (and possibly colliding) market processes set in motion, at different points in time, by the discrepancies, existing at these respective points in time, between actual IVs and the relevant respective equilibrium values for the IVs. These separate market processes run into one another, colliding with or reinforcing each other, so that the actual sequences of IV values are seen as highly complex outcomes of numerous interacting sets of forces. It is the central tenet of market process theory, under this present variant of it, that, despite the complexities thus introduced by continually changing UVs, the essential character of the market process, as a matter of historical experience, does remain largely intact. In fact, it will be our claim, it is this character of the market process which is the dominant feature of real world market economies; it is through our understanding of this market process that we can understand how market economies work.

For the remainder of this chapter we shall use the term 'market process' to connote this meaning of the term, unless we specify otherwise. It may be useful, before proceeding to develop an outline of market process theory (and its significance for the possibility of a prosperous free society), to re-emphasize, in the light of our adopted identification of the notion of market process, how sharply different the market process view of the market economy is from that which we have earlier seen to be the equilibrium theory view of it.

For market process theorists the central thread of change that permits us to understand the market is that of the market process. If we wish to understand the IV values at a given moment, we can do so by referring to the course of the market process until that moment. If we wish to ground our understanding of the market in basic theory, that basic theory must be the theory of what it is that shapes the course of the market process. If we wish to evaluate the significance of the market for human well-being, we must do so by evaluating the impact upon such well-being of the market process. Equilibrium models turn out, for the market process view, to be pictures from which the most important features of the market have been excluded. Such models start by assuming that there is no scope for market processes at all.

THE CHARACTER OF THE MARKET PROCESS

The central feature of the market process, to which we wish to draw attention, concerns the role in it played by ignorance and by discovery. The root insight is that disequilibrium consists in mutual ignorance on the part of potential market participants. We take it for granted that such ignorance cannot persist indefinitely. Sooner or later unexploited opportunities for mutual gain must come to be discovered. It is because the existence of such unexploited opportunities – due entirely to mutual ignorance – are so likely to be eventually discovered that this initial situation is described as a state of disequilibrium.

The market process, then, consists of those changes that express the sequence of discoveries that follow the initial ignorance that constituted the disequilibrium state. We describe this sequence of discoveries as constituting an *equilibrating* process, but we must circumscribe this description by a number of qualifications and cautionary observations. The equilibrating character of the process follows naturally from the circumstance that it is made up, presumably, of corrective discoveries concerning earlier ignorance. Such discoveries lead to the elimination of remaining unexploited opportunities for mutual gain. In the ultimate, when no pockets of ignorance remain, we will be left with a market in full equilibrium. As long as the UVs remain unchanged, the attained absence of ignorance will ensure that all exchanges completed in any one period will be repeated without change in each succeeding similar period. But the equilibrating character of the market process, as we have described it, should not be misunderstood.

First, we emphasize, the fact that the market process is equilibrative does not imply, of course, that equilibrium is in fact ever attained. In any real world, with frequent changes in the UVs, equilibrating processes are continually interrupted by UV changes which initiate fresh, equilibrating processes. None of these processes can be expected to proceed to completion. All that we claim is that the forces for mutual discovery, and for the elimination of ignorance, are constantly at work.

Second, we do not claim that each and every 'discovery' is in fact corrective. Many 'discoveries' turn out to be mistaken; earlier ignorance may turn out to be increased rather than eroded. Some segments of the market process may thus in fact be disequilibrating. If we maintain, nonetheless, that the market process can fairly be described, in general terms, as equilibrating, this is because of a conviction that in the face of initial ignorance there is a systematic tendency for genuine discoveries, rather than spurious ones, to be made.

Third, the possibility of enhanced error rather than of genuine corrective discovery must certainly gain plausibility as a result of the universal circumstance of continual change in the UVs. Genuine discovery of earlier ignorance does not point unambiguously to improved decision making for the future – since the discoverer must now speculate about the likelihood of new changes.

To emphasize the centrality of equilibration in the market process is not, of course, to concede the appropriateness of equilibrium economics. For reasons already given, market process theorists argue that the major features of the market that call for explanation call for process analysis rather than equilibrium theory. A picture of the world as at all times at or in the neighbourhood of equilibrium assumes away far too many important features of reality to be useful for economic understanding. On the other hand, to insist that the real world is unlikely ever to be close to equilibrium is by no means to concede that markets are not powerfully equilibrative. The market process view sees the market as displaying, at all times, the effects of powerful forces encouraging genuine and valuable discovery. This view argues that, to understand how markets work, it is necessary to toe the fine line that rejects both the assumption of constant, instantaneous equilibration and the opposite assumption that the sequence of values of what we have called the IVs is one essentially disengaged from the sequence of UVs.

THE NATURE OF DISCOVERY

In describing the market process as a series of steps correcting earlier ignorance, we do not wish it to be understood that this process consists in a series of deliberate acts of learning. One might indeed describe a sequenced series of deliberate acts of learning as an adjustment process transforming ignorance into knowledge. But the market process is not to be understood on such a pattern. We must distinguish sharply between those acts of discovery of which the market process consists, and the acts of deliberate learning which, unless by accident, form no part of the market process.

A deliberate act of learning occurs when one recognizes one's lack of knowledge, is aware of the way in which this lack can be rectified and at what cost, and believes that the value to be gained by learning more than justifies the costs of learning. The starting point is awareness of one's ignorance – in fact an awareness sufficiently detailed to permit one to identify the specific items of knowledge that one lacks. The endpoint of the learning process is possession of the sought-after knowledge; but such possession involves no essential elements of surprise. When one researches a fact from an encyclopaedia, looks up the meaning and spelling of a strange word in a dictionary or examines a street map of a strange city, one need not encounter anything surprising. One knew one's ignorance; one has not been surprised to discover that one had unknowingly been labouring under a misapprehension, that the world turns out to be quite different from what one had anticipated. The kind of discovery steps we have described as making up the market process, on the other hand, are characterized precisely by the surprise involved by the discovery, and by the corresponding earlier unawareness of the nature of one's ignorance. A simple example will illustrate the point. Consider a market in which two prices prevail for the same commodity in different parts of the same market. Equilibrium theory, of course, would deny such a possibility outright and claim that it can be salvaged only by postulating *different qualities* of commodity (more carefully defined) or the existence of barriers separating the market into *separate* markets. For equilibrium theory such a barrier might be the presence of ignorance that it is costly to remove. Market process theory insists that the possibility of the same commodity selling at different prices within the same market can be entirely accounted for by the phenomenon of costlessly removable unknown ignorance. Unknown ignorance is ignorance concerning which one is unaware. Suppose that one buys fruit for $2, when the same fruit is openly available for $1 in a neighbouring store which one has just passed but overlooked. Then it is clear that one might costlessly have been able to know where to buy the fruit for $1, and in fact paid $2 for it only because one did not know of the possibility of costlessly commanding the needed information – in other words, one has suffered from being unaware of one's costlessly removable ignorance. When one discovers that the fruit for which one has been paying $2 is in fact available for $1, this comes as a surprise. The discovery itself cannot, given the circumstances, have been undertaken deliberately; after all one did not know anything existed to be discovered.

When one theorizes that, pursuant to Jevons's law of indifference, such price differences tend to disappear under the impact of competitive market forces, one is postulating, we wish to assert, a series of spontaneous discoveries that tend to eliminate the price differences. We assume that the existence of a price differential will attract notice. People who paid $2 will notice that others have paid $1: people who accepted $1 will notice that others have received $2. Others may notice the possibility of winning pure profit by buying at $1 and selling at $2; The result of these discoveries – none of which has deliberately been searched for – is increased purchases attempted to be made at $1 and increased sales attempted to be made at $2. This leads to the elimination of price differentials. It is not in general possible, we shall argue, to imagine the elimination of such price differentials in the absence of spontaneous discovery. If, for example, we imagine costly steps deliberately taken to search for better prices, then we face the problem of explaining why such steps had not been taken earlier. (One might of course postulate that the sequence of market events systematically lowers the costs of such deliberate search. But one has then left the realm of general theory for that of *ad hoc* assumptions.) Sooner or later one must have resort to spontaneous discovery – even if only the discovery of the possibility of profitable search itself.

The emphasis we have placed on the discovery (rather than deliberate search) character of the market process is of considerable importance. Processes of deliberate search are, in a definite sense, fully determinate. At each point in the search process one knows, as it were, exactly as much as one has chosen to know. The amount one has chosen to know is completely determined by the value of what one might seek to know and by the costs of search. At each point in time one possesses the optimal degree of knowledge (and thus also the optimal degree of ignorance). Were the market process to be of this character it would be a completely determinate process – one fully explicable in terms of equilibrium theorizing. That is, one would not then describe the market process as following a course from disequilibrium to equilibrium, but rather as following a course from equilibrium with a great deal of (optimal) ignorance to equilibrium with a lesser (but, of course, still optimal) degree of ignorance.

What we have been underlining, on the other hand, is that in the market process view the passage leading from many prevailing prices towards a single price is not at all determined, but nonetheless systematic and expressive of a powerful tendency. There can never be a guarantee that anyone will notice that of which he is utterly ignorant; the most complete rationality of decision making in the world cannot ensure search for that the existence of which is wholly unsuspected. Yet we submit that few will maintain that initial ignorance concerning desirable opportunities costlessly available can be expected to endure indefinitely. We recognize, surely, that human beings are motivated to notice that which it is to their benefit to notice. We identify this general motivation with the alertness which every human being possesses, to greater or lesser degree. This omnipresent human alertness makes it inconceivable that market participants can be expected indefinitely to continue to pay more for an item than they in fact need to; or that they can be expected indefinitely to continue to accept less in payment for an item than they are in fact able to command. We are convinced that specifically unpredictable acts of discovery will add up to a systematic erosion of unjustified price differentials. Because of its non-deterministic, non-mechanical character, this market process of discovery does not lend itself to the kind of modelling central to equilibrium economics. Yet the systematic nature of the process requires that we not permit any methodological predilections in favour of formal modelling techniques to obscure vitally important features of the market economy.

UNDERSTANDING MARKETS

All this provides us, in the market process view, with a sensitive understanding of market phenomena that goes significantly beyond the scope of equilibrium economics. The market process view focuses on the incentives offered by disequilibrium market conditions for those discoveries that add up to systematic equilibrative tendencies. It sees these incentives as continually attracting the attention of potentially new competitors; it recognizes that the attention of such new competitors must take the form of entrepreneurial perception of exploitable profit opportunities.

This understanding of markets, then, refuses to see the constant market agitation initiated by jostling competitors and innovative entrepreneurial upstarts as disturbing elements to be filtered out in order to perceive the underlying stable elements corresponding to market equilibrium positions. Rather the market process view sees in this constant market agitation the essential sets of market forces that permit us to comprehend what is happening in markets. This view sees the apparent chaos of market agitation as not chaotic at all; quite the contrary, it is in this apparently chaotic sequence of market events that the market's orderliness resides. The central meaning of the movements which we continually observe in markets is that discoveries are being made concerning overlooked market gaps. Each such overlooked opportunity constitutes at the same time (a) a disequilibrium feature in the market, and (b) an exploitable opportunity for pure profit. It is the incentive offered in the form of pure profit that inspires and motivates those entrepreneurial discoveries that tend to correct earlier features of disequilibrium.

To be sure, the market process view emphatically recognizes that at any given time the market has not yet eliminated all features of disequilibrium – if for no other reason than the circumstance of continually changing UVs. But this view also insists we recognize the character of the forces at all times impinging on the market – forces inspired by entrepreneurial alertness towards opportunities for pure profits.

This way of understanding the market applies, *mutatis mutandis*, both to the short and to the long run. Pure profit opportunities may offer themselves in three distinct forms, which share in common the applicability of the insights of the preceding paragraphs. Pure profit may occur (a) as a result of pure arbitrage, buying and selling simultaneously at different prices; (b) as a result of 'intertemporal arbitrage', buying an item at a low price and selling it later at a higher price; and (c) as a result of a creative act of production, buying resources at low prices and selling a product innovatively created out of them later at a high price. In each of these cases pure profit occurs because the market had not been fully adjusted to the possibilities it itself contained (either immediately attainable opportunities or subsequently attainable possibilities). The possibility of winning pure profit motivates the alertness of entrepreneurs and inspires judicious and creative decisions to overcome the initial ignorance of which those possibilities are the market counterpart. The entrepreneurial alertness which notices pure arbitrage possibilities today is fundamentally similar to that which presciently envisages the profit possibilities to be obtained through intertemporal arbitrage. And it is analytically parallel, at least, to that alertness to the possibilities that can be opened up through innovation that inspires the creativity and inventiveness of entrepreneurial producers. The market agitation that expresses these kinds of entrepreneurial alertness is of a single pattern. The kinds of equilibrative process which these respective kinds of market agitation initiate achieve corresponding adjustments in the allocation of resources and of products. Pure arbitrage tends to ensure the exploitation of all available opportunities for mutually profitable exchange; intertemporal arbitrage tends to avoid 'wasteful' intertemporal allocation (and thus, where warranted, to build up towards the optimal capital structure); the entrepreneurship exercised in innovative production tends to generate technological progress.

To understand the achievements of the market process in this way should not, we emphasize once again, blind us to the possibilities of entrepreneurial failures. Pure losses, rather than pure profits, may and do emerge. The market process that we have outlined offers a systematic tendency, rather than a sure-fire machine-like trajectory. Moreover the assurance that we feel concerning the overall tendency of the market process is clearly dependent upon the rate at which unanticipated changes in UVs impinge on the market. Were these changes to be so drastic in their volatility and rate of occurrence as to swamp the discovery potential inherent in entrepreneurial alertness, we could hardly expect the market process to manifest itself, in the real world, in a manner able to generate order in the face of apparent chaos. The market agitation thus generated by chaotic change in UVs *could* thus fail to display the underlying tendencies towards orderliness which entrepreneurial processes under less extreme conditions set into motion.

But economic science, from its beginnings, has been moored in the empirical circumstance of markets that do display a certain order. The scientific challenge has been, not to predict an orderliness that has not yet been observed, but to account for the counter-intuitive circumstance of observed market order, in the absence of centralized control. It is in meeting this challenge that market theory, ever since Adam Smith, has grappled to achieve an understanding of markets. The market process approach, fully in line with this scientific tradition, sees a significant advance in the understanding of markets as obtainable from insights into the competitive-entrepreneurial discovery process that constitutes, in this approach, the essential core of market phenomena through time.

MARKET PROCESS AND INDIVIDUAL LIBERTY

The market process approach permits us, in fact, to recognize that the counter-intuitive character of economists' invisible-hand theorems concerning markets masks an even more surprising discovery. Not only is it the case, as traditional economics has demonstrated since Adam Smith, that market efficiency can prevail in spite of the absence of centralized direction. It turns out, as it happens, that the market process approach shows that such absence of centralized direction is in fact *necessary*, if the kind of co-ordination (we have seen to be achievable through the market process) is to be attained at all. It is this insight that Mises and Hayek attempted to enunciate in their expositions of the problems of economic calculation that face socialist planners. As has recently been shown (Lavoie 1985a), the failure of post-Second World War economists to appreciate the force, and even the content of the Mises–Hayek position has much to do with their unawareness of the market process view which these Austrian economists – perhaps unselfconsciously – possessed. From an equilibrium approach, the socialist calculation problem appears far from insoluble; once the market process view is understood, the calculation problem assumes far more formidable proportions.

The calculation problem begins, we now understand, from the inevitable circumstance of unsuspected ignorance. This ignorance, as

Hayek explained over forty years ago (Hayek 1949b), takes the form of *dispersed information*. The point is that at any given moment opportunities exist for socially significant exchange and production activities. The ingredients for such opportunities consist of pieces of information concerning resources and products which, if brought together in a single mind, could present clearly identifiable opportunities. The problem is that they are not, at the moment in question, present to any single mind. The primary function of the economic system, Hayek argued, is not to 'allocate resources efficiently' but, first of all, to overcome the knowledge problem created by dispersed information. The nature of this knowledge problem must, however, be clearly understood; our discussion of the nature of discovery may be helpful in this regard.

The problem created by dispersed information consists, we shall maintain (see also Chapter 8 and 9), not in the circumstance that those who possess some relevant items of information are ignorant of the complementary items of information, but that they are ignorant of their ignorance. Members of an economy possess items of information whose potential value is quite unknown to them, because they have no inkling concerning the availability of complementary inputs, or of complementary information. *This* ignorance means that, even if the costs of search (that might yield the missing pieces of information) are very low, no search will be undertaken. This kind of unknown ignorance, when confronted by central planners, cannot be systematically or deliberately tackled. Planners simply do not know what to look for: they do not know where or of what kind the knowledge gaps are.

And it is precisely this knowledge problem that the decentralized market economy addresses. The existence of unknown ignorance manifests itself in markets as unnoticed opportunities for pure profits. Such opportunities attract the alertness of entrepreneurs. It is the series of discoveries stimulated by such alertness that constitutes the market process. What the market process achieves, then, is systematic co-ordination of dispersed pieces of information available – but languishing undreamed of – throughout the economy.

It turns out, then, that individual liberty is not merely one element in the definition of a market economy. It turns out that individual liberty is that ingredient in that definition upon which the success of the market process depends. Individual liberty is not a circumstance in spite of which markets work; it is the crucial circumstance which permits the market process to work. All this leads one to add several observations concerning the meaning of individual liberty.

THE MEANING OF INDIVIDUAL LIBERTY

The market process which we have described depends, we have seen, on individual alertness. Such alertness, we have seen, is manifested principally through the exercise of entrepreneurship, but is in fact present, to some degree, in all individual activity. We have emphasized the importance of entrepreneurial entry as the driving force in the market process. But, more generally, this process depends on individual freedom to pursue perceived opportunities, within the limits of property rights, without arbitrary obstacles being placed in one's path. The central idea, for an understanding of individual liberty, lies in the individual's freedom *to identify for himself what the opportunities are* which he may endeavour to grasp. While this may seem obvious and even trite, we should notice that it is only within the market process system of thinking about markets that this aspect of individual freedom becomes clearly apparent (Kirzner 1979a: Ch. 13).

Within an equilibrium view of economic activity there really is no scope for this aspect of freedom. For the equilibrium view there is never any question of perceiving opportunities. For this view each individual is assumed, from the very beginning, to find himself confronted by an array of given resources and a ranked series of given objectives. His decision-task is merely the computational one of arranging the disposition of his resources so as to maximize the value of his attained objectives. (Of course this statement of the decision on the equilibrium view recognizes that one of these objectives may be the intermediate objective of obtaining necessary information through search. But we remind ourselves that, on this view, there is no scope for surprise or discovery.) Freedom, under this conception of the individual decision, can mean no more than that it is the decision maker's own preference function, and no one else's, that determines the relevant ranking of objectives. But the market process view that we have articulated points to a far more fundamental feature of freedom, a feature which philosophers have always understood but which economists, under the blinders imposed by equilibrium theory, seem to have lost sight of. This feature is that the free individual has the freedom to decide what it is that he sees. He is free to make his own discoveries (and, of course, to make his own disastrous entrepreneurial mistakes).

The significance of this feature of freedom, for a discussion of the meaning for liberty of the market process, is not difficult to discern.

What a free market does is to offer its participants incentives to make profitable discoveries. This central feature of the free market has *two* implications for individual liberty. First, as already noted, it is able to harness individual freedom to generate the systematic discovery process which is the basis for the co-ordinative properties of the market. Second, by offering the incentive of pure profit opportunities to alert market participants,[5] the market is affording an outlet through which an essential element of individual freedom can be expressed and exercised. If freedom includes, in an important sense, the freedom to recognize hitherto unnoticed opportunities, and if, as argued, one's ability to recognize opportunities depends vitally on one's ability to seize benefit for oneself from such opportunities, then *only* a system that permits the grasping of opportunities for gain is capable of providing scope for individual liberty (other than the kind of liberty enjoyed by Robinson Crusoe).

Not only is it, then, the case that the workings of markets depend on human liberty: it turns out to be the case that only in the context of free markets is there genuine scope for human liberty in society. For the elucidation of *both* these conclusions, we have seen, an understanding of markets in terms of the market process view has been the indispensable intellectual stepping stone.

Part II

The emergence of the Austrian view

Chapter 3

The Austrian School of economics

The birth of the Austrian School of economics is usually recognized as having occurred with the 1871 publication of Carl Menger's *Grundsätze der Volkwirthschaftslehre*. On the basis of this work Menger (hitherto a civil servant) became a junior faculty member at the University of Vienna. Several years later, after a stint as tutor and travelling companion to Crown Prince Rudolph, he was appointed to a professorial chair at the University. Two younger economists, Eugen von Böhm-Bawerk and Friedrich von Wieser (neither of whom had been a student of Menger) became enthusiastic supporters of the new ideas put forward in Menger's book. During the 1880s a vigorous outpouring of literature from these two followers, from several of Menger's students, and in particular a methodological work by Menger himself, brought the ideas of Menger and his followers to the attention of the international community of economists. The Austrian School was now a recognized entity. Several works of Böhm-Bawerk and Wieser were translated into English; and by 1890 the editors of the US journal *Annals of the American Academy of Political and Social Science* were asking Böhm-Bawerk for an expository paper explaining the doctrines of the new school. What follows seeks to provide a concise survey of the history of the Austrian School with special emphasis on (a) the major representatives of the school, (b) the central ideas identified with the school, (c) the relationship between the school and its ideas, and other major schools of thought within economics and, (d) the various meanings and perceptions associated today with the term Austrian economics.

THE FOUNDING AUSTRIANS

Menger's 1871 book is recognized in the history of economic thought (alongside Jevons's 1871 *Theory of Political Economy* and Walras's 1874 *Eléments d'économie politique pure*) as a central component of the 'Marginalist Revolution'. For the most part, historians of thought have emphasized the features in Menger's work that parallel those of Jevons and Walras. More recently, following especially the work of W. Jaffé (1976), attention has come to be paid to those aspects of Menger's ideas which set them apart from those of his contemporaries. A series of recent studies (Grassl and Smith 1986) have related these unique aspects of Menger and the early Austrian economists to broader currents in the late nineteenth-century intellectual and philosophical scene in Austria.

The central thrust of Menger's book was unmistakable; it was an attempt to rebuild the foundations of economic science in a way which, while retaining the abstract, theoretical character of economics, offered an understanding of value and price which ran sharply counter to classical teachings. For the classical economists value was seen as governed by past resource costs; Menger saw value as expressing judgements concerning future usefulness in meeting consumer wants. Menger's book, offered to the German-speaking scholarly community of Germany and Austria, was thus altogether different, in approach, style and substance, from the work coming from the German universities. The latter work, while also sharply critical of classical economics, was attacking its theoretical character, and appealing for a predominantly historical approach. At the time Menger's book appeared, the 'older' German historical school (led by Roscher, Knies and Hildebrand) was beginning to be succeeded by the 'younger' historical school, whose leader was to be Gustav Schmoller. Menger, the 31-year-old Austrian civil servant, was careful not to present his work as antagonistic to that of German economic scholarship. In fact he dedicated his book – with 'respectful esteem' – to Roscher, and offered it to the community of German scholars 'as a friendly greeting from a collaborator in Austria and as a faint echo of the scientific suggestions so abundantly lavished on us Austrians by Germany . . .' (Menger 1981: Preface). Clearly Menger hoped that his theoretical innovations might be seen as reinforcing the conclusions derived from historical studies of the German scholars, contributing to a new economics to replace a discredited British classical orthodoxy.

Menger was to be bitterly disappointed. The German economists virtually ignored his book; where it was noticed in the German language journals it was grossly misunderstood or otherwise summarily dismissed. For the first decade after the publication of his book, Menger was virtually alone; there was certainly no Austrian 'school'. And when the enthusiastic work of Böhm-Bawerk and Wieser began to appear in the 1880s, the new literature acquired the appellation 'Austrian' more as a pejorative epithet bestowed by disdainful German economists than as an honorific label (Mises 1969: 40). This rift between the Austrian and German scholarly camps deepened most considerably after the appearance of Menger's methodological challenge to the historical approach (Menger 1985). Menger apparently wrote that work having been convinced by the unfriendly disinterest with which his 1871 book had been received in Germany that German economics could be rescued only by a frontal attack on the Historical School. The bitter *methodenstreit* that followed is usually (but not invariably, see Bostaph 1978) seen by historians of economics as constituting a tragic waste of scholarly energy. Certainly this venomous academic conflict helped bring the existence of an Austrian School to the attention of the international economics fraternity – as a group of dedicated economists offering a flood of exciting theoretical ideas reinforcing the new marginalist literature, sharply modifying the hitherto dominant classical theory of value. Works by Böhm-Bawerk (1886), Wieser (1884, 1956), Komorzynski (1889) and Zuckerkandl (1889) offered elaborations or discussions of Menger's central, subjectivist ideas on value, cost and price. Works on the theory of pure profit, and on such applications as public finance theory, were contributed by writers such as Mataja (1884), Gross (1884), Sax (1887) and Meyer (1887). The widely used textbook by Philippovich (1893), who was a professor at the University of Vienna (but more sympathetic towards the contributions of the German school), is credited with an important role in spreading Austrian marginal utility theory among German-language students.

In these early Austrian contributions to the theory of value and price, emphasis was placed (as in the Jevonsian and Walrasian approaches) both on marginalism and on utility. But important differences set the Austrian theory apart from other early marginalist theories. The Austrians made no attempt to present their ideas in mathematical form, and as a consequence the Austrian concept of the margin differs somewhat from that of Jevons and Walras. For the latter, and for subsequent microeconomic theorists, the marginal value of a variable refers to the instantaneous rate of change of the 'total' variable. But the Austrians worked, deliberately, with discrete variables (see K. Menger 1973). More importantly the concept of marginal utility, and the sense in which it decreases, referred for the Austrians not to psychological enjoyments themselves, but to (ordinal) marginal *valuations* of such enjoyments (McCulloch 1977). In any event, as has been urged by Streissler (1972), what was important for the Austrians in marginal utility was not so much the adjective as the noun. Menger saw his theory as demonstrating the unique and exclusive role played, in the determination of economic value, by subjective, 'utility', considerations. Values are not seen (as they are in Marshallian economics) as *jointly* determined by subjective (utility) and objective (physical cost) considerations. Rather, values are seen as determined *solely* by the actions of consumers (operating within a given framework of existing commodity and/or production possibilities). Cost is seen (by Menger, and especially by Wieser, whose name came to be associated closely with this insight) merely as prospective utility deliberately sacrificed (in order to command more highly preferred utility). Whereas in the development of the other marginalist theories it took perhaps two decades for it to be seen that marginal utility value theory points directly to marginal productivity distribution theory, Menger at least glimpsed this insight immediately. His theory of 'higher-order' goods emphasizes how both the economic character and the value of factor services are derived exclusively from the valuations placed by consumers upon the consumers' products to whose emergence these higher order goods ultimately contribute. Böhm-Bawerk contributed not only to the exposition and dissemination of Menger's basic subjective value theory, but most prominently also to the theory of capital and interest. Early in his career he published a massive volume (Böhm-Bawerk 1959 [1884]: vol. I) in the history of doctrine, offering an encyclopaedic critique of all earlier theories of interest (or 'surplus value' or 'normal profit'). This he followed up several years later with a volume (Böhm-Bawerk 1889) presenting his own theory. At least part of the renown of the Austrian School at the turn of the century derived from the fame of these contributions. As we shall note later, a number of subsequent and modern writers (such as Hicks 1973; Faber 1979; and Hausman 1981) have indeed seen these Böhm-Bawerkian ideas as constituting the enduring element of the Austrian contribution. Others, taking their cue from an oft-repeated critical remark attributed to Menger (Schumpeter 1954: 847, fn. 8), have seen Böhm-Bawerk's theory of capital and interest as separate from, or even as somehow inconsistent with, the core of the Austrian tradition stemming from Menger (Lachmann 1977: 27). Certainly Böhm-Bawerk himself saw his theory of capital and interest as a seamless extension of basic subjectivist value theory. Once the dimension of time has been introduced into the analysis of both consumer and producer decisions, Böhm-Bawerk found it possible to explain the phenomenon of interest. Because production takes time, and because economizing men systematically choose earlier receipts over (physically similar) later receipts, capital-using production processes cannot fail to yield (even after the erosive forces of competition are taken into account) a portion of current output to those who in earlier periods invested inputs into time-consuming, 'roundabout' production processes.

Böhm-Bawerk became, indeed, so prominent a representative of the Austrian School prior to the First World War that, largely due to his work, the Marxists came to view the Austrians as the quintessential bourgeois, intellectual enemy of Marxist economics (Bukharin 1972). Not only did Böhm-Bawerk offer his own theory explaining the phenomenon of the interest 'surplus' in a manner depriving this capitalist income of any exploitative character, he had emphatically and mercilessly refuted Marxist theories of this surplus. In his 1884 work Böhm-Bawerk had systematically deployed the Austrian subjective theory of value to criticize witheringly the Marxist labour theory underlying the exploitation theory. A decade later (Böhm-Bawerk 1949 [1896]) he offered a patient, but relentless and uncompromising elaboration of that critique (in dissecting the claim that Marx's posthumously published Volume III of *Capital* could be reconciled with the simple labour theory forming the basis of Volume I). This tension between the Marxists and the Austrians was to find later echoes in the debate which Mises and Hayek (third- and fourth-generation Austrians) were to conduct, during the 1920–40 inter-war period, with socialist economists concerning the possibility of economic calculation in a centrally planned economy.

Menger retired from his University of Vienna professorship in 1903. His chair was assumed by Wieser. Wieser has been justly described as

the central figure of the Austrian School: central in time, central in the ideas he propounded, central in his intellectual abilities, that is to say neither the most outstanding genius nor one of those also to be mentioned. . . . He had the longest teaching record. . . .

(Streissler 1986)

Wieser had been an early and prolific expositor of Menger's theory of value. His general treatise on economics, summing up his life's contributions (Wieser 1967), has been hailed by some (but certainly not all) commentators as a major achievement. (Hayek (1968) sees the work as a personal achievement rather than as representative of the Austrian School.) In the decade prior to the First World War, it was Böhm-Bawerk's seminar (begun when Böhm-Bawerk rejoined academic life after a number of years as Finance Minister of Austria) that became famous as the intellectual centre of the Austrian School. Among the subsequently famous economists who participated in the seminar were Josef A. Schumpeter and Ludwig von Mises, both of whom published books prior to the war (Schumpeter 1908, 1934 [1912]; Mises 1980 [1912].

AFTER THE FIRST WORLD WAR

The scene in Austrian economics after the war was rather different from what it had been before. Böhm-Bawerk had died in 1914, Menger, who even in his long seclusion after retirement used to receive visits from the young economists at the university, died in 1921. Although Wieser continued to teach until his death in 1926, the focus shifted to younger scholars. These included particularly Mises, the student of Böhm-Bawerk, and Hans Mayer, who succeeded his teacher Wieser to his chair. Mises, although an 'extraordinary' (unsalaried) faculty member at the university, never did obtain a professorial chair. Much of his intellectual influence was exercised outside the university framework (Mises 1978: Ch. ix). Other notable (pre-war-trained) scholars during the 1920s included Richard Strigl, Ewald Schams and Leo Schonfeld (later Illy). In the face of these changes the Austrian tradition thrived. New books were published, and a new crop of younger students came to the fore, many of whom were to become internationally famous economists in later decades. These included particularly Friedrich A. Hayek, Gottfried Haberler, Fritz Machlup, Oskar Morgenstern and Paul N. Rosenstein-Rodan. Economic discussion among the Austrians was vigorously carried on, during the 1920s and early 1930s, within two partly overlapping groups. One, at the university, was led by Hans Mayer. The other centred around Mises whose famed *privatseminar* met in his Chamber of Commerce office and drew not only the gifted younger economists but also such philosophers, sociologists and political scientists as Felix Kaufmann, Alfred Schutz and Erik Voegelin. It was during this period that British economist Lionel Robbins came decisively under the influence of the intellectual ferment going on in Vienna. A distinctly important outcome of this contact was Robbin's highly influential book (Robbins 1932). It was largely through this work that a number of key Austrian ideas came to be absorbed into the mainstream literature of twentieth-century Anglo-American economics. In 1931 Robbins invited Hayek to lecture at the London School of Economics, and this led to Hayek's appointment to the Tooke Chair at that institution.

Hayek's arrival on the British scene contributed especially to the development and widespread awareness of the 'Austrian' theory of the business cycle. Mises had sketched such a theory as early as 1912 (Mises 1980 [1912]: 396–404). This theory attributed the boom phase of the cycle to intertemporal misallocation stimulated by 'too low' interest rates. This intertemporal misallocation consisted of producers initiating processes of production that implicitly anticipated a willingness on the part of the public to postpone consumption to a degree in fact inconsistent with the true pattern of time preferences. The subsequent abandonment of unsustainable projects constitutes the down phase of the cycle. Mises emphasized the roots of this theory in Wicksell, and in earlier insights of the British currency school. Indeed Mises was tempted to challenge the appropriateness of the 'Austrian' label widely attached to the theory (Mises 1943). But, as he recognized, the Austrian label had become firmly attached to the doctrine. Hayek's vigorous exposition and extensive development of the theory (Hayek 1931, 1933, 1939), and his introduction (through the theory) of Böhm-Bawerkian capital-theoretic insights to the British public, unmistakably left Hayek's imprint on the fully developed theory, and taught the profession to see it as a central contribution of the Austrian School. Given all these developments it is apparent that we must consider the early 1930s as consituting in many ways the period of greatest Austrian School influence upon the economics profession generally. Yet this triumph was to be short-lived indeed.

With the benefit of hindsight it is perhaps possible to understand why and how this same period of the early 1930s constituted, in fact, a decisive, almost fatal, turning point in the fortunes of the School. Within a few short years the idea of a distinct Austrian School –

except as an important, but bygone, episode in the history of economics – virtually disappeared from the economics profession. While Hans Mayer continued to occupy his chair in Vienna until after the Second World War, the group of prominent younger economists who had surrounded Mises soon dispersed (for political or other reasons), many of them to various universities in the United States. With Mises migrating in 1934 to Geneva and later to New York, with Hayek in London, Vienna ceased to be a centre for the vigorous continuation of the Austrian tradition. Moreover many of the group were convinced that the important ideas of the Austrian School had now been successfully absorbed into mainstream economics. The emerging ascendancy of theoretical economics, and thus the eclipse of historicist and anti-theoretical approaches to economics, no doubt permitted the Austrians to believe that they had finally prevailed, that there was no longer any particular need to cultivate a separate Austrian version of economic theory. A 1932 statement by Mises captures this spirit. Referring to the usual separation of economic theorists into three schools of thought, 'the Austrian and the Anglo-American Schools and the School of Lausanne', Mises (citing Morgernstern) emphasized that these groups 'differ only in their mode of expressing the same fundamental idea and that they are divided more by their terminology and by peculiarities of presentation than by the substance of their teachings' (Mises 1960 [1933]: 214). Yet the survival and development of an Austrian tradition during and subsequent to the Second World War, largely through the work of Mises himself and of Hayek, deserves and requires attention.

Fritz Machlup, on several occasions (Machlup 1981, 1982), has listed six ideas as central to the Austrian School prior to the Second World War. There is every reason to agree that it was these six ideas that expressed the Austrian approach as understood, say, in 1932. The ideas were as follows: (a) methodological individualism (not to be confused with political or ideological individualism, but refering to the claim that economic phenomena are to be explained by going back to the actions of individuals); (b) methodological subjectivism (recognizing that the actions of individuals are to be understood only by reference to the knowledge, beliefs, perception and expectations of these individuals); (c) marginalism (emphasizing the significance of prospective *changes* in relevant magnitudes confronting the decision maker); (d) the influence of utility (and diminishing marginal utility) on demand and thus on market prices; (e) opportunity costs (recognizing that the costs that affect decisions are those that express the most important of the alternative opportunities being sacrificed in employing productive services for one purpose rather than for the sacrificed alternatives); (f) the time structure of consumption and production (expressing time preferences and the productivity of 'roundaboutness').

It seems appropriate, however, to comment further on this list. (1) With varying degrees of emphasis most modern microeconomics incorporates all these ideas, so that (2) this list supports the cited Morgenstern–Mises statement emphasizing the common ground shared by all schools of economic theory. However, (3) subsequent developments in the work of Mises and Hayek suggest that the list of six Austrian ideas was not really complete. While few Austrians at the time (of the early 1930s) were perhaps able to identify additional Austrian ideas, such additional insights were in fact implicit in the Austrian tradition and were to be articulated explicitly in later work. From this perspective, then, (4) important differences separate Austrian economic theory from the mainstream developments in microeconomics, particularly as the latter developments proceeded from the 1930s onwards. It was left for Mises and Hayek to articulate these differences and thus preserve a unique Austrian 'presence' in the profession.

LATER DEVELOPMENTS IN AUSTRIAN ECONOMICS

One early expression of such differences between the Austrian understanding of economic theory and that of other schools was Hans Mayer's paper criticizing 'functional price theories' and calling for the 'genetic-causal' method (Mayer 1932). Here Mayer was criticizing equilibrium theories of price that neglected to explicate the sequence of actions leading to market prices. To understand this sequence one must understand the causal genesis of the component actions in the sequence. In the light of the later writings of Mises and Hayek, it seems reasonable to recognize Mayer as having placed his finger on an important and distinctive element embedded in the Austrian understanding. Yet the Austrians themselves during the 1920s (and such students of their works as Lionel Robbins) seemed to have missed this insight. What appears to have helped Hayek and Mises articulate this hitherto overlooked element was the well-known inter-war debate concerning the possibility of economic calculation under central planning. A careful reading of the contributions to that debate suggests that it was in reaction to the 'mainstream' equilibrium arguments of their opponents that Mises and Hayek made explicit the emphasis on process, learning and discovery to be found in the Austrian understanding of markets (Lavoie 1985a).

Mises had argued that economic calculation calls for the guidance supplied by prices; since the centrally planned economy has no market for productive factors, it cannot use factor prices as guides. Oskar Lange and others countered that prices need not be market prices; that guidance could be provided by non-market prices, announced by the central authorities, and treated by socialist managers 'parametrically' (just as prices are treated by producers in the theory of the firm in perfectly competitive factor and product markets). It was in response to this argument that Hayek developed his interpretation of competitive market processes as processes of discovery during which dispersed information comes to be mobilized (Hayek 1949a: Chs 2, 4, 5, 7, 8, 9). An essentially similar characterization of the market process (without the Hayekian emphasis on the role of knowledge, but with an accent on entrepreneurial activity in a world of open-ended, radical uncertainty) was presented by Mises during the same period (Mises 1940, 1966). In the light of these Mises–Hayek developments in the theory of market process (and recognizing that these developments constituted the articulation of insights taken for granted in the early Austrian tradition: Kirzner 1985b; Jaffé 1976), it seems reasonable to add the following to Machlup's list of ideas central to the Austrian tradition; (g) markets (and competition) as processes of learning and discovery; (h) the individual decision as an act of choice in an essentially uncertain context (where the identification of the relevant alternatives is part of the decision itself). It is the latter ideas that have come to be developed in and made central to the revived attention to the Austrian tradition that, stemming from the work of Mises and Hayek, has emerged in the United States during the last decades.

AUSTRIAN ECONOMICS TODAY

As a result of these somewhat varied developments in the history of the Austrian School since 1930, the term Austrian economics has come to evoke a number of different connotations in contemporary professional discussion. Some of these connotations are, at least partly, overlapping; others are, at least partly, mutually inconsistent. It seems useful, in disentangling these various perceptions, to identify a number of different meanings that have come to be attached to the term 'Austrian economics' in the 1980s. The present status of the Austrian School of economics is, for better or worse, encapsulated in these current perceptions.

1. For many economists the term 'Austrian economics' is strictly a historical term. In this perception the existence of the Austrian School did not extend beyond the early 1930s: Austrian economics was partly absorbed into mainstream microeconomics, and partly displaced by emerging Keynesian macroeconomics. To a considerable extent this view seems to be that held by economists in Austria today. Economists (and other intellectuals) in Austria today are thoroughly cognizant of – and proud of – the earlier Austrian School, as evidenced by several commemorative conferences held in Austria in recent years, and by several related volumes (Hicks and Weber 1973; Leser 1986), but see themselves today simply as a part of the general community of professional economists. Erich Streissler, present holder of the chair occupied by Menger, Wieser and Mayer, has written extensively, and with the insights and scholarship of one profoundly influenced by the Austrian tradition, concerning numerous aspects of the Austrian School and its principal representatives (Streissler 1969, 1972, 1973, 1986).

2. For a number of economists the adjective 'Austrian' has come to mark a revival of interest in Böhm-Bawerkian capital-and-interest theory. This revival has emphasized particularly the time dimension in production and the productivity of roundaboutness. Among the contributors to this literature should be mentioned Hicks (1973), Bernholz (1971), Bernholz and Faber (1973), Faber (1979) and Orosel (1981). In this literature, then, the term 'Austrian' has very little to do with the general subjectivist Mengerian tradition (which, as noted earlier, had certain reservations with regard to the Böhm-Bawerkian theory).

3. For other economists (and non-economists) the term 'Austrian economics' has come to be associated less with a unique methodology, or with specific economic doctrines, as with libertarian ideology in political and social discussion. For these observers, to be an Austrian economist in the 1980s is simply to be in favour of free markets. Machlup (1982) has noted (and partly endorsed) this perception of the term 'Austrian'. He has ascribed it, particularly, to the impact of the work of Mises. Mises' championship of the market cause was so prominent, and his identification as an Austrian was at the same time so unmistakable, that it is perhaps natural that his strong policy pronouncements in support of unhampered markets

came to be perceived as the core of Austrianism in modern times. This has been reinforced by the work of a leading US follower of Mises, Murray N. Rothbard, who has also been prominent in libertarian scholarship and advocacy. Other observers, however, would question this identification. While, as earlier noted, many of the early contributions of the Austrian School were seen as sharply antagonistic to Marxian thought, the school on the whole maintained an apolitical stance (Myrdal 1954: 128). Among the founders of the school, Wieser was in fact explicit in endorsing the interventionist conclusions of the German Historical School (Wieser 1967: 490ff.). While both Mises and Hayek provocatively challenged the possibility of efficiency under socialism, they too emphasized the *wertfrei* character of their economics. Both writers would see their free market stance at the policy level as related to, but not central to, their Austrianism.

4. For many in the profession the term 'Austrian economics' has come, since about 1970, to refer to a revival of interest in the ideas of Carl Menger and the earlier Austrian School, particularly as these ideas have been developed through the work of Mises and Hayek. This revival has occurred particularly in the United States where a sizeable literature has emerged from a number of economists. This literature includes, in particular, works by Murray N. Rothbard (1962), Israel Kirzner (1973), Gerald P. O'Driscoll (1977), O'Driscoll and Mario J. Rizzo (1985) and Roger W. Garrison (1978, 1982, 1985). The thrust of this literature has been to emphasize the differences between the Austrian understanding of markets as processes and that of the equilibrium theorists whose work has dominated much of modern economic theory. As a result of this emphasis, this sense of the term 'Austrian economics' has often (and only partly accurately: see White 1984: 9) come to be understood as a refusal to adopt modern mathematical and econometric techniques – which standard economics adopted largely as a result of its equilibrium orientation. The economists in this group of modern Austrians (sometimes called neo-Austrian) do see themselves as continuators of an earlier tradition, sharing with mainstream neoclassical economics an appreciation for the systematic outcomes of markets, but differing from it in the understanding of how these outcomes are in fact achieved. Largely as a result of the activity of this group, many classic works of the early Austrians have recently been republished in original or translated form, and have attracted a considerable readership both inside and outside the profession.

5. Yet another current meaning loosely related to the preceding

sense has come to be associated with the term 'Austrian economics'. This meaning refers to an emphasis on the radical uncertainty that surrounds economic decision making, to an extent that implies virtual rejection of much of received microeconomics. Ludwig Lachmann (1976) has identified the work of G.L.S. Shackle as constituting in this regard the most consistent extension of Austrian (and especially of Misesian) subjectivism. Lachmann's own work (1973, 1977, 1986b) has stressed, in the same vein, the indeterminacy of both individual choices and market outcomes.

This line of thought has come to imply serious reservations concerning the possibility of systematic theoretical conclusions commanding significant degrees of generality. This connotation of the term 'Austrian economics' thus associates it with a stance sympathetic, to a degree, towards historical and institutional approaches. Given the prominent opposition of earlier Austrians to these approaches, this association, as might be expected, has been seen as ironic or even paradoxical by many observers (including, especially, modern exponents of the broader tradition of the Austrian School of economics).

Chapter 4

Carl Menger and the subjectivist tradition in economics

The republication of the facsimile edition of Menger's classic treatise presents a fitting opportunity to re-examine the nature of Menger's revolutionary contribution to economic understanding, and to re-evaluate it critically in the light of the mature insights discovered in the course of a century-long development of the Austrian tradition which Menger initiated. In the present commentary we shall focus on Menger's central 'vision', the new way in which he persuaded economists to 'see' the economic system as a whole. Menger himself, in the preface to the *Grundsätze* (1981 [1871]: x), pointed to his having placed 'alle Preiserscheinungen (somit auch den Kapitalzins, den Arbeitslohn, den Grundzins, u.s.f.) unter einem einheitlichen Gesichtspunkte zusammenfassenden Preistheorie'. We shall maintain that this 'point of view' reflects Menger's subjectivist vision of the system as a whole, a vision that forms the very core of his contribution.

In a now classic passage Hayek, probably the most famous twentieth-century representative of the Austrian tradition initiated by Menger, has drawn attention to the role of subjectivism in the development of economic thought. Writing at mid-century Hayek (1955: 31) suggested 'that every important advance in economic theory during the last hundred years was a further step in the consistent application of subjectivism'. We shall argue in these pages that, measured against this criterion, Menger's vision represented a major step forward in the history of economics – but one which, we can now recognize with hindsight, fell short of exploiting its own full potential. The same preface in which Menger referred to his unified point of view – the point of view expressing, as we shall see, Menger's subjectivist understanding of market forces – reveals Menger's conviction that he had discovered 'die Gesetzmässigkeit *der von dem menschlichen Willen gänzlich unabhängigen* Erscheinungen gelten, welche den Erfolg der wirthschaftlichen Thätigkeit der Menschen bedingen' (Menger 1981 [1871]: ix, emphasis added). Our interpretation of this conviction of Menger will illustrate the sense in which his own understanding of the economic system failed to appreciate later steps taken in the development of subjectivist economics – a development which was unquestionably initiated entirely and solely by Menger himself. Let us first set out what we believe Menger's central vision to be.

THE MENGERIAN VISION

In his highly critical introduction to the 1950 English translation of the *Grundsätze*, Frank Knight focused attention on what he believed to be the 'most serious defect in Menger's economic system' (Knight 1950: 25). This, Knight claimed, is Menger's 'view of production as a process of converting goods of higher order into goods of lower order'. Now, we do not at all agree that Knight has put his finger here on any defect in Menger; but we do believe that he has identified, in this view of production, the root insight that nourished Menger's understanding of the economic process.

For Menger the entire economic system is seen as a complex of activities directly or indirectly inspired by the goal of satisfying consumer needs. Every single item or service bought and sold in the market is valued only in so far as it can, in the purchaser's judgement, contribute valuably, directly or indirectly, towards the satisfaction of consumer needs. An act of production, in the Mengerian view, is an act which brings such valued items or services closer to the fulfilment of this ultimate goal of satisfying consumer needs – it is an act of 'converting goods of higher order into goods of lower order'. No act of production, by definition, can fail to result in goods of 'lower order' than those utilized in that act of production.

With this teleological perspective Menger, in a revolutionary manner, was liberating economics from the strictly physical view of production which had dominated classical economics. In that view production could easily be discussed as if its output had its own economic significance, quite independently of its designed function in the ultimate promotion of consumer satisfaction. Knight objected to Menger's view of production that 'in the technical production process, the typical relation is the use of both iron and coal to produce both iron and coal' (Knight 1950: 25). Exactly. For the non-Mengerian view the typical process of production does not, in any necessarily obvious way, reveal itself as bringing us nearer the satisfaction of ultimate consumer needs. Menger recognized that we must refine our vision of each act of production to see how it fits into an overall, unified process of deploying given nature-endowed resources, in a systematic fashion, towards the satisfaction of consumer needs. All the phenomena of the market, Menger saw, can be understood from this perspective. All 'Preiserscheinungen (somit auch den Kapitalzins, den Arbeitslohn, den Grundzins . . .)' fall into place, from this perspective, as expressive of the acts of valuation generated by and concurrent with the opportunities for, and acts of, production. It is this one, unified point of view which illuminates all these phenomena, explaining them all as the systematic reflection, direct and indirect, of consumer needs, as they impinge on the given complex of society's resources.

For Menger, therefore, production is not simply a physical process in which the combining of inputs results in desired outputs; rather it is a process in which the importance of needed valuable prospective outputs – ultimate outputs needed for their own sakes – imposes itself upon, and enforces the appropriate deployment of, available given resources, no matter how remote these resources may be from the finally desired output. The web of market transactions is not so much one which, in Walrasian terms, permits a complex of interdependent intertwined acts of exchange and of production coherently to be consummated. Rather that web of transactions is seen as the network of forces through which the various relative strengths of different consumer needs exercise their power over the discovery and deployment of relevant goods of highest order and their systematic conversion in patterns leading ultimately to the provision of the goods of lowest order.

To be sure, we find iron and coal used in production processes yielding iron and coal. Menger would see nothing at all strange in this. But he would point out the superficiality of the view which fails to recognize the difference between the two sets of iron and coal – between means and ends (including intermediate ends!). At least part of the produced iron and coal must be designed for utilization in further steps of production (other than the generation of iron and coal). And as for that portion of produced iron and coal destined for use in yet further processes of iron and coal production, at least part of *its* iron and coal output must be designed to be used in further steps of production (other than the generation of iron and coal). What inspires the production of iron and coal cannot be *solely* the goal of commanding inputs for the production of additional iron and coal *ad infinitum.* What inspires the production of producing iron and coal, what confers economic significance – Mengerian economic *value* – upon any input unit of iron or coal, is the degree of importance associated with ultimate consumer needs directly or indirectly dependent upon that unit. For Menger an act of production cannot be understood except in teleological terms – as an act of deploying means towards ultimate, or at least intermediate ends.

THE SUBJECTIVISM OF MENGER'S VISION

There is no doubt that Menger's vision constituted one of those steps in the application of subjectivism of which Hayek wrote. Every textbook in the history of economic thought recognizes Menger as the founder of Austrian subjectivism. But we wish to draw attention to a subjectivist element in Menger's contribution which is not always appreciated.

Standard accounts of the early years of Austrian economics focus on the discovery of the principle of diminishing marginal utility and on the Austrian marginal utility theory of value.[1] Important though these aspects of Menger's work certainly were, however, it seems to us that they do not go to the heart of Menger's subjectivist perspective. For us, Menger's subjectivism reveals itself in his vision of the entire economic system – every single act of production and every transaction of exchange – as inspired by the deliberate attempts of economizing individuals to promote, in the light of their own knowledge and understanding, the satisfaction of ultimate consumer needs. This perspective transmutes all the phenomena of the economy from being simply physical transformations, relationships or ratios into direct or indirect expressions of human valuations, preferences, expectations and dreams. This subjectivist perspective of Menger extends far beyond an understanding of diminishing marginal significance and its implications, and far beyond the narrow confines of the utility-based theory of value. This perspective suffuses the Austrian understanding of every single facet of the economy.

It is widely recognized that Menger's vision included – already in 1871 – the ideas essential for a marginal productivity understanding of factor prices and of the theory of functional income distribution. Where the other pioneers of the marginal utility revolution confined their early insights to the theory of product price (with two decades to elapse before the extension to the theory of factor price), Menger presented his understanding of the principles of factor pricing in the same 1871 work in which he offered his theory of product price. For Menger the marginal productivity theory of factor value is not an *extension* of the marginal utility theory of product price, but part of the very same, seamless whole. The very same vision which saw product price as the expression of the marginal valuations of consumers saw factor prices as the indirect expression of those very same valuations. Although Knight at one point belittles Menger's theory of distribution ('We find in Menger barely the germ of a theory . . . of distribution . . .' (Knight 1950: 23)), he does recognize that 'the "marginal utility" doctrine, with its application to indirect and complementary goods, "logically" covers all there is to say about distribution theory' (p. 15). The truth surely is that Menger's central insight is precisely this, that distribution theory is to be seen as simply an implication of the marginal utility theory of consumer goods prices. Marginal utility value theory is not the pinnacle of Menger's subjectivist achievement, but its foundation.

THE INCOMPLETENESS OF MENGER'S SUBJECTIVISM – THE ADVANTAGE OF HINDSIGHT

Revolutionary though Menger's subjectivist vision of the economic system undoubtedly was, we can now see its limitations very clearly. The consistent development of Austrian economics since 1871 permits us to identify the key weaknesses in the *Grundsätze*. Somewhat paradoxically, these weaknesses turn out to be inadequacies in Menger's subjectivism. The subjectivist perspective which Menger's disciples learned from their master has enabled them to pursue a line of discussion and to grasp insights which eluded the master himself.

As was the case in our discussion of the positive features of the subjectivism of Menger's contribution, our assessment of the limitations of that subjectivism will differ from the conventional wisdom concerning Menger. The standard accounts of the development of subjectivist insights following Menger focus principally on the inadequacies of Menger's theory of needs. While not disagreeing on the unfortunate (and non-subjectivist) character of Menger's theory of needs, we shall emphasize a different set of limitations surrounding the subjectivism of his vision.

As is well known, Menger's utility theory took as its point of departure the existence of a set of individual needs, for each consumer, which seem disturbingly objective and concrete. It is as if the physiological and psychological make-up of the individual generates definite requirements with definite degrees of urgency – quite apart from any choices made freely by that individual. What is emphasized in Menger is not freely exercised preferences, purposes spontaneously and independently pursued, but rather the inevitable adjustment of economic behaviour to meet the requirements imposed by these given sets of individual needs.[2] One begins to understand Menger's reference to 'die Gesetzmässigkeit der von dem menschlichen Willen gänzlich unabhängigen Erscheinungen gelten. . .'. It is as if these given sets of individual needs exercise their own force upon the system, constraining the allocation of resources and determining economic values, entirely without as it were the intermediation of the human will. Commentators have justifiably seen this view as somewhat primitive, at least as judged from the perspective of the more developed and sophisticated subjectivism of the later Austrians. We wish to draw attention to a different sense in which we must point out the inadequacy of Menger's subjectivism. It turns out that this inadequacy is to be found precisely in that overall vision of the economic system which we noted for the revolutionary subjectivist nature of its understanding of the system. It will be helpful for us to recall, by way of introduction, a fascinating little episode involving Hayek's sharp criticism of a position taken by Joseph Schumpeter.

At the end of his celebrated 1945 paper 'The use of knowledge in society' Hayek referred to a passage, in *Capitalism, Socialism and Democracy* (1950), in which Schumpeter belittled the problem of economic calculation under a centrally planned system. Mises had argued that, in the absence of markets for factors of production, socialist planners would have no indexes of the relative social importance of the various resources and would hence be unable to plan rationally. Schumpeter maintained that economic rationality can none the less be attained in a planned society. For the theorist, Schumpeter argued, 'this follows from the elementary proposition that consumers in evaluating ("demanding") consumers' goods *ipso facto* also evaluate the means of production which enter into the production of those goods' (Schumpeter 1950: 175). Hayek found this pronouncement 'startling'. Only for a single mind to which would be simultaneously known not only 'the valuation of the consumers' goods but also . . . the conditions of supply of the various factors of production' (Hayek 1949b: 90) would it be valid to claim that consumers' valuations logically imply corresponding evaluations of the productive services. Schumpeter, Hayek charged, has fallen victim to an approach which 'habitually disregards . . . the unavoidable imperfection of man's knowledge and the consequent need for a process by which knowledge is constantly communicated and acquired' (p. 91).

Clearly what Hayek found wanting in Schumpeter was an appreciation for the market process through which the scattered information, concerning resource availabilities and consumer valuations, is mobilized and brought to bear upon the decisions governing production and the allocation of resources. What needs to be introduced into Schumpeter's vision of the economic system is recognition of the role of entrepreneurial alertness and imagination, in inspiring and driving this market process of knowledge mobilization – in the face of the stark uncertainties of an unknown future. It was Schumpeter's failure – towering pioneer though he was in understanding the entrepreneurial role – to grasp the subjective dimension of this market process which led him to believe that consumers' valuations automatically translate into valuations of productive factors (Kirzner 1979a: Ch. 4, especially pp. 68f.).

This lapse in Schumpeter's subjectivism, we wish to submit, parallels precisely a corresponding lapse in Menger's subjectivism. The Schumpeterian vision of consumer valuations automatically generating valuations of productive factors is identical, we shall see, with Menger's vision in which consumers' needs generate results that are 'von dem menschlichen Willen gänzlich unabhängig. . .'. Precisely that vision in which Menger saw how the economic system transmits consumer judgements of economic significance to the arrays of goods of higher order is, we wish to suggest from the perspective of modern subjectivism, flawed in failing to recognize the entrepreneurial steps – taken imaginatively, daringly and spontaneously, in the face of the impenetrable fog of the uncertain future – through which these judgements must necessarily be transmitted. These entrepreneurial steps represent the imagination and vision of the entrepreneurs peering into the unknown. Any claim to the effect that consumers' preferences dictate the allocation of resources can have validity only to the extent that these preferences are sensed and transmitted by market entrepreneurs. Menger's recognition of the way in which market phenomena reflect the active imprint of consumer valuations (rather than the passive constraints of the physical environment) was indeed a pioneering step in the

development of subjectivist economics. This recognition would
eventually point the way to an understanding that this imprint (in so
far as it relates to the markets for higher order goods and the decisions
through which they are allocated) is achieved through human actions
expressing the alertness and the expectations of the entrepreneurs.
But this complete subjectivist understanding, we argue, escaped
Menger. For him, we submit, it was indeed as if the economic regularities that link consumer preferences to relevant shifts in the allocation of resources operate automatically and mechanically. In this
fundamental respect Menger's subjectivism must, from the perspective afforded by a century's hindsight, be judged incomplete. Let us
look more closely at Menger's overall vision.

MENGER AND THE ASSUMPTION OF PERFECT KNOWLEDGE

We have cited several times Menger's reference in his preface to
economic laws as being independent of the human will. This theme is
raised again by Menger in the body of his book, especially in the
context of his theory of price. In explaining the formation of price in a
monopolized market, for example, Menger concludes: 'Fassen wir
das in diesem Abschnitte Gesagte zusammen, so ergibt sich, dass . . .
die hiebei zu Tage tretenden ökonomischen Erscheinungen demnach
durchaus keinen zufälligen, sondern einen streng gesetzmässigen
Charakter haben . . . es bieten uns somit die Erscheinungen des
Monopolhandels in jeder Beziehung das Bild strenger Gesetzmässigkeit.' He then adds the following intriguing afterthought: 'Irrthum
und mangelhafte Erkenntniss können wohl auch hier Abweichungen
zu Tage förden, es sind dies indess dann pathologische Erscheinungen der Volkswirthschaft, welche ebensowenig gegen die Gesetze
der Volkswirthschaftslehre beweisen, als die Erscheinungen am
kranken Körper gegen die Gesetze der Physiologie' (Menger 1981
[1871]: 200. Clearly Menger confined the scope of economic law to
the range of human activity unaffected by error and imperfect knowledge. A careful examination of his entire Chapter 5, on the theory of
price, confirms that for Menger the inescapable laws which, given
consumer valuations, determine prices are deduced strictly on the
assumption that each economizing individual is in fact fully aware of
the circumstances relevant to his decisions.

We have here then a clear statement of an important feature of
Menger's economics. For Menger what economic theory explains is

the determination of 'economic prices', the prices that would emerge under conditions free of the 'pathological' influence of error and imperfect knowledge. In his 1883 *Untersuchungen* Menger elaborated on this theme: 'Dass . . . die *realen* Preise von den *ökonomischen* (den der ökonomischen Sachlage entsprechenden) demnach der Regel nach mehr oder minder abweichen, bedarf kaum der Bemerkung' (Menger 1985 [1883]: 56). Menger attributed this discrepancy to various considerations, especially to vagueness and error on the part of market participants concerning what they want and how to achieve their goals, and to incomplete knowledge concerning the economic situation.

It is clear, then, that the economic laws, operating independently of human will, which Menger saw as governing all market phenomena pertain, strictly speaking, only to a world of omniscient economizing individuals. The Mengerian vision which sees the values of the services of land, labour and capital as being but 'die nothwendige Consequenz ihres ökonomischen Charakters' (Menger 1981 [1871]: 143) proceeds by presuming that the economic system indeed permits actual prices to approximate the true economic prices. 'Die Preise der obigen Güter (die Bodenrente und der Capitalzins) sind demnach das nothwendige Product der ökonomischen Sachlage, unter welcher sie enstehen *und werden dieselben um so sicherer entrichtet, je ausgebildeter der Rechtszustand eines Volkes und je geläuterter dessen öffentliche Moral ist*' (pp. 143–4, emphasis added).

What Menger clearly believes (although he does not appear to present an argument to support this belief, nor even to articulate it explicitly) is that the assumptions required for the emergence of economic prices are sufficiently reasonable to permit us to conclude that the understanding of the laws of economics provides an understanding of the real world. Although Menger, more perhaps than any other economist of his time, refers again and again to the effects of error and uncertainty, none the less he seems prepared to assume them away in arriving at his overall understanding of the economic system (Kirzner 1979a: Ch. 4).

All this is not a serious flaw, perhaps, in Menger's theory of prices, understood as an abstract system. While it certainly seems highly desirable to have an understanding of the dynamic market process through which prices emerge, there is certainly also scope for the (separate) theory of the factors governing the position towards which these prices may be gravitating. There is room for both a theory of the equilibrating process and the theory of equilibrium itself. There is a legitimate place for enquiry as to what would be implied by perfect knowledge.

But when the perfect knowledge assumption is transferred (as Menger's overall vision of the economic system apparently requires it to be transferred) to the proposition that consumer valuations are in fact substantially transmitted to the markets for the services of land, labour and capital, we have reason to be worried. For we now, over a century later, understand that if such transmittal indeed occurs, it can only be as the result of the competitive pressures exerted by alert entrepreneurs. Nowhere does Menger display awareness of the need to introduce the operation of these competitive-entrepreneurial pressures. Nowhere does he display appreciation for the circumstance that such pressures cannot be understood as mechanical or automatic, but must be understood as made up of the spontaneous discoveries of alert human beings. Nowhere, in brief, does Menger display a sensitivity to this dimension of the subjectivism upon which market forces in fact depend.

The situation is, in one sense, even worse than merely a lack of awareness by Menger of the scope for subjectivism in understanding the maket process through which relative consumer preferences are transmitted throughout the system. When Menger refers to error and imperfect knowledge as 'pathological' phenomena, he portrays a most unfortunate (if widely shared) understanding of the operation of markets. The truth, however, is surely that it is *only* through entre- preneurial incentives (for winning pure profit) *created by error* that we can hope to attain any approximation at all to that state of omniscience which Menger treats as normal for a healthy body economic. Appreciation for the possibility that subjectively based errors may drive a wedge between real prices and economic prices does not begin to equal a recognition that such subjectively based errors are in fact to be seen positively as *stepping stones* towards any real world relevance for these economic prices – and for the overall Mengerian vision which they make possible. Having recognized this incompleteness in Menger's subjectivism, let us now return to appreciate certain often overlooked features of those major steps towards subjectivism which Menger's vision so daringly represented.

A METHODOLOGICAL DIGRESSION – THE ESSENTIALISM OF MENGER

Professor Hutchison has drawn attention to a much neglected methodological feature of Menger's contribution. Menger, he explains, 'insisted that what the economist is after is not only relationships between quantities (*Grössenverhältnisse*) but the essence (*das Wesen*) of economic phenomena: "How can we attain" he asks Walras [in an 1884] letter, "to a knowledge of this essence, for example, the essence of value, the essence of land rent, the essence of bi-metallism &c by mathematics?" ' (Hutchison 1953: 148).

Emil Kauder, too, appreciated Menger's methodological essentialism. 'Menger claimed that the subjects of science are not the constructions of our mind but are rather the social essences. Essence means the reality underlying a phenomenon' (Kauder 1965: 97). Kauder took note of the Aristotelian character of Menger's approach: 'Menger's theory deals with the Aristotelian essences, with exact types, and typical relations. . . . Like his Greek master, Menger searched for a reality hidden behind the observable surface of things. This X-ray technique of investigation is far removed from the way in which Walras, Jevons, and their followers worked' (pp. 97–8). Most recently Uskali Mäki has intensively explored the epistemological character of Menger's essentialism (see especially Mäki 1990). Our present purpose is the modest one of reminding ourselves of this feature of Menger's work, and of pointing out its relationship to the subjectivist tradition he pioneered in Austrian economics. Once again a critical comment by Frank Knight alerts us to what is going on.

Knight refers disparagingly to Menger's treatment both of demand theory and of cost and supply theory. In particular he deplores what he believes to be the neglect (by Menger especially, but to some extent also by the other leading economic theorists of his time) of the *interrelationships* between demand and supply. Knight describes some observations by Menger on the impact of marginal utility on production cost expenditure as lame, and 'a far cry from recognition of the true relations of mutual determination between these variables' (Knight 1950: 23). For Knight the 'comparative roles of (relative) utility and (relative) cost in determining price depend on the comparative elasticities of demand and supply' (fn.; see also Knight 1931). Menger presents no such a theory, and is therefore seen by Knight as having only a crude understanding of the theory of price determination. I think it is fair to say that this Knightian criticism expresses an unarticulated, perhaps unperceived – but none the less highly important – difference between Knight's own understanding of what a theory of price is supposed to explain and Menger's understanding of that same task. It will be helpful to refer to a somewhat similar disagreement between Böhm-Bawerk and Irving Fisher concerning the task of providing a theory of interest.

Irving Fisher cites Böhm-Bawerk as having postulated '*two* questions involved in the theory of the rate of interest, viz. (1) why any rate of interest exists and (2) how the rate of interest is determined' (Fisher 1930: 13f.; see also p. 474). Fisher argued that there is only one question 'since to explain how the rate of interest is determined involves the question of whether the rate can or cannot be zero'. Fisher sees no point in any separate explanation for the *existence* of the phenomenon of interest. Böhm-Bawerk, on the other hand, was most vigorous in maintaining the distinction which Fisher wished to deny. Böhm-Bawerk distinguished, specifically, between 'originating forces' and 'determining forces'. An explanation for the origin of interest may be sought separately from an explanation for the interest *rate*. Böhm-Bawerk employed an illuminating analogy to drive his point home. 'When we inquire into the causes of a flood we certainly cannot cite the dams and reservoirs built to prevent or at least mitigate inundations. But they are a determining factor for the actual water-mark of the flood' (Böhm-Bawerk 1959: vol. III, 192). In the same way, we are to understand, an enumeration of all the interest-rate-determining forces would be misleading as an explanation for the phenomenon of interest. It seems very clear that the difference between Fisher's understanding of the task of a theory of interest and that of Böhm-Bawerk parallels most faithfully the difference we are discussing between a Mengerian and a Knightian theory of price.

If we have identified all the factors which jointly determine the rate of interest, we have, for Fisher, provided a theory of interest. We know, in principle, what is responsible for the particular rates of interest we observe. No other task (such as explaining why the phenomenon of interest is to be found) calls for our attention (since our theory will have explained why the rate of interest is what it is).

Quite similarly for Knight what is being sought in the theory of price is a complete identification of those factors which in fact determine price. If we know the demand curve and the supply curve, we have identified the forces which, through the mutual determination of the relevant variables, establish the equilibrium price. And, unless we have completely identified these variables and the way in which they determine each other (for equilibrium to prevail), we have not fulfilled our responsibilities as price theorists. For Knight a theory of price is not a theory to account for the phenomenon of market value, but a theory to explain, in principle, why any particular price is what it is. Of course Knight's understanding of the task for price theory is very much the view which pervades neoclassical economics. Fisher's view on the task of a theory of interest was merely part of this general neoclassical outlook on the function of price theory. Yet, once we grasp Menger's essentialist perspective, it appears clear that Menger's view was quite different.

For Menger, it appears, the prime responsibility of a theorist explaining prices is not that of identifying the forces, and the relative strengths of these forces, which are jointly responsible for the level of prices. Rather the theorist, in his search for the essence of price, is looking for the root causes which are responsible for the phenomenon of price. Menger would presumably not deny the truth of Knight's often repeated contention (in criticism of the Austrian theory of value) that in the long run the relative prices of beaver and deer cannot (whatever their relative utilities) systematically differ from the ratio of physical inputs respectively needed to acquire them. But he would still have maintained that prices do not arise because of needed inputs, but because consumers' needs for these goods impel them to offer other goods in exchange. The number of pounds of deer flesh paid as the price of beaver does not *essentially* express the relative difficulty of their capture (even if this price cannot indefinitely diverge from that ratio). Rather, the essential reality underlying this price phenomenon is that it expresses the intensity of the need felt for beaver (relative to the intensity of the need felt for deer). The essence of a price is that it expresses the intensity of consumer needs. All kinds of circumstances, including especially the physical circumstances surrounding supply possibilities, will help determine the particular volume of goods which a consumer will feel constrained to offer as the price of the good he wishes to buy. But if the focus of our theoretical interest is (as the essentialist would maintain) to account for the phenomenon of price (rather than for its level) then once we have identified the root cause for this phenomenon (and explained how this root cause impinges on the environment in which production and exchange take place), we will have fulfilled our task.[3] From this perspective the explanations given in Menger's Chapter 5 on the theory of price, in which he explains the limits within which the actual level of prices is determined, must not be misunderstood. What Menger is showing in this chapter is not so much what determines the level of prices but how the level of prices expresses in fact the root cause (i.e. the intensity of consumer need) of prices. What from Knight's perspective must indeed have appeared as not much better than a valiant but crude pioneering effort towards a complete explanation for the determination of prices appears quite differently when seen from the perspective of the rather different essentialist agenda.

That Böhm-Bawerk, as we have seen, appears to have shared in Menger's understanding of the theorist's task is surely significant. A distinct, entirely valid, task of a theory of interest is to identify its essence, the underlying reality causing the phenomenon to come into existence. This task is to be distinguished from that of accounting for the height of interest rates. The root underlying cause for a flood is not to be looked for in the existence of dykes, important though dykes may certainly be in the determination of the water level. That Böhm-Bawerk (quite unselfconsciously) shared Menger's perspective in this regard seems to suggest that this perspective has something to do with the subjectivist perspective which these founders of the Austrian tradition shared.

We have argued earlier in this comment that the key contribution of Menger, and the kernel of his subjectivism, lay not in his theory of marginal utility but in his revolutionary vision of the economy. In that vision Menger saw the entire system as a complex of activities directly or indirectly inspired by the goal of satisfying consumer needs. Of course this complex of activities occurs against the background of the relevant resource constraints and technological possibilities, but that background remains – background. To be sure the concrete activities will reflect the specific character of that background, but the essential nature of these activities remains that of serving consumer desires. In one physical environment consumer need for bread may generate a labour-intensive mode of agriculture; in another environment that same need may be responsible for a land-intensive mode of agriculture. For Menger the essence of both agricultural regimes is their being inspired by (and explained by) consumer needs for bread. The specific price of bread in any set of production constraints will certainly depend, in a functional sense, upon the specifics of those constraints. But the 'underlying reality' accounting for the phenomenon of bread prices is, for the Mengerian view, to be seen in the consumer needs which they express.

That such an essentialist understanding of the task of economic theory is so strange to modern ears is a measure, surely, of the distance which modern economics has moved away from Menger's subjectivism. It was the subjectivism of Menger's vision of the economy which shaped his understanding of the goal of price theory. It was that subjectivism, surely, which shaped Böhm-Bawerk's understanding of the goal of a theory of interest. From this vantage point the contemporary rediscovery of Menger's essentialism seems to offer scope for renewed appreciation of the subjectivism of Menger's vision.

MENGER – THE SUBJECTIVIST PIONEER

We have seen (a) that Menger's core contribution was the subjectivism of his vision of the economy and (b) that this subjectivism is bound up with Menger's essentialist agenda for economic theory. We have also taken note of the incompleteness of Menger's subjectivism. We conclude by pointing out briefly how Menger's contribution was the pioneering step in an Austrian tradition which substantially completed the subjectivist perspective which Menger initiated.

Menger's *Grundsätze* served, of course, as the foundation for the Austrian School that is recognized in the history of economic thought. When Hayek wrote his 1934 introduction to Menger's *Collected Works*, he could say, after referring to Menger's 'brilliant followers, Eugen von Böhm-Bawerk and Friedrich von Wieser', that 'it is not unduly to detract from the merits of these writers to say that [the Austrian School's] fundamental ideas belong fully and wholly to Carl Menger' (Hayek 1981: 12). At the time that Hayek wrote these words the state of Austrian economics was somewhat stagnant and self-satisfied. Its principal protagonists believed (with much validity) that not very much beyond style of exposition separated the substance of Austrian economics from that of other schools of economic theory; that the insights of Austrian theory had been successfully absorbed into economics generally. Yet certain features of Menger's sub-jectivism, set forth in his *Grundsätze*, were pointing the Austrian tradition in a direction sharply diverging from mainstream neo-classicism.

It was undoubtedly Menger's teachings which inspired Ludwig von Mises and Friedrich Hayek in their long and arduous journey of articulating the Austrian vision systematically in non-equilibrium terms – in terms which emphasize the subjectivism of ignorance and discovery, of entrepreneurship and dynamic competition. This long journey began with Mises' 1920 critique of the possibilities for rational economic calculation in the centralized economy (Mises 1920). It proceeded via the brilliant papers of the 1930s and 1940s, published in the course of the ensuing debate, in which Hayek unravelled the subtle roles of dispersed knowledge and dynamic competition.[4] And that journey led to Mises' most complete formulation of the Austrian subjectivist view, in his 1949 *Human Action* (Mises 1966). By the end of this journey the Austrians had travelled far indeed from the contemporary mainstream. An appreciation for the profound vision which the Mises–Hayek formulations presented must surely proceed through appreciation for the subjectivism and the essentialism which shine through Carl Menger's *Grundsätze der Volkswirtschaftslehre*.

Chapter 5

Menger, classical liberalism and the Austrian School of economics

A series of valuable recent papers has reflected increasing current interest in the political and ideological stance of the founding economists of the Austrian School. What is particularly intriguing about this literature is that it offers what appears, at least superficially, to be a set of sharply differing readings and assessments of this politico-ideological stance. Especially with regard to Carl Menger, we are offered apparently contradictory assessments. He was a champion of *laissez-faire*; he favoured substantial state economic intervention; he had no clearly defined and articulated political position at all – each of these views of Menger and the early Austrians is to be found expressed somewhere in the literature. Each of these views is supported by citations from the early Austrians. The purpose of the present chapter is to reconcile the apparent inconsistencies presented in these earlier papers.

Our conclusions will be (a) that the early Austrians, especially Menger, occupied a position which recognized both the efficacy of markets and scope for useful governmental economic intervention; (b) that this half-full, half-empty position was not articulated in any deliberate, integrated fashion, so that individual remarks can be cited that might suggest more extreme positions than the one in fact occupied; (c) that this half-full, half-empty position none the less expressed an understanding of markets which, *taken by itself*, strongly suggested a more radical appreciation for free markets than the early Austrians themselves in fact displayed. It is the latter circumstance, we surmise, which explains how, when later Austrians arrived at even more consistently *laissez-faire* positions, they were seen by historians of thought as somehow simply pursuing an Austrian tradition that can be traced back to the founders.

As must be apparent, the development of this thesis, while at first

glance in conflict with the various contributions to the current literature on this topic, in fact differs from them only in matters of
emphasis. Indeed the present chapter contains very little that is new:
it draws most of its ideas from the existing literature, merely weaving
these ideas into what makes up, we wish to maintain, a more acceptable, integrated story. Writers have pointed out that the cup was not
full; writers have pointed out that the cup was not empty; writers
have even pointed out that the cup was half-full and half-empty. We
will not merely confirm the half-full, half-empty reading but help
explain, perhaps, why the cup could seem quite full to some observers
while appearing quite empty to others.

MENGER, THE AUSTRIANS, AND *LAISSEZ-FAIRE:* SOME PARADOXES

Stephan Boehm has drawn our attention to one strand of the conventional wisdom with regard to the Austrian School from the time of
Menger onwards, namely the identification of the Austrians as
'rigorous defenders of *laissez-faire* and outspoken apologists of the
capitalist system' (Boehm 1985: 249). Against this traditional view of
the Austrians Boehm marshals powerful evidence from Menger's
own writings: 'Menger presents a list of five legitimate tasks ascribed
to the state, respectively ''improvement of the situation of the working
class, just distribution of income, encouragement of individual
ability, thrift and entrepreneurial initiative'' ' (p. 250, citing Menger
1891). If this (ambitious!) list of governmental responsibilities were
not sufficiently impressive, Boehm cites both Menger and Böhm-
Bawerk as emphatically, even vehemently, rejecting charges that they
followed a *laissez-faire*, 'Manchester' approach to social policy.
Menger, Boehm cites, maintained explicitly that 'nothing could be
more opposed to his school than to vindicate the capitalist system. In
fact, the only thing that he appreciated in Schmoller was his passionate
concern for the poor and weak.'[1]

Yet the view that the Austrian economists were indeed uncompromising advocates of *laissez-faire* – and certainly the view that they were
perceived as such – cannot be summarily dismissed. Erich Streissler,
particularly in his recent work, has drawn our attention to newly
available material supporting this view of Menger. As is well known,
Menger spent several years as tutor to Crown Prince Rudolph of
Austria. Rudolph was required to prepare essays setting forth the
lectures he had heard from Menger. These lecture notes, with

corrections by Menger, have recently been rediscovered by Brigitte Hamann, who provided typewritten copies to Streissler. From these essays Streissler has concluded that Menger taught Rudolph 'a liberalism possibly even more rigorous than that of Adam Smith. In "normal" cases economic action of the state is always harmful: it is only to be allowed in "abnormal" cases.'[2]

Perhaps even more persuasive, with regard to the perception of the Austrian School as champions of non-interventionism, are the personal reminiscences of Ludwig von Mises. Mises studied at the University of Vienna in the very early years of this century, and he became one of Böhm-Bawerk's best-known disciples. His name is invariably cited as a prominent participant in Böhm-Bawerk's famous seminar at the University. There can be little doubt that Mises was thoroughly familiar with the political stance of the members of the Austrian School, Although he did not study under Menger, he could not but have been aware of what Menger's political views were understood to be. For Mises there seems to have been not a shadow of doubt that the Austrians saw themselves (and were seen by their contemporaries) as vindicating not merely an abstract science of economics (against historicist challenges), but also at the same time the effectiveness of the market economy (against its socialist and statist detractors).

In a chapter entitled 'The political aspects of the *Methodenstreit*' Mises describes the alliance between Schmoller and his Historical School, and the Bismarckian policies in Prussia which 'began to inaugurate its Sozialpolitik, the system of interventionist measures such as labor legislation, social security, pro-union attitudes, progressive taxation, protective tariffs, cartels, and dumping' (Mises 1969: 30). It is true that Mises recognized that when 'Menger, Böhm-Bawerk and Wieser began their scientific careers, they were not concerned with the problems of economic policies and with the rejection of interventionism by Classical economics. They considered it as their vocation to put economic theory on a sound basis and they were ready to dedicate themselves entirely to this cause' (p. 18). But this passage is followed by the flat assertion that 'Menger heartily disapproved of the interventionist policies that the Austrian Government . . . had adopted'. A sceptic might be tempted to wonder if Mises (writing in 1969) was not perhaps independently reading into his teachers' attitudes the *laissez-faire* stance which he himself came to adopt in his own career. But a fair-minded reader of Mises' many references to the political implications of the *Methodenstreit* will find it difficult to avoid concluding that Mises is simply expressing the generally held perception of the Austrians as being strongly opposed to the statist intervention espoused by the Historical School.

And yet, as cited by Boehm (1985: 248) we find Gunnar Myrdal describing the Austrians as being the rare nineteenth-century economists who did not inject political motives into their economics: 'In Austria, economics has never had direct political aims' (Myrdal 1954: 128). Apparently Myrdal's reading of Austrian economics found it neither tendentiously interventionist nor seeking to promote *laissez-faire*.

To round out our sketch of perceptions of the Austrian School's political stance (or lack of such) we must refer to a most explicit statement by Nikolai Bukharin, the eminent Marxist theorist and economic scholar, who spent time as a participant in Böhm-Bawerk's seminar and wrote a book-length, trenchantly Marxist critique of Austrian economic theory. In his preface to the Russian edition of this book Bukharin refers to his having chosen to attack the Austrian School (rather than other schools of modern economics): 'Our selection of an opponent for our criticism probably does not require discussion, for it is well known that the most powerful opponent of Marxism is the Austrian School' (1972: 9). Of course, to be a power-ful opponent of Marxism is not yet to be a champion of *laissez-faire*. Yet it seems clear that the Austrians were seen as providing a strong intellectual defence of capitalism.[3] Nothing in their writings, it appears, could suggest any principled reasons for doubting the effectiveness of capitalist institutions in promoting human economic welfare.

This, then, is the situation in which we find ourselves. Evidence apparently exists to support the view that the Austrians were pro-ponents of *laissez-faire*, the view that they were sympathetic to inter-ventionism, and the view that they were unconcerned with the political implications of their doctrines. Let us consider independ-ently, quite apart from any of the cited evidence, what one might *expect* to conclude, in terms of political implications, from the economic theory of the Austrian School, especially in its initial, Mengerian incarnation.

MENGER AND THE MARGINAL UTILITY REVOLUTION

A certain ambiguity has come to surround the question of the degree to which Menger's *Grundsätze* represented a revolutionary, pioneering contribution to the economics of his time. The traditional view among historians of thought has seen Menger's work as one of the three basic contributions to the 'marginal utility revolution' (besides being a manifesto upholding the theoretical method in economics, in opposition to the historical method that had become entrenched in German economics). From this traditional reading of Menger, his book was a frontal, pioneering, revolutionary attack on classical orthodoxy. Yet at the same time Menger's book, and especially its preface, freely acknowledged profound indebtedness to earlier writers, particularly to the 'foundation laid by previous work that was produced almost entirely by the industry of German scholars' (Menger 1981: 49). Indeed Streissler has in recent work (1990) drawn attention to a mid-nineteenth-century German 'protoneoclassical' tradition in which Menger's work should be recognized as a contribution offering continuity of forward development, rather than providing any revolutionary departure. Although Menger emphasized themes central to the marginal utility revolution, Streissler argues, Menger saw himself as a reformer rather than a revolutionary.

Yet this ambiguity concerning possible links between Menger's *Principles* and this German 'protoneoclassical' tradition must surely relate strictly to specific features of Menger's system, especially his subjective theory of value. There seems little doubt concerning Menger's awareness that he was offering, in his *Principles*, a perspective on the economic system which was entirely new. Menger's emphasis, in his preface, on the need to balance 'careful attention to past work in all the fields of our science thus far explored' against criticism, 'with full independence of judgement, [of] the opinions of our predecessors, and even [of] doctrines until now considered definitive attainments of our science', (1981: 46) suggests his very clear sense of breaking sharply with the past. Hayek has told us that Menger is said to have 'remarked that he wrote the *Grundsätze* in a state of morbid excitement' (Hayek 1981: 16). It seems reasonable to attribute this excitement to Menger's conviction that he was writing a path-breaking book.

Menger's acknowledgement of debt to German scholars and his dedication of his book to Wilhelm Roscher, the famous leader of the (older) German Historical School, should not be misunderstood. These references are surely to be understood, not as reflecting any failure to perceive the novelty of his own work, but as expressing his meticulous sense of propriety towards earlier scholars whose contributions he valued (as well as being prudent strategic policy in seeking to ally himself with the most influential scholars of his time, in his effort to dislodge the classical orthodoxy). This interpretation is entirely consistent with the measured criticism which Menger accorded the work of Roscher himself a dozen years after the *Grundsätze* (Menger 1985: 185–9). The difference in tone (in regard to Roscher and the other pre-Schmoller German economists) that separates Menger's *Untersuchungen* from the *Grundsätze* need not be attributed to a change of heart, or of opinion, on these matters (to be explained perhaps by the coolness with which the *Grundsätze* was received in Germany). Menger still warmly acknoweldged (in 1883 as in 1871) the 'virtues of the scientific personality of the learned Leipzig scholar; his outstanding merits and his advancement of the historical understanding of a number of important economic phenomena; the incomparable stimulation which his studies in the literature of our science have given to all younger colleagues' (1985: 189). The criticisms of Roscher in 1883 may rather be understood as expressing Menger's recent realization that his own success in fashioning his new understanding of the economic system depended crucially on his own theoretical orientation, with which the now-dominant German approach must be sharply contrasted. (Moreover, the cool reception accorded to the *Grundsätze* in Germany may have convinced Menger that no strategic alliance with the German economists could now realistically be anticipated.)

So Menger's work in 1871 is surely to be read as quite deliberately offering an entirely fresh perspective on the economic system as a whole. It is true that important elements (concerning subjectivism, utility and so on) were drawn from earlier German writers, as Streissler (and Hayek 1981: 13–14, 17) have pointed out. Yet the overall vision of the economy as a system driven entirely and independently by the choices and valuations of consumers – with these valuations transmitted 'upwards' through the system to 'goods of higher order', determining how these scarce higher-order goods are allocated among industries and how they are valued and remunerated as part of a single consumer-driven process – was one which Menger surely (and correctly) sensed as being wholly new.

And if this, rather than any technical innovations in marginal utility theory, is to be seen as Menger's self-recognized original contribution, then it seems reasonable to understand Menger as perceiving a correspondingly original implication of his vision for normative economics. This assertion calls for brief elaboration.

MENGER AND THE EFFICIENCY OF THE MARKET ECONOMY

Menger's vision of the economic system as one controlled entirely by consumer preferences, valuations and choices has significant welfare implications. Against a given background of scarce resources (potential goods of higher order) consumer preferences and choices set in motion an ever-widening ripple series of entrepreneurial productive activities which result in market valuations of factor services, and corresponding allocations of them among industries. From this vision there emerges a clear sense of *consumer sovereignty* – a concept with obviously important normative implications.

This vision of consumer sovereignty offers a normative criterion which differs sharply from the classical basis for *laissez-faire*. Classical economists saw the free market economy producing (under the incentives afforded by the invisible hand) the *greatest possible volume of material wealth*. Menger's view of the market pointed, not so much to a maximization of aggregate output, as to a pattern of *economic governance exercised by consumer preferences*. This aspect of Menger's vision suggests an appreciation for the outcomes of free markets that differs subtly from more standard neoclassical welfare theorems concerning the social optimality of *laissez-faire*. For Marshall and Pigou the sense in which free markets can be argued (in the absence of externalities) to be economically optimal is one which focuses on the *maximization of aggregate welfare*. For Walras and other continental neoclassical welfare economists, markets achieve welfare ideals by achieving *an optimal allocation of resources* (equivalent, in a world of interpersonal utility comparisons, to maximization of aggregate welfare). It is true that such optimality is predicated upon the welfare primacy accorded to the need to respect consumer preferences; but this still-standard mainstream perspective of welfare economics does not focus on the effective control exercised by consumer choices. For mainstream welfare theory what is important is the pattern of allocation achieved by the market (measured against the yardstick of the structure of consumer preferences). But from Menger's vision of the economy appears the insight that it is in fact solely the series of choices taken by consumers which create the market values and determine the entrepreneurial valuations which control the actual allocation of resources.

It is difficult to avoid the conjecture that Menger's appreciation for the achievements of the free market economy (as expressed, let us say, in Rudolph's essays) is to be attributed in large measure to this novel Mengerian insight concerning consumer sovereignty. It seems plausible in the extreme that it was in this insight, thoroughly absorbed into the economics of Menger's younger colleagues and followers, Böhm-Bawerk and Wieser, that Marxists saw their principal conflict with Austrian economics. For Bukharin, steeped in the Marxian perception of the capitalist economy as a system of exploitation, the claim that the pure capitalist economy is one in which consumer preferences dictate all, in which the capitalist assignment of income shares is that pattern 'required' and imposed by consumers, must have appeared dangerous indeed. No wonder that he saw Austrian economics as the most powerful opponent of Marxism. And there can be no doubt that it was this tenet of consumer sovereignty, so central to Austrian economics, which subsequently inspired Mises' critique of socialism. As Mises was to emphasize throughout his career, the key to economic literacy is the understanding that entrepreneurial decision making is grounded entirely in the incentive to anticipate consumer preferences: 'By themselves the producers, as such, are quite unable to order the direction of production. This is as true of the entrepreneur as of the worker; both must bow ultimately to the consumers' wishes. And it could not well be otherwise. People produce, not for the sake of production, but for the goods that may be consumed' (Mises 1936: 443). It was this thoroughly Mengerian insight which nourished Mises' lifelong polemic against socialist and interventionist misunderstandings of the market economy.

Yet, as we shall see, this insight of Menger's, his pioneering perception of the role of consumer sovereignty, was not by itself sufficient to require him unambiguously to subscribe to a policy of pure *laissez-faire*. Certainly the appreciation for consumer sovereignty carries normative implications. But for a mind as careful, as sensitive to subtle distinctions and as thorough as Menger's, his understanding of the paramountcy of consumer valuations in the structure of an economic system can hardly have guaranteed unqualified endorsement of pure *laissez-faire*. Menger's own economic theory left a number of openings for conceivable arguments, economic or social, in favour of specific interventions. Let us see how this must have been the case.

MENGER, CONSUMER SOVEREIGNTY AND SCOPE FOR GOVERNMENT INTERVENTION

We wish to identify three circumstances which rendered Menger's vision of the consumer-driven market economy an insufficient basis for *Manchestertum*, for a policy insisting on unblemished *laissez-faire*. There is every reason to assume that Menger was alive to these circumstances (and for us to explain the various conflicting strands of evidence concerning his position by reference to these circumstances and the extent to which he articulated the social implications of them). Streissler has emphasized externalities as a basis for Menger's concessions to interventionism (1988: 201). We wish to suggest three other circumstances that are likely to have been at the basis of Menger's list (cited above from Stephan Boehm's discussion) of legitimate tasks for the state.

First, we have every reason to believe that Menger recognized that his vision *assumed* a *given* structure of property rights and property law. When Menger discussed the scarcity-based reasons for the institution of private property, he referred to the arbitrariness of such an institution. A 'new social order', he explained, 'could indeed ensure that the available quantities of economic goods would be used for the satisfaction of the needs of different persons than at present.' But such redistribution would never eliminate scarcity; it would not avoid the need for the institution of property itself. Any 'plans of social reform can reasonably be directed only toward an appropriate distribution of economic goods but never to the abolition of the institution of property itself' (1981: 97–8). Nothing in Menger's theory suggested that the status quo, with regard to the distribution of resource ownership, is socially optimal. It seems highly plausible to understand much of Menger's sympathy for 'Schmoller's passionate concern for the poor and weak'[4] as reflecting this extra-economic dissatisfaction with the status quo. Menger's vision of consumer sovereignty, logically speaking, was entirely consistent with a social conscience which preferred a different set of effective consumers to be in control.

Second, although Menger emphasized the role of consumer preferences, he was certainly of the opinion that consumers may be 'mistaken' as to what is in fact in their own best interest. Menger dwelt explicitly on the possibility that consumers may erroneously assign value to primitive medicines, love potions and the like (1981: 53). He noticed the weakness which people display for 'overestimating the importance of satisfactions that give intense momentary pleasure but contribute only fleetingly to their well-being' (p. 148) and so on. This paternalistic attitude on his part might easily suggest state policies to correct consumer errors in valuation. It is plausible to read Menger's reference to the need for state action to encourage thrift (Boehm 1985: 250) as expressing his paternalistic urge to counteract the circumstance that 'men often esteem passing, intense enjoyments more highly than their permanent welfare, and sometimes even more than their lives' (Menger 1981: 148). Third, we must emphasize that Menger distinguished sharply between the 'economic prices' explained by his theory of exchange (based, in turn, on marginal utility foundations for consumer valuation and demand) and real world prices. The former are the prices which would prevail in the absence of error, if economizing individuals acted in their own best mutual interests without the hindrance of incomplete information (see Kirzner 1979b). In the real world, error clouds human decision making, considerations of goodwill towards others affect the economic character of transactions, and other causes complicate the outcomes: 'A definite economic situation brings to light precisely *economic* prices of goods only in the rarest cases. *Real* prices are, rather more or less different from economic' (Menger 1985: 69). The sense in which Menger's overall view of the economic system saw it as governed entirely by consumer valuations is confined to the model in which the effects of error and similar complications are ignored. Only if economic prices – prices which 'correctly' reflect the underlying realities of 'correct' consumer valuations – were to prevail would it be true that resource allocation indeed expresses, faithfully and efficiently, the wishes of the sovereign consumers. I have elsewhere (Kirzner 1979b) expressed bafflement at the absence, in Menger, of any *analysis* of a market process through which, possibly, errors on the part of market participants might be systematically eliminated. Be this as it may, it can confidently be asserted that while Menger did indeed apparently assume that markets will, sooner or later, tend toward an array of economic prices, he certainly did not claim that at all times such an array can be assumed to be already in place. It is plausible to read his reference to the need for state action to encourage entrepreneurial initiative (Boehm 1985: 250) as expressing a fear that circumstances may arise where entrepreneurial error or otherwise-founded lack of initiative will lead to pathologically uneconomic prices (and allocations of resources) unless state action to spur corrective entrepreneurial initiatives is introduced.

THE MENGERIAN REVOLUTION AND THE CASE FOR *LAISSEZ-FAIRE*: SUMMARY ASSESSMENT

We are now in a position to sum up discussion thus far. Menger had introduced a revolutionary view of the operation of a market system, in which he saw consumer valuations governing the entire structure of production and rigorously determining the allocation of resources and the corresponding market remunerations of scarce resource services. This perception of consumer sovereignty certainly carried with it important implications for the social assessment of the efficiency of the capitalist system.

There can be little doubt that (as we have seen to be the case for Mises) acceptance of the Mengerian vision carries with it a powerful defence of capitalist results. These results can be seen as rigorously necessary and desirable, *if* we indeed wish to respect the wishes of consumers as they themselves express them, and *if* we wish to treat existing property and other rights and endowments as given and not subject to challenge. What we have seen, however, is that for Menger himself it was not necessarily the case that the expressed wishes of consumers are to be seen as requiring respect; nor was it the case that any given initial pattern of property endowment be invested with title to moral approbation. More to the point, we have seen that Menger's insight into the nature of consumer sovereignty was circumscribed by his awareness that entrepreneurial errors and other aberrations may easily serve as a wedge separating the real world economy from Menger's consumer-governed 'economic' model of that reality.

What we wish now to submit is that these considerations serve adequately to account for the conflicting strands of evidence (concerning Menger's attitude towards state intervention in the market economy) cited at the outset of this chapter. We should not be at all surprised to find passages in Menger consistent with pure *laissez-faire*; we should not be surprised to find passages in Menger consistent with thoroughgoing interventionism; we should not be surprised to find passages in Menger consistent (as Gunnar Myrdal read them) with a complete detachment from policy issues. And we should certainly not be surprised to find Marxist writers such as Bukharin perceiving in Mengerian economics a powerful enemy of any exploitation theory of capitalism.

RECONCILING THE CONFLICTING EVIDENCE

There can surely be no mystery concerning the widespread perception (cited by Boehm) of the early Austrians as stout defenders of the
free market system. As we have seen, Menger's basic vision of the
market economy, a vision never totally lost sight of in the subsequent
Austrian tradition, certainly does have to it a strong classical–liberal
ring. It shows how, with error and aberration absent, markets may
faithfully express consumer sovereignty rather than entrepreneurial
control. Markets are not only not seen as chaotically discoordinated,
they are seen as systematic, efficient servants of the consuming
public. It is easy to see how the centrality of this vision could lead
subsequent historians of thought (as well as subsequent Austrians
themselves) to conclude – without reference to the Mengerian fine
print[5] – that Austrian economics vindicates the free market as a
requirement for the achievement of consumer sovereignty.

But as we have seen, the Mengerian fine print is indeed there to be
read and taken account of. When we move from the realm of
economic theory to that of social policy, the apparently clear message
arising out of the Mengerian view becomes cloudy, complex and
ambiguous. Not only may one harbour doubts as to the applicability
of the theory to the real world (since in the real world the array of
'economic' prices is likely to be absent – with an inefficient,
erroneous array of 'non-economic prices' in place instead); in
addition the social policy maker may legitimately question the moral
acceptability of the pattern of resource ownership which the economic
theory had simply taken for granted. Moreover, once one moves
from the value-free desk of the economic theorist to the paternalistic
podium of the policy maker, it becomes necessary to consider the
extent to which freely made consumer choices may appear mistaken
and wrong, not consistent with the 'true' well-being of the consumers. All these considerations are amply sufficient to account for
the statements adduced by Boehm and others testifying to Menger's
willingness to assign important interventionist responsibilities to the
state.

And, again, an observer such as Gunnar Myrdal could legitimately
cite the Austrians as having no political or ideological axes to grind.
Menger's exposition of his central vision of the market did not
attempt to articulate any *laissez-faire* policy implications – and, as we
have seen, did not in fact preclude adoption of a moderately interventionist programme. So while Bukharin quite correctly read the

Austrian theory as a powerful threat to the Marxist vision of the capitalist economy, Myrdal could equally correctly commend the Austrians for pursuing a programme of scientific research untainted by any political agenda. A number of further observations need to be made in order to complete our story, reconciling the apparently conflicting strands of evidence concerning Menger and the early Austrians.

CONCLUDING CONSIDERATIONS

Our reconciliation of the conflicting strands of evidence has depended upon our being able to distinguish sharply between Menger's central vision of the economic system, on the one hand, and complicating considerations regarding error and property rights on the other. It is because the context in which Menger articulated his central vision was one into which the latter complicating considerations did not have to be explicitly introduced that apparently conflicting conclusions concerning Menger's views on economic policy could come to be drawn. Certain additional circumstances combined to create this somewhat confusing situation.

Streissler has pointed out that the tradition in German and Austrian universities was for there to be 'two chairs of economics in each university: a chair of economic theory and a chair of economic policy' (1988: 200). Menger and the early Austrian economists held chairs of theory; they were not responsible for the teaching of economic policy. Their research and their books dealt almost exclusively with positive theory. This circumstance must have encouraged followers of the early Austrians, as well as historians of thought, to draw their own conclusions concerning the policy direction to which Austrian theory was pointing. This tendency can only have been strengthened by the fact that the centrality of Menger's new vision of the economic system was given so much emphasis in his theoretical work, while the 'fine print' acknowledging the legitimacy of state intervention found its way into the more peripheral, even journalistic, contributions of the founders. It is plausible that Menger himself may have seen his 'fine print' as having distinctly less impact on practical policy considerations. This would explain his being able to lecture to Rudolph along lines which, to a first approximation, so to speak, permitted him to avoid emphasis on his own 'fine print'.

As Boehm has reminded us (1985: 256–7), the principal frontier of ideological and political conflict in late-nineteenth century Austria was not that which separated proponents of pure *laissez-faire* from those of aggressive state intervention. Rather it was between the champions of the older, entrenched privileges of the clergy, artistocracy, army and bureacracy and the exponents of '*Josephinismus*, the Austrian version of enlightened absolutism'. The Austrian economists endorsed a 'liberalism . . . deeply rooted in Josephinic traditions, whose primary [purpose] was to do away with feudal privileges and guilds' (1985: 256–7). Menger's scientific work did not need to address these concerns. His openness towards state interventionism could quite easily be relegated to the fine print. When, in the course of decades, the frontier shifted, so that the principal policy issues among economists revolved around the degree of desirable state intervention, it became easy to focus almost exclusively on Menger's central, consumer sovereignty vision of the economic system and to draw one's own conclusions.

Moreover, as Austrian economics entered its second and third generations, the focus of public policy inquiry shifted towards the feasibility of socialism. Here Mises, as noticed above, was able to draw on both the Böhm-Bawerkian and Mengerian roots of Austrian economics to restate the case for the free market with a new sharpness of focus. It is not surprising, therefore, that in light of this twentieth century concern of the Austrians their tradition has come, in the view of historians of thought, to be identified with a consistent support for the free market economy.

Our conclusions are therefore that each of the postions cited at the outset of this chapter can be defended but that an understanding of the complexities surrounding the policy positions of the early Austrians permits us to see how this involves no necessary inconsistencies, either with regard to what the Austrians themselves maintained or with regard to what they were perceived to have maintained.

Chapter 6

The economic calculation debate: lessons for Austrians

The thesis of this chapter is that the celebrated debate over economic calculation under socialism that raged during the inter-war period was important for the history of economic thought in a sense not generally appreciated. Not only was the debate an important episode, of course, for its own sake. It was, in addition, I shall claim, important as a catalyst in the development and articulation of the modern Austrian view of the market as a competitive-entrepreneurial process of discovery. Professor Karen Vaughn has written of her conviction that 'the most interesting results of the controversy . . . were the further developments of economic theory to which it gave rise' (1976: 107). It will be my contention here that the crystallization of the modern Austrian understanding of the market must be counted among the most significant of these 'further developments of economic theory'. I shall argue that it was through the give-and-take of this debate that the Austrians gradually refined their understanding of their own position; the Mises–Hayek position at the end of the 1940s was articulated in terms far different from those presented in the Misesian statements of the early 1920s. Moreover, this more advanced Mises–Hayek position pointed beyond itself towards (and decisively helped generate) the more explicit Austrian statements of the 1970s and 1980s.

Now it may at first glance appear that my thesis contradicts the view of the most eminent historian of the calculation debate. Don Lavoie (1985a), in his definitive account of the debate, has exhaustively explored the debate as what we have referred to as 'an important episode for its own sake'. His position with regard to the debate emphasizes two related points. First, Lavoie emphatically denies that, as a result of the thrust and parry of the debate, the Austrian side found it necessary 'to retreat' from or otherwise modify its originally stated case challenging the feasibility of economic calculation under socialism. For Lavoie, the later statements of Mises and Hayek do no more than restate – in better, clearer, fashion – the originally presented arguments. Second, Lavoie has demonstrated with admirable clarity and thoroughness that the Mises–Hayek arguments, from the very beginning, reflected the Austrian understanding of the market as a competitive discovery process. (He furthermore has shown that it was failure by the socialist economists to recognize this that led to confusion during the debate itself, while it was failure by later historians of the debate to recognize this that led to the widespread misinterpretations of the debate by post-Second World War writers.) Thus it may appear that my contention that the debate was itself responsible for the distillation of that Austrian understanding runs sharply counter to both these elements in Lavoie's thesis. It will perhaps be helpful to explain briefly why, in my view, there is no contradiction here.[1] In fact, such a brief explanation permits me usefully to introduce further the central ideas to be offered in this chapter.

THE ARTICULATION OF THE DISCOVERY-PROCESS VIEW

Professor Lavoie is entirely correct, I believe, in interpreting the original 1920 argument by Mises as reflecting the characteristically Austrian understanding of the market as an entrepreneurial process.[2] And, as Lavoie shows, once this is recognized, there is no reason whatever to read the later statements by Mises and Hayek as 'retreating' from the original argument. My position, however, is that neither Mises nor (in his earlier papers on the topic) Hayek was aware of how sharply their Austrian view of the market differed from that implicit in the views of other contemporary schools of thought. Accordingly, the earlier statements of the Austrian position failed to articulate sufficiently clearly the 'process' perspective that Lavoie (correctly) perceives as underlying those statements.

The truth is that, among most economists (Austrian, Marshallian or Walrasian) in the early twentieth century, there was a superficial, shared understanding of markets that submerged important distinctions that would become apparent only much later. In this shared understanding, there coexisted elements of appreciation for dynamic market processes and elements of appreciation for the degree of balance – the degree of equilibrium – held to be achieved by markets.

To be sure, the Mengerian background of the Austrian version of this common understanding pointed unquestionably to the predominance of the process view, while the Walrasian version of this common understanding pointed consistently towards a strictly equilibrium view, but these conflicting signposts were simply not seen at the time. Mises' earlier statements, while they indeed adumbrated the process elements central to the Austrian tradition, did not emphasize these elements (and, as Lavoie suggests, a case can be made that for his immediate purposes in 1920 it was not at all necessary for Mises to emphasize these elements) so that when economists such as Lange came to consider the Misesian challenge from their own equilibrium perspective, they failed to recognize how seriously they were misunderstanding that challenge.

What occurred as a result of the vigorous inter-war debate was that the Austrians were inspired, not to retreat, but to identify more carefully the aspects of their understanding of market processes that their critics had failed to recognize. This process of increasingly precise articulation was not merely one of improved communication; it was a process of improved self-understanding. It is upon this process of improved self-understanding that I wish to focus in this chapter. While my own principal concern here is with the gradually developing articulation of the modern Austrian position, we should recognize at the same time that the debate was contemporaneous with a parallel process of the development of a more consistently articulated Walrasian neoclassical position. While it would probably be an exaggeration to see the calculation debate as significantly responsible for the development of a more explicit neoclassical perspective, it seems quite plausible to see the Lange–Lerner position in the calculation debate as at least a significant episode in that development.

What occurred, then, in the quarter century following Mises' original paper on socialist calculation is that a single, blurred picture of the market, common to most economists, came to be resolved into its two separate, distinct and well-focused components. The one component came to be perceived as the completely static general equilibrium market model; the second component came to be perceived as the dynamic process of entrepreneurial discovery. It was in the course of the debate that it gradually became apparent to the Austrians – but not to their opponents in the debate – that their position represented a critique of socialism only because and to the extent that markets under capitalism indeed constitute such a dynamic process of entrepreneurial discovery. Lavoie has himself put the matter as follows: 'I have concluded that the Austrian economists have learned much by "living through" the calculation debate. Because they have had to cope with criticisms in past debates, they now have much better, clearer ways of putting their arguments' (1985a: 26f). My contention is that what the Austrians learned was more than a technique of exposition; they learned to appreciate more sensitively how their own tradition understood the market process.

We can distinguish several distinct (but, of course, related) lines of development that occurred during this gradually improved articulation of the Austrian position. First, there was development in the positive understanding of the market process. Second, there was development in understanding the 'welfare' aspects of the market process (in particular, in understanding the social function of economic systems or the nature of the 'economic problem' facing society). Third, there was development in understanding the role of prices in grappling with this now better understood 'economic problem' facing society. I shall be discussing each of these lines of development in this chapter. (There were, of course, parallel developments in neoclassical economics with regard to the positive understanding of markets in equilibrium, with regard to appreciation for the welfare properties of general equilibrium and with regard to the role of equilibrium prices in promoting complete dovetailing of decentralized decisions.)

SIMULTANEOUS LEVELS OF ECONOMIC UNDERSTANDING

My story of the developing articulation of the modern Austrian perspective is complicated, especially with regard to the calculation debate, by the circumstance that from that perspective there appear to be *three* distinct levels of economic understanding with regard to the price system. It may be useful for me to spell these out at this point. They are, respectively, (1) the recognition of scarcity, (2) the recognition of the role of information and (3) the recognition of the role of discovery.

1 The foundation of economic understanding consists, of course, in the recognition of scarcity and of its implications. At the individual level, the recognition of scarcity informs individual allocative, economizing activity. In society, the phenomenon of scarcity implies the social benefits that arise from a price system that

translates the relative scarcities of particular resources or products into a price structure that encourages correspondingly effective 'economic' utilization of these scarce resources by potential users, whether producers or consumers.

2 A deeper appreciation for the social usefulness of a market price system stems from the insight that prices may be efficient means of communicating information from one part of the economy to another. Where prices do in fact fully reflect the bids and offers made by market participants throughout the market, such prices afford a highly effective system of signals that obviate the need for the transmission of detailed, factual information to decision makers. If the source of supply of an important raw material has suddenly been destroyed, the jump in its market price will effectively convey the impact of this disaster to potential users, with great rapidity. Those who have themselves learned of the disaster do not have to inform potential users that it has occurred, the price rise suffices.

3 Finally, and building upon these two previous levels of economic understanding, the modern Austrian perspective decisively draws attention to the manner in which the price system promotes alertness to and the discovery of as yet unknown information (both in regard to existing opportunities for potential gains from trade with existing techniques and in regard to possibilities for innovative processes of production).

The complications introduced by Austrian recognition of the simultaneous relevance of all these levels of economic understanding should be fairly obvious. From the vantage point of today's explicit modern Austrian position, it is clear that full appreciation of the social benefits provided by the price system involves all three of these levels of understanding. That is, while an understanding of the social *consequences* of scarcity need not involve an understanding of the subtleties of information and discovery, Austrian recognition of the way in which the market price system effectively *grapples* with the scarcity confronting society depends very much upon the recognition of the function that prices play in communicating existing information, and of the function that prices play in alerting market participants to hitherto unglimpsed opportunities. On the other hand, however, neoclassical economics, which certainly recognizes the role of the price system in contending with scarcity, is likely to refer to this role without any recognition of the discovery process of the market (and, until recently, without recognition of the role of the market in

communicating information). Because the earlier Austrian statements in the calculation debate did not distinguish between the
various levels of economic understanding, and did not emphasize the
discovery process upon which their own understanding of the market
depended, it was quite easy (for the Austrians themselves as well as
for onlookers) to believe that the Austrian critique of socialist calculation indeed proceeded from an understanding of how markets work
that was shared by their neoclassical opponents. This was particularly
the case because Mises found himself, in the earlier stages of the
debate, contending with proponents of socialism who seem not at all
to have understood the social problems raised by the phenomenon of
scarcity, at the most fundamental level.

It was only after more competent economists – who *did* understand
the economic problem created by scarcity – came to argue that Mises'
reasoning failed to establish his case that the Austrians were compelled to articulate more carefully the basis of their understanding of
the market process (and, hence, their contention that the socialized
economy is unable to provide any counterpart to that process). Thus,
Mises refers specifically to H.D. Dickinson and Oskar Lange as two
socialist writers on the calculation problem who did appreciate the
economic problems involved (1966: 702n.).

It is against the background of these complications that I now turn
to consider, in somewhat greater detail and in more systematic
fashion, the developing self-awareness on the part of the Austrians
that came to be induced by the various stages of the economic calculation debate. As I have suggested, I shall pay separate attention to
developments (a) in the positive understanding of how markets work,
(b) in understanding the welfare and normative aspects of the
economic problem facing society and (c) in understanding the role of
prices in helping to deal with that economic problem.

THE MARKET AS A PROCESS OF DISCOVERY

With the benefit of hindsight, we now understand that, in the
Austrian view of the market, its most important feature is (and was)
the dynamic entrepreneurial-competitive discovery process. We
know now that, for Mises, the idea of a price that does not reflect and
express entrepreneurial judgement and hunch is virtually a contradiction in terms. (It is for this reason that Mises rejected Lange's
contention that socialist managers may be able to take their bearings
from – and to calculate on the basis of – centrally promulgated non-

market prices.) We know now that for Mises the description of states of market equilibrium is mere byplay (1966: 251) – the description of something that will never in fact occur and that provides us with little of direct relevance to real world conditions (conditions that at all times display the characteristics of markets in disequilibrium). We know now that for Mises competition is an entrepreneurial process, not a state of affairs (1966: 278f.). We know these matters because they have formed a central theme in Misesian economics since the publication of *Nationalökonomie* in 1940. And we have every reason to agree with Lavoie and others that these insights were, at least implicitly, an integral element in the Austrian heritage from before the First World War. (Surely it is for this reason that Schumpeter's views on competition are so similar to those of Mises and Hayek.)

But, despite all this, it must be acknowledged, after a careful study of Mises' 1920 paper, that a first reading of that paper might easily lead to a quite different conclusion. It might easily be concluded from a reading of that paper (and of the corresponding passages in Mises' 1922 original German edition of *Socialism*) that the central feature in Mises' appreciation for markets was their continual ability to generate prices that, to a reasonable extent, approximated their equilibrium values. In his discussion of how market values of commodities enter into economic calculation, it does not seem important to Mises to point out that such market values may be seriously misleading (1920: 97ff.). He does at several points emphasize that 'monetary calculation has its limits', its 'inconveniences and serious defects' (pp. 98, 109), but the weaknesses that Mises identifies seem to consist almost exclusively in the inability of money prices to capture the significance of non-pecuniary costs and benefits and in the measurement problems arising out of the fluctuations in the value of money. He does not draw attention to the possibility that disequilibrium money prices may inspire market participants to make responses that are mutually inconsistent (e.g. an above-equilibrium price may inspire producers to offer goods that buyers will not buy at that price) or that cause them to overlook opportunities for mutually gainful trade (e.g. where a commodity is being sold at different prices in different part of the same market). It might easily appear to the superficial reader that Mises was satisfied that market prices are (subject to the limitations to which he refers) reasonably accurate expressions of relative social importance; and that it is this that constitutes the achievement of markets that could not be duplicated under socialism. Under 'the economic system of private ownership of the means of production', Mises asserts, 'all goods of a higher order receive a position in the scale of valuations in accordance with the immediate state of social conditions of production and of social needs' (1920: 107).

It is true that Mises already in his 1920 paper drew attention to the special problems generated by *changes* in the basic data, with respect to which economic calculation is called for. Thus, it might be argued that for Mises in 1920, a central achievement of the market is its ability to inspire entrepreneurial alertness to such changes, so that, perhaps, his appreciation for the market did, after all, recognize it as 'discovery procedure'. But it seems difficult to make this claim. Certainly, we can feel confident that Mises in 1920 would have accepted the insight that markets inspire entrepreneurial discovery; but he did not, in his 1920 paper, refer to the problems raised by changing data in a way that presented markets as being essentially on-going processes of discovery. His references to change were merely in order to point out that, although a newly socialized economy might well usefully take its bearings from the patterns of production that had characterized the previously prevailing market economy, changes in underlying conditions and goals would rapidly render those patterns obsolete and inefficient (1920: 109). These brief references by Mises would not prevent a reader from concluding that Mises believed that markets are continuously close to equilibrium, even in the face of changing data. This failure to draw attention to the market as a process of discovery seems to exist in all of Mises' writings published before *Nationalökonomie*.

But in his 1940 *Nationalökonomie* (later to be translated and revised to become *Human Action*), Mises emphasized the importance of seeing the market as an entrepreneurial process with unsurpassable clarity. By that year, Hayek, too, had drawn explicit attention to the problems of equilibration that are somehow, to some degree, apparently successfully overcome in the course of market processes (1949c). Moreover, by 1940, Hayek, like Mises, was pointing out that some of those who were arguing in the 1930s for the possibility of socialism based on centrally promulgated non-market prices were guilty of 'excessive preoccupation with problems of the pure theory of stationary equilibrium' and failed to understand how real world markets are likely to have the advantage in regard to the rapidity of 'adjustment to the daily changing conditions in different places and different industries' (1949d: 188).

There seems to be little doubt that what led Mises and Hayek to emphasize these dynamic aspects of markets at the close of the 1930s was the position taken up by their opponents such as Lange, Lerner and Dickinson in the calculation debate. Where Mises' original statements were directed at those who were completely innocent even of the most fundamental level of economic understanding (involving at least an appreciation for the implications of scarcity), his challenge had now been picked up by competent economists – but economists whose understanding of the market was limited by 'preoccupation with equilibrium theory'. It was in restating their case in the face of the arguments of these economists that the Austrians were led to make explicit some of the 'process' elements in their understanding of markets which they had hitherto not been impelled to emphasize.

This developing process of greater self-awareness among the Austrians continued during the 1940s. Mises' contribution in this period consisted of his revision and translation of *Nationalökonomie* into *Human Action*. It was the latter statement of his vision of the market process that was to have the most far-reaching influence on the further development of the Austrian view. It was this magisterial work that presented a dynamic interpretation of the market process in a manner so emphatic and clear as to render it henceforth impossible to overlook the profound differences between the Austrian and the mainstream neoclassical perspectives.

But it was Hayek who, in two celebrated papers during the 1940s, articulated certain key elements in the Austrian view in an exceptionally lucid and seminal fashion. In the first of these papers, 'the use of knowledge in society' (1945), Hayek drew attention to the role of the market in communicating information. In doing so, he explicitly linked his discussion with the socialist calculation debate. (I shall return later to further consideration of the part this paper has played in the crystallization of the modern Austrian position.) In the second of these two papers, 'The meaning of competition' (1946), Hayek was able to enunciate with great clarity the Austrian understanding of what competition really means and how the contemporary mainstream developments in treating competition in terms of the perfectly competitive state of affairs must be deplored as obscuring understanding of how markets work.

To treat competition exclusively as the perfectly competitive state of affairs, Hayek pointed out, is to confine attention exclusively to states of complete adjustment, to states of equilibrium. But to do this is already *to assume* 'the situation to exist which a true explanation ought to account for as the effect of the competitive process' (1949e: 94). In other words, Hayek was in this second paper *attributing to dynamic competition the central role in providing a true explanation of how markets generate tendencies towards mutual adjustment of decentralized decisions.*

There seems no doubt that Hayek was led to these insights concerning the severe limitations surrounding the usefulness of the notion of perfect competition by his experience with the proposals of the proponents of 'competitive socialism' during the 1930s. It became very clear that the illusion of transplanting competition to the environment of the socialized economy could have made its appearance only as a result of the mistaken belief that the role of competition in markets is best portrayed by the model of perfectly competitive equilibrium. Indeed, there are rather clear signs that Hayek's insights concerning the competitive processes were developed as a result of the calculation debate. Thus, in his 1940 essay, 'Socialist calculation III: the competitive "solution" ', Hayek pointed out that preoccupation with equilibrium analysis had led the socialist economists to misunderstand the role of competition. Apparently, Hayek wrote, 'the concept of perfect competition . . . has made them overlook a very important field to which their method appears to be simply inapplicable'. This important field includes much 'machinery, most buildings and ships, and many parts of other products [that] are hardly ever produced for a market, but only on a special contract. This does not mean that there may not be intense competition in the market for the products of these industries, although it may not be "perfect competition" in the sense of pure theory' (1949d: 188f.). This passage is not as explicit in its understanding of the problems of the perfectly competitive model as Hayek's 1946 paper, but it is clearly pointing towards the latter paper – and it has clearly been motivated by the effort to dispel the misunderstandings of the proponents of 'competitive socialism'. And from the 'Meaning of competition' (1946) to 'Competition as a discovery procedure' (1968) was but a small step for Hayek (1978a: Ch. 12). Thus, the linkage between the unfolding of the calculation debate and Hayek's most advanced statement concerning the market as a process of discovery seems not merely eminently plausible, but quite unmistakable.

THE UNFOLDING OF THE DISCOVERY VIEW

What seems to have been the case is something like the following. The earlier Austrians were simply not aware of their own implicit acceptance of a process view, rather than an equilibrium view, of markets.

One is not always aware that one is speaking prose or, perhaps more to the point, one is not always aware that one is breathing. If Jaffé found it necessary to 'dehomogenize' the economics of the Walrasian, Jevonsian and Austrian schools (Jaffé 1976), this was not merely because outside observers failed to recognize the important distinctions that separated their respective views, but also because leading protagonists of these schools failed to do so as well. Consider the following statement – one is tempted to describe it as an astonishing statement – made by Mises in 1932:

> Within modern subjectivist economics it has become customary to distinguish several schools. We usually speak of the Austrian and the Anglo-American Schools and the School of Lausanne. . . . [The fact is] that these three schools of thought differ only in their mode of expressing the same fundamental idea and that they are divided more by their terminology and by peculiarities of presentation than by the substance of their teachings.
>
> (Mises 1960: 214)

Clearly, the major opponents of Austrian economic theory, in 1932, were perceived by Mises not as being the followers of Walras or of Marshall but as being the historical and institutionalist writers (as well as a sprinkling of economic theorists) who rejected marginal utility theory. Mises lists these opponents as including Cassel, Conrad, Diehl, Dietzel, Gottl, Liefmann, Oppenheimer, Spann and Veblen (Mises 1960: 215). Against the views of these writers, Mises saw the three major schools of economics united in their support of the subjectivist theory of value, which for Mises was synonymous with 'the theory of the market' (p. 207). Differences between an emphasis on process, as against an emphasis on equilibrium, were simply not seen.

Between 1932 and 1940, however, the eyes of Mises and Hayek were, at least partially, opened. The work of the socialist economists, particularly Durbin, Dickinson, Lange and Lerner, was based on an understanding of how the market system works, which revealed and expressed the perceived primacy of equilibrium in the workings of that system. In confronting the arguments of these writers, based on this understanding that a parallel non-market price system can be devised for the socialist economy, Mises and Hayek felt called upon to draw attention to the primacy of the entrepreneurial-competitive process that they themselves associated with the market system.

Certainly, the mathematicization of mainstream microeconomics that was occurring (as Walrasian ideas became merged the Marshallian tradition) during this period helped crystallize the equilibrium emphasis that came to characterize mainstream theory. What helped crystallize the process emphasis of the Austrians was the dramatic use made by the socialist economists of mainstream price theory, to refute the Misesian challenge – a challenge that Mises had believed to be based solidly on that very mainstream theory of price. It was this confrontation, one now sees, that provided much of the impetus for Mises' repeated attacks, in later years, against the misuse of mathematics in economics, the misuse of equilibrium analysis and the misunderstandings embodied in mainstream treatments of competition and monopoly.

It would be a mistake to suppose that the crystallization of the Austrian process view was completed by the early 1940s. In the writings of neither Mises nor Hayek were the differences between their own approach and that of the neoclassical mainstream clearly stated. I can attest to the difficulties that the graduate student studying under Mises in the mid-1950s had in achieving a clear understanding of precisely what separated the two approaches. It was extremely tempting at that time to set down the Mises–Hayek approach as simply old-fashioned, imprecise and non-rigorous. In helping the student appreciate the foundations of the Austrian approach, Hayek's papers cited in the preceding section were especially helpful. But the gradually achieved clarification of the Austrian process approach – a clarification still not completed – can be traced back unerringly to those first reactions by Mises and Hayek to the contentions of the brilliant socialist writers of the 1930s.

THE DEVELOPMENT OF AUSTRIAN WELFARE ECONOMICS

With the benefit of hindsight, it is possible to recognize that for Austrians a normative evaluation of the achievements of the market (or of alternative economic systems) must apply criteria for judgement that differ substantially from those that are encountered in mainstream welfare economics. Now, of course, it was during the course of the inter-war debate on socialist economic calculation that modern mainstream economics developed those major features that have characterized it since the Second World War. And it is difficult to avoid the conclusion that the developments in mainstream welfare economics owe much to clarifications attained during the course of the debate. This was probably most especially the case with A.P. Lerner, but appears to be true of welfare economics in general (see also Hutchison 1953: Ch. 18; Little 1957: Ch. 14). What I wish to argue in the present section of this chapter is that in the case of the Austrian approach to normative economics, too, it was the debate on socialist calculation that triggered the process of clarification and articulation.

From the vantage point of the 1980s, it is clear that for Austrians none of the several notions that economists over the past two centuries have had in mind in evaluating the economic 'goodness' of policies or of institutional arrangements can be accepted. Classical ideas that revolved around the concept of maximum aggregative (objective) wealth are clearly unacceptable from the subjectivist perspective. Neoclassical attempts (by Marshall and Pigou) to replace the criterion of aggregative wealth by that of aggregate utility came to grief, for Austrians, in the light of the problems of interpersonal utility comparisons. Modern concepts of social efficiency in resource allocation that seek to avoid interpersonal comparisons of utility, based on notions of Paretian social optimality, are now seen as not being very helpful after all. Not only does the concept of the allocation of social resources imply a notion of social choice that is uncongenial, to put it mildly, to Austrian methodological individualism,[3] it turns out that the concept offers a criterion appropriate almost exclusively to the evaluation of *situations* (rather than processes). Following on Hayek's path-breaking (and now generally celebrated) papers on the role of markets in mobilizing dispersed knowledge, modern Austrians have converged on the notion of *co-ordination* as the key to normative discussion (Kirzner 1973: Ch. 6; O'Driscoll 1977). As we shall see, this notion fits naturally into the Austrian understanding of the market process. Let us see how this modern Austrian idea developed, in large measure, as a consequence of the economic calculation debate.

In Mises' 1920 statement (pp. 97f.) and its almost verbatim repetition in his 1922 book (Mises 1936: 115), Mises was very brief in his assessment of the economic function of market prices. Economic calculation carried on in terms of market prices expressed in money, he stated, involves three advantages. First, 'we are able to take as the basis of calculation the valuation of all individuals participating in trade'. This permits comparisons across individuals where direct interpersonal utility comparisons are out of the question. Second, such calculations 'enable those who desire to calculate the cost of complicated processes of production to see at once whether they are working as economically as others'. Inability to produce at a profit proves that others are able to put the relevant inputs to better use. Third, the use of money prices enables values to be reduced to a common unit. The statement of these advantages refers, it is conceded, to economic calculation as such, rather than to the broader issue of the social advantages of the price system. None the less, they seem to express a view of social 'economy' that does not differ from a perspective of social allocation of scarce resources. And the same seems to have been the case with Hayek at least as late as 1935. He defined 'the economic problem' as being the 'distribution of available resources between different uses' and pointed out that this is 'no less a problem of society than for the individual' (1949f: 121). Here, we have a clear idea of the textbook extension of Robbins's famous criterion of economizing activity from the level of the individual to that of society as a whole. What is important for my purposes is that both Mises and Hayek were judging the usefulness of the price system in terms that treat society as if it were compelled to choose between alternative patterns of use for given scarce resources.

Yet as early as 1937 Hayek was already beginning to draw attention to the economic problem raised by dispersed knowledge. He asserted that the 'central question of all social sciences [is]: How can the combination of fragments of knowledge existing in different minds bring about results which, if they were to be brought about deliberately, would require a knowledge on the part of the directing mind which no single person can possess?' (1949c: 54). In 1940, Hayek applied this insight to criticize the socialist economists in the calculation debate. The 'main merit of real competition [is] that through it use is made of knowledge divided between persons which, if it were to be used in a centrally directed economy, would all have to enter the single plan' (1949d: 202). But it was in 1945 that Hayek emphatically denied what he had himself apparently previously accepted – that the economic problem facing society was that of achieving the solution to an optimum problem, that of achieving the best use of society's available means:

The economic problem of society is thus not merely a problem of how to allocate 'given' resources – if 'given' is taken to mean given to a single mind which deliberately solves the problem set by these 'data'. It is rather a problem of how to secure the best use of resources known to any of the members of society, for ends whose relative importance only these individuals know. Or, to put it briefly, it is a problem of the utilization of knowledge which is not given to anyone in its totality.

(Hayek 1949b: 77f.)

Moreover, Hayek was explicit in linking the economic calculation debate with this rejection of the idea that the economic problem facing society was the simple optimization problem. A year later, Hayek again referred to his new normative criterion in the course of his criticism of perfect competition theory. Referring to the assumption, central to that theory, of complete knowledge of all relevant information on the part of all market participants, Hayek comments that 'nothing is solved when we assume everybody to know everything and . . . the real problem is rather how it can be brought about that as much of the available knowledge as possible is used' (1949e: 95).

Here then we have the strong assertion to the effect that standard approaches to welfare analysis are assuming away the essential normative problem. There can be little question that this assertion has revolutionary potential for welfare analysis. Although these implications for welfare analysis have been all but ignored by the economics profession (despite a fair degree of understanding of Hayek's related interpretation of the price system as a network of information communication), the truth is that Hayek opened the door to an entirely new perspective on the 'goodness' of economic policies and institutional arrangements. Instead of judging policies or institutional arrangements in terms of the resource allocation pattern they are expected to produce (in comparison with the hypothetically optimal allocation pattern), we can now understand the possibility of judging them in terms of their ability to promote discovery. This innovative insight, whose importance seems difficult to exaggerate, was very clearly a direct by-product of the calculation debate.

As we found in regard to the positive recognition of the market as constituting a discovery process, progress in regard to the normative aspects of discovery has not ceased since the mid-1940s. It has been pointed out that emphasis on fragmented knowledge is not quite enough to dislodge mainstream welfare concepts. 'Co-ordination' (in the sense of a *state* of co-ordination), while it may refer to co-ordination of decentralized decisions made in the light of dispersed knowledge, still turns out to involve standard Paretian norms. It is only 'co-ordination' in the sense of the process of co-ordina*ting*

hitherto *unco*-ordinated activity that draws attention to the discovery
norm identified through Hayek's insights (see Chapters 8 and 9).
Hayek has himself deepened our understanding of the problem of dispersed knowledge as going far beyond that of 'utilizing information
about particular concrete facts which individuals already possess'. He
now emphasizes the problem of using the abilities that individuals
possess *to discover* relevant concrete information. Because a person
'will discover what he knows or can find out only when faced with a
problem where this will help', he may never be able to 'pass on all the
knowledge he commands' (1979: 190). All this focuses attention on
the more general normative criterion of encouraging the *elimination of
true error* in the individual decentralized decisions impinging on the
uses made of society's resources. Clearly, this criterion is pre-
eminently relevant to appreciation for the character of market *processes*
(in which entrepreneurship and competition spur continual discoveries). Once again, therefore, we see how the socialist calculation
debate was responsible for a very fruitful line of development that
relates to modern Austrian economics.

THE FUNCTION OF PRICES

As Don Lavoie's history of the debate demonstrates, modern
Austrian economics is able to comprehend the various stages in the
debate with a clarity not hitherto attained. From the vantage point of
our present understanding of the nature of dynamic competition, of
the role of entrepreneurship and of the social significance of error discovery, we can see what Mises and Hayek 'really meant' – even
better, perhaps, than they were themselves able to do at the time they
wrote. We can see how the inability of the socialist economists to
comprehend what Mises and Hayek really meant stemmed from the
mainstream neoclassical paradigm within which the socialist
economists were working. And we can see how all this led to confusion and misunderstanding. What is important for the approach in
this chapter is that it was the calculation debate itself that generated
those key developmental steps in modern Austrian economics that
were ultimately responsible for our contemporary improved Austrian
understanding of 'what it was all about'. We turn now to review
briefly the development of greater clarity within the Austrian
tradition in regard to the function of market prices.

We have noticed Mises' brief 1920 reference to the role that market
prices play in permitting economic calculation in the competitive

market economy. It would be easy for a superficial reader of the 1920 paper (and of the 1922 book) to conclude that market prices play their part in achieving social efficiency through confronting each market participant with social valuations that reflect the activities of all other market participants and which, again, impose relevant efficiency constraints on the decisions of each market participant these prices now confront. Clearly, such an understanding of the role of market prices would not be greatly different from that understood by Lange in his now notorious reference to 'the parametric function of prices, i.e. on the fact that, although the prices are a resultant of the behavior of all individuals on the market, each individual separately regards the actual market price as given data to which he has to adjust himself' (1964: 70).

As Lavoie has extensively documented, the true role of price in the Austrian understanding of the market economy is quite different from that understood by Lange. For Austrians, prices emerge in an open-ended context in which entrepreneurs must grapple with true Knightian uncertainty. This context generates 'precisely the kind of choice that stimulates the competitive discovery process' (Lavoie 1985a: 137). In this context, the entrepreneur 'does not treat prices as parameters out of his control but, on the contrary, represents the very causal force that moves prices in coordinating directions' (1985a: 129).

Mises paints the picture of the entrepreneurially driven market and of the role that prices play within it as follows:

> There is nothing automatic or mechanical in the operation of the market. The entrepreneurs, eager to earn profits, appear as bidders at an auction, as it were, ... Their offers are limited on the one hand by their anticipation of future prices of the products and on the other hand by the necessity to snatch the factors of production away from the hands of other entrepreneurs competing with them. . . . The entrepreneur is the agency that prevents the persistence of a state of production unsuitable to fill the most urgent wants of the consumers in the cheapest way. . . . They are the first to understand that there is a discrepancy between what is done and what could be done. . . . In drafting their plans the entrepreneurs look first at the prices of the immediate past which are mistakenly called *present* prices. Of course, the entrepreneurs never make these prices enter into their calculations without paying regard to anticipated changes. The prices of the immediate past are

for them only the starting point of deliberations leading to forecasts of future prices. . . . The essential fact is that it is the competition of profit-seeking entrepreneurs that does not tolerate the preservation of *false* prices of the factors of production.

(Mises 1966: 332–5, emphasis in original)

This 1949 statement (presumably based on a similar passage in *Nationalökonomie*, 1940) appears to attribute a role to prices that differs sharply from that which the superficial reader might have gathered from Mises' 1920 or 1922 statements. The contrast is between the role of prices that are assumed *already* to express with reasonable accuracy all relevant information and the role of prices seen as stimulating entrepreneurial anticipations for the future. It is difficult to escape the conclusion that what led Mises to his more profound articulation of the role that prices play in the entrepreneurial process was his dismay at the Lange–Lerner misunderstandings concerning the 'parametric function of prices'. His earlier statements concerning market prices had not been made primarily in order to explain the operation of the market system; they had been made in order to illustrate the kind of economic calculation that market prices make possible. These statements were directed primarily at those who fail to recognize how market prices, precisely or crudely, do enforce the constraints implied by scarcity. The experience during the calculation debate not only sensitized Mises to the existence of more sophisticated proponents of socialism, it also sensitized him to the more subtle insights embodied in his own, Austrian, appreciation of the way in which markets work.

In regard to the function of market prices, too (as we found in regard to the appreciation for the discovery procedure of the market and for the emergence of the 'co-ordination' criterion for normative evaluations), the development of the modern Austrian position was not completed in the 1940s. Hayek's seminal 1945 paper 'The use of knowledge in society', which drew explicit attention to the role of prices in communicating information, did not succeed in distinguishing between two quite different communication functions. It is one thing to recognize the role of equilibrium prices as economic signals which permit instantaneous co-ordination of decentralized decisions, based on dispersed bodies of knowledge. It is quite another thing to recognize the role of *dis*equilibrium prices in stimulating entrepreneurial discoveries concerning the availability of dispersed information (whose existence had hitherto escaped relevant attention).

The statements of both Mises and Hayek during the 1940s, stimulated by the calculation debate, betray sure signs of appreciation for the latter role. But precisely because of Hayek's pioneering and carefully presented insights into the first role (that relating to the signalling function of equilibrium prices), it is doubtful whether he came to recognize the sharp distinction that today's Austrians would surely with to draw between the two roles (see Chapter 8).

Be this as it may, the modern Austrian recognition of prices as *stimulating discovery* must be seen as a further development in an unfolding series of advances that must surely be judged as having been set in motion, in significant degree, by the calculation debate.

THE CONTINUING DEBATE

It would be a mistake to believe that the calculation debate has ended. Lavoie has stated the main purpose of his work as being 'to rekindle the fires of the calculation debate' (1985a: 179). There are signs that a new round in the debate is indeed called for. From the perspective of the present chapter, these signs must be read as calling for restatement of the Austrian position with even greater clarity and sensivity. The appearance of an important paper by Richard R. Nelson exemplifies this need (Nelson 1981). Nelson's critique of the market and his implied (moderate) defence of central planning were written with a fairly extensive familiarity and understanding of the Austrian literature in the calculation debate. None the less, it is this writer's opinion that Nelson's paper betrays insufficient understanding of the Austrian position. We have seen that the Austrian position has required successive stages of clarification. Nelson's contention illustrates very well how the most recent clarifications – and more still need to be contributed – are vital in this continuing debate.

Chapter 7

Ludwig von Mises and Friedrich von Hayek: The modern extension of Austrian subjectivism

Much has been written about Ludwig von Mises.[1] And a great deal has been written about Friedrich von Hayek.[2] However, not much seems to have been written about Mises and Hayek as a linked pair in the development of modern economics. In particular their decisive role in the post-Second World War continuation of the Austrian tradition has not received its scholarly due. It is true that, in their accounts of the development of the Austrian School of economics, historians of economic thought have routinely cited Mises and Hayek as being modern representatives of the Austrian School. But such citations have generally tended to view them more as representing the last gasps of a dying tradition (or, indeed, the post-expiration twitches of one already dead) than as authentic contributors to a still-unfolding series of fresh intellectual developments. Furthermore these brief discussions have not explored the degree to which the work of Hayek indeed represents a continuation and extension of that of Mises, in the face of the important disagreements that separate the two. The purpose of the present chapter is to fill, to some degree, these gaps in the literature concerning the role of Mises and Hayek in the twentieth-century history of Austrian economics.

THE PARADOX OF MISES AND HAYEK

The truth is that something of a paradox surrounds the conventional pairing of these two economists. There can be no doubt that, on key elements in the Misesian system, Hayek is no Misesist at all. For Mises the possibility of economic understanding rests entirely on insights achieved *a priori*; his *praxeological* view of economic science expresses this apriorism in consistent and unqualified fashion. Yet at a relatively early and pivotal stage in his career as economist, Hayek made it clear that he was unable to follow his mentor in this regard.[3] For Hayek the possibility of economic regularities capable of being comprehended by science rests squarely on an empirical basis. Unaided human logic, for Hayek, is able to generate no systematic truths concerning economic processes. If historians of thought have paired Mises and Hayek in their accounts of twentieth-century economics, it almost seems as if this is based (beyond the purely personal and academic bonds linking the two from the inter-war Vienna milieu) entirely on certain key similarities in their views concerning some rather narrowly focused theoretical issues, specifically (a) the possibilities for economic calculation under central planning (see Hayek 1935, 1949: Chs 7, 8, 9) and (b) the malinvestment theory of the business cycle (see for example Mises 1980: 357–66; Hayek 1931, 1933). Perhaps the important commonalities in the political/ideological implications seen as flowing from their shared views on these specific theoretical topics has been responsible for their names being linked in the literature. But for historians of the Austrian School of economics these common positions seem not sufficient to justify treating Hayek's economics as a seamless further development of Misesian economics. To justify such a treatment it would be necessary to go beyond agreement on a few specific issues and to demonstrate a uniquely shared overall understanding of the economic system. Can such a uniquely shared understanding be postulated for Mises and Hayek in the face of the fundamental methodological and epistemological differences that separate them?

It is our contention in this chapter that the correct answer to this question is in the affirmative. The apparent paradox of Mises and Hayek can, we maintain, be resolved in a manner that illuminates the contribution each has made to the advancement of the Austrian tradition in economics. Since elaboration of this assertion is to be the theme of this chapter, it will be understood that no attempt is made to survey the entirety of the enormously prolific scholarly output of these two eminent economists, during three-quarters of a century. Our concerns here are strictly limited to a discussion of (a) the important continuity that links the contributions of Mises and Hayek, as (b) this continuity has represented a consistent development of the Austrian School (and has, indeed, nourished a significant current revival of interest in the School). It may be helpful at this point to provide a concise preliminary overview of our proposed discussion.

MISES, HAYEK AND SUBJECTIVISM

We shall argue that the development of the Austrian tradition is to be assessed in terms of the *subjectivism* which has traditionally informed the Austrian approach to economic understanding. Subjectivism in economics did not, we submit, spring full blown into fully articulated existence with Menger's *Grundsätze*. What is common, we shall claim, to both Mises and Hayek is a readiness to extend subjectivist economics *beyond the relatively unsophisticated stage represented in the work of Austrians (and others) during the 1920s*. As we shall see, the advances for subjectivism contained in the work of Mises are rather different from those present in Hayek's contributions. Yet it is by drawing upon *both* of these complementary sets of contributions towards a more sophisticated subjectivism that the contemporary Austrian revival has been able to carry forward those continuing refinements in subjectivist economic understanding that have, arguably, constituted the history of Austrian economics since Carl Menger.

Our argument therefore will (a) have to establish the inadequacies in the subjectivism of the earlier writers, (b) will have to identify the separate advances in this regard contained in the work, respectively, of Mises and Hayek and (c) will have to show how these separate advances can be integrated in such a fashion as to permit us to talk sensibly about a joint Mises–Hayek contribution to the development of the subjectivist Austrian tradition in economics.

In an oft-quoted passage, Hayek many years ago underscored the significance which he attaches to the progressive deepening of subjectivist influence upon economic analysis. 'It is probably no exaggeration to say', he wrote in 1952, 'that every important advance in economic theory during the last hundred years was a further step in the consistent application of subjectivism' (1955: 31). And in a footnote he paid glowing tribute to Mises in this regard: 'This is a development which has probably been carried out most consistently by L. v. Mises and I believe that most peculiarities of his views which at first strike many readers as strange and unacceptable are due to the fact that in the consistent development of the subjectivist approach he has for a long time moved ahead of his contemporaries' (p. 210, n. 24).

In this chapter we propose that it is indeed this shared dedication to subjectivism on the part of Mises and Hayek that represents the thread of continuity that links their work together. Moreover, as we shall see, the sum total of the insights which emerged as a result of this shared dedication to subjectivism have constituted a significant historical episode in the modern development of that intellectual tradition in economics for which subjectivism has always been the central idea – the Austrian School of economics.

SUBJECTIVISM AND SUBJECTIVISM

From its very beginning, of course, the Austrian School was identified as being 'subjectivist'. Whereas the classical theory of value had sought explanations in terms of the objective conditions surrounding physical production, the Austrians emphasized the market processes initiated by the actions of valuing, choosing, consumers. But explorations of subjectivism in recent years have drawn our attention to several quite different levels at which individual choice may be discussed. In particular *two* levels have been identified: one terminology identifies them as (a) 'static subjectivism' and (b) 'dynamic subjectivism' (Buchanan 1982; O'Driscoll and Rizzo 1985: Chs 2, 3; Ebeling unpublished). (After the late Professor Machlup's delightful survey of the numerous different uses made in economic terminology of the static–dynamic distinction, it is of course wholly unnecessary to spell out which of these two levels is to be considered the more profound' (Machlup 1963). There are some differences between different formulations of the distinction. But a useful criterion for such a classification is supplied by the well-known contributions of G.L.S. Shackle to the analysis of human decision making. In a stream of works over the course of some two decades,[4] Shackle has been concerned to emphasize the radical *creativity* and *indeterminacy* of the human decision. Each decision is a spontaneous new beginning, not at all the inexorable outcome of some previously given configuration of preferences and obstacles. Social history is a fabric woven out of the continual emergence of such mutually interacting new beginnings. These decisions are made in the face of the need to speculate on the course of future events, when the future is shrouded in ineradicable uncertainty. Moreover the essential unpredictability of the future is itself partly the consequence of our complete certainty that the future will be shaped, in large part, by intrinsically unpredictable future human decisions. From this Shacklean perspective, a 'dynamically' subjectivist view of social history sees it as being governed by forces that must be traced back to choices being made, at each and every moment, by individual market participants *whose decisions can in no manner or form be treated as flowing inexorably out of the objective circumstances* prevailing at the instant prior to these respective decisions.

This view of the subjective character of human choice is contrasted sharply with that other ('static') level of subjectivist analysis in which the creativity and inherent indeterminacy of decision making is, at least tacitly, suppressed. The 'statically subjectivist' view portrays the decision as indeed expressing the subjective preferences of the decision maker, but makes it appear as if these preferences are somehow separate from (and even, in some versions, chronologically prior to) the decision itself, and as if these preferences then 'determine' the specific decision taken. The course of social history is then seen as the 'inexorable' flow of events emerging from these interacting decisions (it being understood that such 'inexorability' is strictly relative, of course, to the independent, 'subjective' preferences of potential decision makers).

As Shackle and others have pointed out, the human decision envisaged in such a 'statically' subjectivist view hardly constitutes a genuine *choice* at all (Shackle 1972: passim; Kirzner 1979a: Ch. 13). The very circumstance that the 'chosen' course of action is seen as already inexorably implied in the given configuration of preferences and constraints, of ends and means, makes the choice 'mechanical' or 'automatic' – and thus not a true choice at all. True choice surely requires the realistic possibility of more than one alternative; but for the statically subjectivist view the rejected alternative is *already, before* (or at least apart from) the moment of decision, an option declared to be a suboptimal (and thus a quite unthinkable) alternative. The circumstance that, in this statically subjectivist view, the scales of individual preference, or the relevant indifferent maps, are declared to be the expression of independent subjective likes and dislikes does not suffice to invest this 'mechanical' model of decision making with the characteristics of genuine choice. A machine can calculate a required optimal option; we would not wish to say that the machine can *choose*.

Now, a plausible view of doctrinal history might see the contemporary neoclassical mainstream as representing the legacy of 'static subjectivism' stemming from the approaches of Jevons, Walras, and especially Pareto. (Pareto's notorious remark to the effect that the 'individual can disappear, so long as he leaves us a photograph of his tastes'[5] concisely but accurately captures his extremely limited concern with the subjectivism of individual choice.) On the other hand, this view would suggest, the Austrian School from Menger to Mises has been much closer to 'dynamic subjectivism'. From Menger's emphasis on independent consumer *valuation* of the signifi-cance of commodities (and, indirectly, of factor services) to Mises' concern with purposeful human action in an open-ended, uncertain world, the Austrian tradition has refused, it would appear, to treat choice as if it were inexorably determined by 'given' preferences. While not entirely wrong, this view of the Austrian School is, we shall see, rather seriously oversimplified. The truth is that, despite signifi-cant elements of 'dynamic subjectivism' in Menger (and perhaps in several of his followers), the early post-First World War develop-ments in Austrian economics were generally in the direction of being 'static' rather than 'dynamic' in their subjectivism. That this was the case can be perhaps most effectively conveyed by briefly considering the Austrian provenance of that extremely influential work, Lionel Robbins's 1932 *Essay on the Nature and Significance of Economic Science*.

LIONEL ROBBINS, THE AUSTRIANS, AND NEOCLASSICAL ECONOMICS

If modern neoclassical microeconomics sees itself as based upon the analysis of *choice*, this is in no small measure due to the influence of Robbins's book. When a modern textbook devotes an entire (admit-tedly brief) chapter to credit Robbins with the breakthrough leading up to the contemporary view that 'the core of pure economic science is the general theory of choice' (Walsh 1970: 17), this is by no means an exaggeration. What is now a commonplace was, in 1932, some-thing of a revolutionary idea; since then this idea has decisively governed the direction of mainstream economic thought. What is important for our purposes in this chapter is to recognize (a) the Austrian influence on Robbins in this regard and (b) the circum-stance that this influence came to be transmitted to the neoclassical mainstream (via Robbins) in 'statically', rather than 'dynamically', subjectivist terms. The latter circumstance will suggest rather strongly that the Austrian literature that influenced Robbins so powerfully was itself perhaps closer to the Paretian, rather than the Mengerian, brand of subjectivism.

In a recent paper Mark Addleson (1984) has reminded us of the pervasive Austrian influence which Robbins's book reflects (and which was widely recognized at the time of its appearance). He cites

R.W. Souter's scathing 1933 review of the book, in the course of which Souter described it as a 'scholarly and succinct account of the main tenets of "The Austrian School"'' (Souter 1933, cited in Addleson 1984: 509). As Addleson points out the '*Essay* is steeped in the Austrian tradition. This is reflected in the author's acknowledgement of his "especial indebtedness to the works of Professor Ludwig von Mises . . .". The names of economists like Schönfeld, Hans Mayer, Strigl, Carl Menger, Fetter, Hayek, Böhm-Bawerk, Morgenstern and Machlup, are evoked time and time again. . . .'[6]

So that, if the 'static subjectivism' that is so characteristic of modern neoclassical choice theory is significantly attributable to Robbinsian influence, we must not be surprised to discover evidence of such limited subjectivism not only in Robbins himself, but also in at least part of the Austrian literature that he cited.

For Robbins, of course, the role of choice was indeed central for the economic side of human life. 'Economics is the science which studies human behavior as a relationship between ends and scarce means which have alternative uses' (Robbins 1935: 16). 'When the time and the means for achieving ends are limited *and* capable of alternative application, *and* the ends are capable of being distinguished in order of importance, then behaviour necessarily takes the form of choice. . . . It has an economic aspect' (p. 14). But Robbinsian choice offers little scope for what we have called 'dynamic' subjectivism.

The outcome of a Robbinsian act of choice, it appears, is inescapably implied in the given pattern of ends and of means the relationship between which is the prerequisite for Robbinsian choice. This outcome emerges, it seems to be asserted, in a manner almost beyond the control of the decision maker – it is instead 'the resultant of conflicting psychological pulls acting within an environment of given material and technical possibilities (Robbins 1935: 35). To be sure the ends themselves, while given, are not fixed for all time. Ends can and do change: 'sybarites become ascetics' (p. 26). But the replacement of one set of given ends by a second set occurs *before* (or at least *outside*) Robbinsian choice itself. Whatever the process through which Robbinsian man comes to be endowed with the system of ends with respect to which he must allocate his finite array of given means, this process not only lies wholly outside the scope of economic science, it lies outside the realm of economic choice itself. Economic choice, for Robbins, is circumscribed entirely by the framework of given ends and given means that makes systematic allocative behaviour necessary. As Talcott Parsons pointed out at the time (1934: 512), this unfortunate mechanical picture of choice is a consequence of the way in which Robbins treats ends as given, suppressing the futurity of the very notion of a human purpose.

But a 'dynamically' subjectivist viewpoint must surely recognize that in expressing his purposes man must choose between alternative imagined future scenarios. His imagination of these alternative futures is very much an intrinsic element of choice. At the moment of choice ends are not all 'given'; they are nailed down only through the act of choice itself. Whatever it is that accounts for the particular ends that are thus chosen to be aimed at, it cannot be the solution of a problem in constrained maximization for which these ends themselves are data.[7] A fully subjectivist treatment of choice could not, as Robbins does, avoid discussion of these matters. A fully subjectivist treatment of choice must grapple with the way the decision maker, with all his spontaneous creativity in the face of a radically uncertain world, *chooses* which of the infinite possible pictures of the future he adopts as the basis for the alternative scenarios among which he undertakes the path he is to pursue. Despite all its virtues, all its Austrian credentials, Robbinsian choice is portrayed in abstraction from (if not in complete denial of) the insights of dynamic subjectivism.

But, as Richard Ebeling has recently shown in an unpublished paper, the writings of leading Austrian economists during the 1920s, including especially Hans Mayer, Richard Strigl (whom Robbins had cited prominently) as well as Rosenstein-Rodan, expressed a conception of choice *which is precisely as limited in its subjectivism (as 'static') as that of* Robbins. If it is reasonable to judge the work of Robbins as pointing towards a synthesis of the various post-1870 marginalist schools of economic thought, then it must be stated that the subjectivism which Robbins brought to the synthesis from Vienna was severely limited to the 'static' aspects of subjectivism.

Here, then, we find the basis for our earlier claim that by the early 1930s the development of the Austrian tradition had produced a seriously limited variety of subjectivism. We shall now argue that the work of both Mises and Hayek can be illuminatingly viewed as introducing (separate) elements of dynamic subjectivism. It will prove useful for this purpose, however, first to re-examine the theoretical model of a market economy populated entirely by 'economizing men'.

THE WORLD OF ROBBINSIAN ECONOMIZERS:
A RECAPITULATION OF MISGIVINGS

We shall find it convenient to identify *two* distinct aspects of this world that must appear very troublesome for any realistic attempt to understand markets. It will turn out, not at all accidentally, that the Misesian 'dynamically subjectivist' contribution entails an alteration of this world in so far as concerns one of these two offending aspects; the Hayekian subjectivist contribution would transform this world in the second of these two aspects. Taken together, we shall see, the two contributions successfully replace a statically subjectivist view of the market with a dynamically subjectivist view. It is this circumstance, it is our thesis in this chapter, which (a) justifies the traditional pairing of Mises and Hayek and (b) recognizes their important joint contribution in extending the vision of the Austrian School of economics.

The world populated entirely by Robbinsian economizers is in fact the world of contemporary neoclassical microeconomics. Thus the demonstration of how the Mises–Hayek subjectivist contributions together drastically transform that world offers at the same time a glimpse of how the contemporary Austrian theoretical vision, informed by those contributions, differs sharply from the dominant neoclassical view.

Economizing man, we have seen, 'chooses' within a framework rigidly circumscribed by the pattern of ranked ends and available means assumed to be perceived as given (for the moment of economizing choice). His strictly allocative choice does not encompass the perception or identification of the elements making up this rigid framework. Now, in the market economy, neither the ranking of ends nor the availability of means can be considered as given to any agent apart from the decisions of other (similarly 'economizing') individuals. No producer, for example, can treat output of his product as equivalent to the achievement of ends of given importance without specific expectations concerning the market prices to be offered for that output, and so on. No producer can treat inputs as available means without specific expectations concerning the market prices to be asked by the sellers of those inputs. But surely recognition of this circumstance, that a world of economizing individuals presupposes definite anticipations concerning the choices which the other (similarly economizing) individuals are in fact now in the process of making, presents us with a very serious dilemma.

Either the economizing choices actually being made are 'correct', in the sense that they sustain the anticipated frameworks of ranked ends and available means identified respectively by market participants; or these choices fail to confirm these anticipated ends–means frameworks. On the first of these two alternatives all the allocative decisions being made can in fact be successfully, and without generating regret, carried out as planned – since the selected courses of action deemed optimal indeed turn out to be both feasible and most preferred. The feasibility and optimality of any chosen course of allocative action has not been frustrated by failure of any of the anticipated choices of others to occur as expected. On the second of these alternatives, on the other hand, things are quite different. On the second alternative decision makers find themselves unable to complete their chosen courses of action (because those courses of action presupposed decisions of others that turn out not to have been made); or else they discover that their chosen courses of action turn out – for symmetrical reasons – to have been by no means the truly optimal allocative programmes in the light of the actual hierarchy of ranked ends and available means which the pattern of market decisions in fact generates. Each of these alternative possibilities appears to raise serious difficulties.

If we are to assume that all the economizing decisions are indeed 'correct', we have necessarily confined ourselves to the fully co-ordinated, equilibrium world – something imaginable only on the basis of universal mutual omniscience concerning what market participants can and will choose to do. To *confine* ourselves and our economic analysis to the context of full mutual omniscience is not merely to accept a wildly unrealistic assumption; it is to confess that our model of the economizing world *is unable to throw light upon any process of adjustment through which, perhaps, an approach towards the fully co-ordinated state of affairs (or, indeed, of any specific state of affairs) might occur* in the real world of imperfect knowledge. But the second alternative is no less troublesome in this regard.

We may indeed easily imagine a world in which a large proportion of attempted economizing decisions turn out to be disappointed in execution (because the necessary anticipated decisions on the part of others have not in fact been made) or turn out to be regretted (because hindsight reveals that the true relevant patterns of ends and means would have suggested even more desirable courses of allocative action). *But it is not at all clear how, in a world of exclusive economizers,* such disappointments *can be held to generate systematic modifications* in the allocative decisions to be made by market participants in subsequent time periods. We must remember that our economizers are not endowed with any propensities that might systematically modify expectations concerning the decisions being made by others. Economizers are, so to speak, *endowed* with given ends–means frameworks. There is *nothing* within the scope of the analysis of economizing activity that permits us to postulate a systematic series of modifications in the ends–means frameworks held to be relevant by market participants. Unless we transcend the assumption of purely Robbinsian economizers, our second alternative indeed results in frustrated economizing attempts – but such disequilibrium chaos cannot be held to result in *any* systematic modifications of choices, let alone any *equilibrating* sequences of such modifications (see Kirzner 1973: 36).

To use a model made up of economizing individuals in order to arrive at an explanation for systematic market adjustments (that might be generated by initial disequilibrium) it is clearly necessary to assume that market participants do indeed come to know where market events have shown their previously assumed frameworks of ends and means to require revision. But to do this is to jeopardize the integrity of the model by importing into it a totally arbitrary modifying feature, i.e. endowing the population of economizers with the propensity to replace discredited assumed ends–means frameworks by new frameworks revealed to be relevant by market experience. To postulate such an endowment is not only sharply to modify the scenario of pure economizers (who were, after all, supposed to have *given* endowments of ends–means frameworks). It is to leave unexplained how market experience communicates to these economizing individuals sudden awareness of exploitable opportunities *which already existed but which were previously overlooked by the same economizing individuals*.

Here, then, we have before us the two separate aspects of this purely economizing world that must surely engender grave misgivings. First, the model of such a world is clearly seriously deficient in its failure to pay attention to the role played by *knowledge* and *learning* in the initial endowment of assumed ends–means frameworks, and in subsequent modification of these endowments as a result of market experience. Second, the make-up of the model, in terms of a population consisting solely of pure economizers, is in fact inconsistent with the kinds of learning sequences which one would have to postulate in order to account for systematic market processes. We shall see that while the 'dynamic' subjectivism expressed in Mises' writings opened up the possibility of dealing with the second of these difficulties, it was not until Hayek's contributions to the deepening of subjectivism that the first of these two inadequacies was eliminated. Misesian subjectivism replaced the mechanical, allocative activity of the rather wooden economizer by the dynamics of human action. Hayek's work compelled the economics profession to address explicitly the role of knowledge and learning in economic process. Together, the Mises–Hayek contributions offer a truly 'dynamically' subjectivist understanding of market processes.

LUDWIG VON MISES AND THE SCIENCE OF HUMAN ACTION

For Mises economics is a *science of human action*. Every conclusion of economic theory is, for Mises, the outcome of the circumstance that economic life consists of interacting human *agents*. It is human action that is the basic unit of analysis. Although Mises never did, to this writer's knowledge, spell out the distinction between his own notion of *human action* and the Robbinsian concept of 'economizing', there can be no doubt that the difference is a fundamental one. Human action is a far broader concept than that of economizing; while the allocation of scarce means among multiple competing ends may be an *example* of human action, human action need not be allocative at all. 'Human action is purposeful behavior' (Mises 1966: 11). What acting man seeks to do is 'to substitute a more satisfactory state of affairs for a less satisfactory' (p. 13). Nothing in these formulations confines them to the calculative allocation of scarce means with respect to competing goals.

We may distinguish two subjectivist elements contained in the Misesian concept that are absent from the narrower notion of Robbinsian economizing choice. First, human action is essentially *purposive*; its objective is not *maximization* (of, say, utility or profit) subject to side constraints, but the removal of felt uneasiness, the attainment of a better future state of affairs. No one could accuse Mises (as some had accused Robbins) of suppressing the sense of purposefulness that suffuses human activity; no one could accuse him of suppressing the subjectively felt sense of *futurity* that human beings attach to the goals they seek to achieve through their actions. Not only does the concept of human action emphasize its purposefulness; the notion of purposefulness really does exhaust its essence. For Mises human action may consist of deliberately remaining completely idle (Mises 1966); *in*action may be an example of action. The *essential* element in action is goal pursuit, not maximization, not allocative efficiency, or anything else. There is no possibility of abstracting from the subjective element in human action without completely eroding the very concept.[8] Second, the concept of human action (unlike that of Robbinsian economizing) contains within it an essential *entrepreneurial* element. 'In any real and living economy every actor is always an entrepreneur' (Mises 1966: 252). The human agent 'is endowed not only with the propensity to pursue goals efficiently, once ends and means are clearly identified, *but also with the drive and alertness to identify which ends to strive for and which means are available*' (Kirzner 1973: 34, emphasis added). Thus subjectivism in the analysis of decision making means more than merely the recognition that the ends–means framework relevant to a particular decision maker is that with which he has been peculiarly endowed. It means more, even, than the recognition that the decision maker is consciously pursuing his purposes, that his activity is suffused with the sense of driving to attain his objectives. Subjectivism in the analysis of Misesian human action includes the insight that any ends–means framework relevant to a human action has *itself been actively chosen* in the course of that very action – and that that choice expresses and reflects that agent's dreams, aspirations and imagination, his expectations and his knowledge, his hunches and his biases.

Once our picture of the economic agent has, following Mises, been broadened from that of a constrained maximizer (in the context of an endowed ends–means framework) to that of the human being actively following his own hunches, his own vision (as to what is worthwhile pursuing and as to what is the best available relevant course of pursuing action), the way is open for incorporating *learning by discovery* into our understanding of market processes. We are now no longer bound to a mode of theorizing in which the unit of analysis precludes us from serendipitous changes in relevant knowledge. We are no longer confined to a world in which everything deemed worthwhile knowing is either *already* known to agents or is now confidently planned to be learned, sooner or later, in the course of already-fully-envisaged systematic search procedures. We can now find scope, within the market process, for the *spontaneous discovery* of hitherto unnoticed opportunities, or for the realization that earlier anticipations have proved to have been over-optimistic. We can now look for a possibly systematically unfolding series of such discoveries, made possible by the changing arrays of opportunities which these sequences of discoveries themselves generate.

To put this somewhat differently, we can now, possibly, explain a changing pattern of decisions over time as the systematic outcome of changing patterns of knowledge, with the latter changes themselves being the result of discoveries stimulated, in turn, by the steadily shifting sets of interpersonal opportunities created through time by these very sets of changing decisions. In other words this implication of the Misesian contribution contrasts sharply with one of the two disquieting features of the Robbinsian world noted in the preceding section of this paper, namely that a world of economizers is inconsistent with the kinds of learning sequences needed to account for systematic market processes.

To state these systematic implications of the Misesian subjectivist contribution is not, however, to claim that Mises himself explicitly enunciated the character of market processes in these terms. In fact Mises himself did not emphasize the role of changing arrays of knowledge as constituting the unfolding market process. It was Hayek's contribution to a deepened subjectivism that brought this role into unmistakably clear focus. To that contribution we now turn.

FRIEDRICH VON HAYEK AND THE ROLE OF KNOWLEDGE

Hayek's contributions to modern economics (quite apart from his prolific work in other disciplines) extend across a formidable range of areas within the subject. His bibliography in economics alone includes now classic works in monetary theory, business cycle theory, capital theory, doctrinal history, the theory of socialist planning, economic methodology and other important areas. Yet it seems correct to state that the portion of Hayek's work most frequently cited (if not always adequately understood) in contemporary economic discussion is that which concerns *the role of knowledge*. In this section we briefly refer to this celebrated Hayekian contribution and cite it as constituting, in our view, a decisive, explicit extension of subjectivism in modern economics.

Hayek's definitive introduction of knowledge into economics involved two separate (but certainly related) series of insights. The first (represented most clearly by his famous 1937 paper 'Economics and knowledge'[9]) demonstrated (a) the nature of market equilibrium constructs as the working out of the implications of complete mutual knowledge on the part of market participants and (b) the nature of hypothesized equilibrating market processes as consisting of specific patterns of mutual *learning*. The second set of insights concerning knowledge (introduced already in the 1937 paper, and spelled out definitively in Hayek's equally famous 1945 paper, 'The use of knowledge in society' (Hayek 1949b)) drew attention to the positive and normative implications of the circumstance that the sum total of knowledge available in an economy 'never exists in concentrated or integrated form but solely as the dispersed bits of incomplete and frequently contradictory knowledge which all the separate individuals possess' (p. 77).

To recognize market processes as consisting of systematically changing patterns of individual knowledge about one another, to recognize the normative significance of social institutions that make possible the fullest utilization by members of society of 'knowledge which is not given to anyone in its totality' (Hayek 1949b: 78), is to threaten revolution in both microeconomic theory and the theory of welfare economics. Modern neoclassical theories of microeconomics and welfare economics, as suggested earlier, have remained at the lower (or 'static') level of subjectivism. Hayek's insights concerning knowledge pointed to a comprehensive fully (or 'dynamically') subjectivist revolution of understanding in these areas. That these threatened revolutions somehow never succeeded in dislodging the neoclassical dominance is mute evidence of the very limited extent to which the modern profession has been hospitable to extensions of subjectivism.

Hayek himself drew explicit attention to the subjectivist character of his work on the role of knowledge. In his most detailed discussion of the importance of subjectivism for the social sciences, Hayek wrote of 'the more complex phenomena with which economic theory is concerned and where in recent years progress has been particularly closely connected with the advance of subjectivism'. He cited in particular 'the new problems which these developments make appear more and more central, such as the problem of the compatibility of intentions and expectations of different people, of the division of knowledge between them, and the process by which the relevant knowledge is acquired and expectations formed' (1955: 33). For the purposes of this paper it is important to notice that these subjectivist contributions of Hayek contrast sharply with that other disquieting feature of the model of the Robbinsian world noted earlier in this chapter, namely its failure to focus on the role of knowledge and learning (both in the initial specification of the model and in the manner in which the model can be put through its paces in accounting for market processes).

MISES, HAYEK AND SUBJECTIVIST ECONOMIC UNDERSTANDING

We have taken note of the separate contributions to the extension of subjectivism made by Mises and Hayek. For Mises economics came to be transformed into a science of (radically subjectivist) human action; Hayek outlined the translation of economic theorems into new forms of understanding concerning human knowledge. We wish to argue here that these separate contributions together not only make up a decisive step from static to dynamic subjectivism but also, at the same time, help articulate a subjectivist understanding of market processes that constitutes an authentic extension of the work of economists of the Austrian School, in a tradition going back to Menger. If our argument in this regard is accepted, it will have vindicated the references in the literature to a strong linkage between Mises and Hayek, in the face of the very important differences that separate them. It will moreover add significance to the references in the literature to this pair of economists as being latter day representatives of the classic Austrian School.

Carl Menger decisively changed the orientation of economic understanding. His subjectivist insight demonstrated how economic phenomena can be most successfully perceived as the reflection and expression of valuing and economizing individuals. Menger's own subjectivism appears, on a number of accounts, to have been refreshingly 'dynamic'. Menger's successors carried many of these insights and brought them into contact with the work of marginalist economists from other schools. But in the very course of refining Austrian marginal analysis, a certain 'static' quality seems to have crept into the subjectivism which that work expressed in the immediate post-First World War period. (To state this is not to criticize the writers involved. There are unquestionably certain aspects of Austrian economics for which articulation of dynamically subjectivistic insights is simply not necessary.) As a consequence it became possible for a brilliant synthesist such as Robbins to inject key Austrian insights into mainstream neoclassical economic theory (to which 'dynamic' subjectivism was virtually a complete stranger) without transcending the level of static subjectivism at all. Thus the subsequent advances in neoclassical microeconomics, enriched by Robbinsian–Austrian injections, continued along a line which is, in fact, starkly *incompatible* with a dynamically subjectivist perspective. It is no surprise, therefore, to find some modern exponents of dynamic subjectivism, such as Professors Shackle and Lachmann, compelled to reject the neo-classical paradigm virtually in its entirety. Mises and Hayek took a different path.

The importance of the contribution of Mises and Hayek consists, in fact, not merely in their drawing attention to subjectivist elements absent from the earlier Robbins–Austrian formulations. Their intro-duction of these new elements enabled the traditional Austrian approach to be extended by suggesting a deepened understanding of market process. While indeed sharply differing from the neoclassical mainstream on many crucial substantive and methodological points, this deepened understanding yet preserved those important areas of overlap which from Menger's time onwards, were shared in common by the Austrians and the other marginalist schools. What Mises and Hayek preserved was a vision of the market which firmly recognizes its *systematic* (rather than chaotic or haphazard) character while never losing sight of the 'open-endedness' of the decision making environ-ment – an open-endedness generated by the imminent passage of time, by the imperfect knowability of the future and by the consequent omnipresence of radical uncertainty. This feat they accomplished by pointing the way to an understanding of market processes as syste-matic 'discovery procedures'[10] – i.e. spontaneous mutual learning procedures – continually being set in motion by entrepreneurial human agents. The drive, the alertness and the incentives which spur human action tend to guide these unmodellable entrepreneurial discoveries in the direction of enhanced mutual knowledge, of enhanced interpersonal co-ordination. Despite continual buffeting by unpredictable exogenous changes in the basic data, it is still possible, on this modern Austrian view, to perceive the powerful co-ordinative forces of entrepreneurial alertness, as they manifest themselves in the ceaseless agitation of the market. To be sure, the disruptive effect of those continual buffetings manifests itself more seriously in some markets than in others. Thus while this deepened modern Austrian understanding provides insights relevant to *all* markets, their deploy-ment to arrive at concrete forecasts or judgements in *particular* markets calls for close attention to the relevant empirical and insti-tutional detail.

All this surely does vindicate the widespread linkage associated with the names of Mises and Hayek. There is every ground for believing that their vision of the market is indeed basically a single one, and that the subtlety and power of this vision derives from the sophisticated character of their contributions to subjectivism. From this perspective the shared critique of the possibility of centralized economic calculation (enunciated by both Mises and Hayek during the inter-war years) is no accident at all. That shared critique derived, we can now clearly perceive, from that shared understanding of market processes as processes of spontaneous entrepreneurial discovery (see Lavoie 1985a). For this shared understanding, we have argued in this chapter, their separate contributions to a deepened subjectivism can be seen as providing crucially important ingredients. For all these reasons, therefore, the linked contributions of Mises and Hayek may be seen, in the broad sweep of twentieth-century economic-intellectual history, as representing a vigorous spurt of new progress in a still-very-much-alive tradition of Austrian subjectivism.

Part III

Some new explorations in the Austrian approach

Chapter 8

Prices, the communication of knowledge and the discovery process

Among the fundamental contributions that Professor Hayek has made to economic science, certainly one of the most significant and far-reaching must be judged to be his path-breaking articulation of the nature of the 'economic problem which society faces' (Hayek 1949b: 77). It was in this context that Hayek decisively drew the attention of the economics profession to the unique problems that arise from the *dispersal of knowledge*.

> The economic problem of society is . . . not merely a problem of how to allocate 'given' resources – if 'given' is taken to mean given to a single mind which deliberately solves the problem set by these 'data'. It is rather a problem, of how to secure the best use of resources known to any of the members of society, for ends whose relative importance only these individuals know. Or, to put it briefly, it is a problem of the utilization of knowledge which is not given to anyone in its totality.
>
> (Hayek 1949b: 77–8)

Hayek's insight represented a breakthrough, of course, in the modern history of welfare economics, as well as providing a brilliant new way of stating the crucial arguments making up the 'Austrian' side of the socialist economic calculation debate (see particularly Lavoie 1985a). In addition, however, Hayek's emphasis on the role of knowledge constituted an important step forward in our understanding of the way in which markets work, and of how the price system in fact tends to solve the economic problem which society faces. Indeed it seems to be this aspect of Hayek's contribution that has attracted the most attention in the economics profession. While accounts of modern developments in welfare economics rarely refer to Hayek's dismissal of the allocative-efficiency criterion (in favour of the co-ordination' perspective), and while accounts of the socialist economic calculation debate have, notoriously, thoroughly and unforgivably muddled it up (Lavoie 1985a), Hayek's insights into the role of prices in solving the knowledge dispersal problem have been widely cited, and often by the most orthodox of neoclassical economists. I shall argue in this chapter that, in spite of its citation of Hayek's work in this regard, the economic literature has regrettably failed to do justice to the full significance of that work. As a result professional concern with problems of knowledge dispersal has tended to remain, unfortunately, at a rather superficial level. In demonstrating the validity of this assertion it will be necessary to distinguish sharply between two quite different 'communications' challenges arising out of knowledge dispersal, and (consequently) two quite different functions that markets may possibly fulfil in the context of the 'economic problem which society faces'. It may perhaps be helpful to start with an analogy drawn from a rather different context, that of automobile traffic through a busy urban street intersection.

AUTOMOBILES AND THE PROBLEM OF DISPERSED KNOWLEDGE

Consider cars approaching the intersection of two urban streets, the one north–south and the other east–west. The driver of a car approaching from (say) the north must decide whether or not to stop before proceeding south across the east–west street. The driver's decision will depend on his knowledge or expectations concerning the decisions that the drivers of other cars (that may possibly be driving towards the intersection from the other directions) will make when *they* reach the cross-roads. In order for traffic to move smoothly and safely through the intersection it is clearly necessary that these various decisions be somehow co-ordinated. Absence of co-ordination may, rather obviously, result in regrettable, costly (because perhaps quite unnecessary) delays at the intersection before proceeding through it, or in even more regrettable and costly automobile collisions. It is easy to see that such regrettable events are to be attributed at least in part to the dispersal of knowledge: the driver of one car knows, at the moment when he makes his decision, what he has decided to do, but the drivers of other cars do not know what the first driver has decided (or perhaps even that there *is* this first driver). *Their* decisions are then likely to fail to be co-ordinated as well as is possible with that of the first driver, and so on. Were an omniscient single mind to make the decisions for *all* the drivers, that mind might arrange the drivers' actions in smooth and safe fashion. In the absence of such a central omniscient mind, a well-designed (and fully enforced) system of traffic signals can achieve co-ordination by providing each driver of a vehicle with confident assurance as to what the other driver will decide to do. The green light beckoning a southward-bound driver is in fact assuring him that cars proceeding in the east–west street will not cross the intersection in the immediate minute or minutes ahead. A red light directs him to stop, while at the same time it provides conviction (in a well-designed system) that the waiting is not wasted (since it implies that cars are being permitted to proceed east and west). By timing the light changes appropriately, smoothly co-ordinated traffic conditions can be achieved. Let us analyse what we mean when we say that a signal system 'achieves co-ordination'. It will be convenient to focus on the manner in which the system eliminates *unnecessary delays*. (Rather similar considerations apply to the system's elimination of avoidable collisions.)

A successful traffic signalling system will not only succeed in avoiding collisions, it will avoid requiring cars to wait needlessly (such as at times when traffic along the other direction is extremely light). Superior co-ordination would permit the timing of light changes to reflect the relative intensities of traffic along the two inter-secting streets. 'To achieve co-ordination' is thus a phrase which, in the context of the automobile example, can have two quite distinct meanings.

First, a traffic signal system may be said to be achieving co-ordination when its timing, from the very installation of the system, is such as in fact to control the flow of traffic in some optimal manner. No undesired collisions, no unjustified waiting, result from unanimous obedience of the traffic signals. This successful achieve-ment of co-ordination has clearly involved the efficient communica-tion of correct information. The information fed to the drivers of cars has been such as (a) correctly to inform each of them of the conse-quences of the decisions of other drivers, leading them, in turn (b) to make those decisions that permit this above property (a) to hold, with the resulting set of drivers' decisions being such as (c) to result in no unnecessary waiting. This is certainly a valid sense of the phrase 'to achieve co-ordination'. But a second possible meaning may be intended by use of this phrase.

For this second meaning consider a traffic signal system that, when installed, is timed suboptimally. Southbound drivers find themselves waiting at red lights, let us say at 3.00 in the afternoon, for several minutes during which no traffic flows at all in the east–west directions. Clearly this waiting is unnecessary; it means that north–south drivers are compelled to act in a fashion that is not co-ordinated with the decisions of east–west drivers (since the latter have decided not to pass through the intersection at this time, yet the former have been prevented from taking advantage of those east–west decisions). But imagine now that the signal system is programmed in a manner that, at the beginning of each day, alters the system's timing to reflect yesterday's actual time-profile of traffic experience (registering not only the dearth of traffic in the east–west direction at 3.00 in the afternoon, but also the heavy volume of traffic in the north–south direction). Then the very experience that results today from the as-yet-imperfectly co-ordinated system plays its part in bringing about a revision in the system's timing, in a way that substitutes a better co-ordinated system in place of the less co-ordinated one. This kind of signal system (including its property of improving itself by 'learning' from the unfortunate results of its earlier imperfections) may also be described as one that 'achieves co-ordination'. However, here the phrase refers to the property of the system that permits it to identify and begin to correct its earlier weaknesses. The system begins its co-ordinating task at the very time when its signals promote *un*coordinated activity on the part of drivers – since it is that very uncoordinated activity that provides the information necessary for improved timing. The system's ability to achieve co-ordination, in this sense, certainly does *not* mean that, at the outset, it achieved the sets of results (a), (b) and (c) described in the preceding paragraph. Drivers proceeding south who have been directed to wait needlessly at the red light have, in effect, been informed *incorrectly* concerning the rate of traffic flow in the east–west direction. Yet, as we have seen, the system, from the very outset, has possessed the property of 'achieving co-ordination' in the sense of incorporating a feedback mechanism that deploys the results of its own inadequacies towards their systematic elimination. Here too the co-ordinating property of the system arises from the way that it provides information – but in a sense quite different from that relevant to the system that is *already* perfectly timed. In this second, initially faulty, system, the co-ordinating properties arise from its ability *to communicate information concerning its own faulty information communication properties.*

Let us return to the role of the price system in coping with the problems arising from dispersed knowledge – the 'economic problem which society faces'. We shall find (a) that prices tend to 'achieve co-ordination' in *both* the senses we have noticed in the traffic signal example, while (b) the literature has in fact recognized (and cited Hayek in regard to) only one of these two senses.

EQUILIBRIUM PRICES AND MARKET CO-ORDINATION

Economists often speak, nowadays, of the competitive equilibrium price system as an effective way in which the individual decisions of many market participants can be co-ordinated. Prices are, indeed, often compared with signals. Without knowing the details concerning the preferences of other market participants or concerning the conditions surrounding production processes, decision makers, through the guidance of these price signals, are led – economists explain – to that pattern of attempted activities that permits all of them to be carried out without disappointment and without regret.

In the Marshallian market for a single commodity, for example, the equilibrium market price for that commodity inspires the pattern of market clearing bids and offers. The price is such as to motivate potential buyers to ask for exactly that aggregate quantity of the commodity that potential suppliers have been motivated – by that same price – to produce. No buyer has been misled by the lowness of the price to seek to buy *more* than is in fact offered for sale. (And no buyer is discouraged from bidding for what is in fact available to him at a price he is prepared to pay.) No supplier has been misled by the height of this price to seek to produce more than is in fact being sought to be bought. (Nor is any supplier discouraged from offering that for which a price acceptable to him can be obtained.) No buyer need in fact know anything at all about the conditions of supply, the availabilities or the costs of inputs, and the like. Nor need the seller know anything about the preferences of consumers, the availability to them of substitute commodities, and the like. All that market partici-pants need to know, for the Marshallian market to co-ordinate buying and selling conditions perfectly, is the prevailing equilibrium price of the commodity. By offering to buy all they wish to buy at this price, buyers find that their offers smoothly dovetail with the offers of sellers to sell (with the latter merely offering to sell all they wish to sell at this same prevailing equilibrium price). The equilibrium price co-ordinates. All this is of course well understood, and is part of the basic equipment common to all economists.

Hayek's emphasis on knowledge is frequently cited in the context of this understanding of what equilibrium prices can achieve. Equilibrium prices are explained to be communicating to potential buyers and sellers, in highly economical fashion, the information necessary for co-ordinated decisions to emerge. It is because the detailed information concerning the preferences of individual potential buyers, and concerning the peculiar productive capabilities of individual sources of potential supply, is so scattered and dispersed that the co-ordinative ability of the equilibrium price system is so valuable and impressive.

This kind of co-ordinative ability recognized as being possessed by equilibrium prices is clearly analogous to the ability of an optimally timed traffic signal system smoothly and safely to co-ordinate traffic.[1] Equilibrium prices, like optimally timed signal changes, correctly communicate the information that (by virtue of the very notion of 'correctness' in this context) motivates and enables individual decision makers to generate a smoothly dovetailing set of decisions; a set that will entail neither disappointment nor regret. We must now show that, in addition to this possible sense in which prices may be said to achieve co-ordination (i.e. when the prices are already equilibrium prices – analogous to the already optimally timed signal system), there is also a much more important other possible sense in which prices may be said to achieve co-ordination. This sense refers to the possible ability of *dis*equilibrium prices to generate systematic changes in market decisions about price offers and bids, in a way that, by responding to the regrettable results of initially *un*coordinated sets of decisions, tends to replace them by less uncoordinated sets. (Here, of course, the analogy is to the non-optimally timed traffic signal system that contains a feedback mechanism through which the regrettable results of initial poor timing generate a tendency towards improved timing.)[2]

DISEQUILIBRIUM PRICES AND MARKET CO-ORDINATION

Consider the market for a single commodity (say, a given quality of tea) that has *not* attained equilibrium. Imagine, for example, that in different parts of this market there have occurred during the past 'day' sales of tea at widely differing prices. Imagine, moreover, that by the end of the day the total quantity of tea that has changed hands is far less than that which the realities of supply and demand conditions in fact warrant, so that potential suppliers remain holding inventories of tea which could, in truth, have been reduced by sale to eager buyers at prices that these suppliers would have found attractive. These market conditions express the co-ordination failures that have occurred: prices have failed to clear the market. The signals offered by bids and offers have failed to generate completely dovetailing sets of decisions; market participants, because of inadequate information concerning each other's attitudes, preferences and capabilities, have failed to take advantage of existing opportunities for mutually gainful exchange.

These unfortunate market conditions can be expected to result, sooner or later, in both disappointment and regret. Disappointment and regret may occur because sooner or later buyers will, perhaps, realize that, had they offered higher prices, they could have obtained more tea (and that they would have been happy to do so, even at the higher price, rather than go without tea because they foolishly believed it would be forthcoming at lower prices). Or sellers may realize that they might, had they only offered to sell at lower prices, have sold more tea (and that they would have preferred to do so rather than refusing to sell because of a mistaken belief that higher prices were available). In these cases disappointments arise as buyers (sellers) discover that their hopes to buy (sell) at low (high) prices were unrealistic. Regrets arise at not having realized that they would have been better advised to have offered to buy (sell) at higher (lower) prices. In addition, of course, since tea was sold at many different prices during the same day, many of those who sold (bought) at the low (high) prices will regret not having done so at the higher (lower) prices at which in fact tea exchanged elsewhere in the very same market.

These disappointments and regrets may generate sharp changes in the decisions made by potential buyers and sellers (even in the absence of change in the sets of 'real' determinants of their preferences and productive capabilities). Buyers who paid the high prices and sellers who accepted the low prices may revise their market attitudes, so that a tendency towards a uniform price may occur. Buyers (or sellers) who had overestimated the willingness of potential suppliers (or buyers) to sell (or buy) will realize their earlier errors and adjust their offers to the realities. In fact it is precisely because all these adjustments are likely to cause the initial sets of prices to give way to a different set (a set perhaps less divergent, and perhaps less likely to generate disappointments and regrets) that the initial market must be described as having been in disequilibrium. Without any outside

forces whatever (such as changes in preferences or in supply conditions) the initial sets of buying and selling offers are likely to give
way to different sets. Where the changes generated in this way are
systematically in the direction of better co-ordinated sets of decisions
(than in the initial period), we may surely describe the market (even
in its early, grossly discoordinated state) as possessing, to some
degree, an ability to achieve co-ordination. The very disappointments and regrets that result from initial co-ordination failures
systematically bring about improved sets of market decisions. Here
the appropriate analogy, surely, is to the initially faulty traffic signal
system.[3]

It should be noticed that here too the 'co-ordinative properties' of
the (disequilibrium) market derive from the ability of prices to communicate information, *but in a sense quite different from that in which
equilibrium prices may be said to co-ordinate through the accurate communication
of information*. Equilibrium prices co-ordinate because they are *already*
so adjusted ('pre-reconciled') that decisions that take these prices into
account turn out to be mutually reinforcing. Disequilibrium prices
can, if at all, be described as 'co-ordinating' only in the sense that
they reveal, to alert market participants, how *altered* decisions on their
part (from those that contributed to the emergence of these disequilibrium prices) may be wiser for the future. Thus disequilibrium prices
that are 'too low' (and which therefore generated excess demand)
suggest to some disappointed buyers that they should offer to pay
higher prices. Or again, to the extent that disequilibrium has
manifested itself in the emergence of many prices in the same market
for tea, this very spread between high and low prices suggests to some
alert entrepreneurs that arbitrage profits may be won through offering to buy at somewhat higher (that the lowest) prices and simultaneously offering to sell elsewhere at somewhat lower (than the
highest) prices. The information that inspires these 'co-ordinating'
changes is indeed information that is supplied by the initial structure
of prices, but so supplied only through alert *realization of the failures* of
those initial prices to achieve the kind of co-ordination that we found
in the case of equilibrium prices.

DISPERSED KNOWLEDGE, THE PRICE SYSTEM AND ECONOMIC LITERATURE

We have thus seen that the Hayekian insights into the nature of
the economic problem facing society permits us to recognize the

co-ordinative role of prices in a sense far more important than that played by equilibrium prices. The circumstance that information is dispersed offers society a 'communication' challenge not only because even the most fully co-ordinated set of decentralized decisions must *presuppose* and *contain* an effective signalling system. The circumstance that information is dispersed offers society a far more important 'communications' challenge – that of generating flows of information or of signals that might somehow stimulate the *revision* of initially *un*cordinated decisions in the direction of greater mutual co-ordinatedness.

So long as economists saw the economic problem to be one of achieving an efficient allocation of social resources (in the same way as the individual economizer faces the problem of private resource allocation), there could, of course, hardly be appreciation for the 'co-ordinative' contributions to social well-being that a price system can offer in helping overcome the problem of dispersed knowledge. As is by now fairly widely understood, as a consequence of what we have learned from Hayek, to talk of the problem of efficiently allocating society's resources is completely *to assume away and thus to overlook* the dispersed knowledge problem.

What is disappointing, in the way in which the profession has absorbed the Hayekian lesson, is that the literature appears to have failed to grasp the way in which the price system meets the 'communications' challenge, offered by the circumstance of dispersed knowledge, that we have described as being by far the more important one. Instead it appears to have focused entirely on the more superficial sense in which a price system may be said to communicate information, namely on the signalling role fulfilled by equilibrium prices.

Now, for textbook purposes this limited exploitation of the Hayekian insights is arguably understandable and defensible. Thus a number of contemporary textbooks[4] cite Hayek's well-known example of the tin market.

Assume that somewhere in the world a new opportunity for the use of . . . tin, has arisen, or that one of the sources of supply of tin has been eliminated. It does not matter for our purpose – and it is significant that it does not matter – which of these two causes has made tin more scarce. All that the users of tin need to know is that . . . they must economize tin. There is no need for the great majority of them even to know . . . in favor of what other needs they ought to husband the supply. . . . The mere fact that there is one price for any

commodity . . . brings about the solution which . . . might have
been arrived at by one single mind possessing all the information
which is in fact dispersed among all the people involved in the
process.

(Hayek 1949b: 85f.)

It is certainly true that this particular example of Hayek's is concerned only with the communication-of-information function fulfilled
by equilibrium prices. (This is quite clear, for example, from the
concluding sentences referring to the single price and to the coincidence between the results of there being a single price for tin
throughout the market, and the solution that might be arrived at by a
single omniscient mind.) This example does not focus on the communication problem that confronts a price system in which, as yet,
the bewildering arrays of market prices reflect only highly *uncoordinated* decisions on the parts of potential buyers and sellers. Yet
there is no need to criticize the textbooks for not going beyond the
simplest communication function of prices. There can be no doubt
that an understanding of this simpler Hayekian lesson at the beginning of one's study of economics can be profoundly beneficial.

What is more puzzling is that the deeper implications of the
Hayekian lesson have somehow failed to be noticed, not only in the
textbooks, but also in the more advanced literature that has referred
to Hayek's contribution. Thus, a considerable mathematical literature has emerged exploring the extent to which market prices convey
information in the face of stochastic supply and/or demand conditions
(see, for example, Grossman 1976; Grossman and Stiglitz 1976,
1980; Frydman 1982). The questions asked in this literature concern
whether or not uninformed market participants can derive correct
information from market prices themselves. Nowhere is there
enquiry as to whether entrepreneurial alertness and motivation may
perhaps be 'switched on' by the configuration of market prices, to
conjecture (and to try out!) hunches that may in fact be closer to the
truth (than the information that the prices themselves reflect).
Similarly, in what surely must be regarded as the most extensive and
wide-ranging development of the implications of the Hayekian
insights, Thomas Sowell's monumental *Knowledge and Decisions*, one
looks in vain for any discussion of the way in which prices and price
differences may stimulate a deployment of existing information that
might be superior to that which these prices themselves express.

To emphasize, as Sowell does throughout his work, that prices *summarize* economic knowledge (see especially Sowell 1980: 38) is of unquestioned value. But this insight into the relationship between prices and knowledge ignores the far more important truth that it is the very *inadequacies* that cloud the manner in which these price-summaries express existing knowledge that create the market incentives for their modification. The profit opportunities embedded in existing prices are thus extraordinarily effective communicators of knowledge (in a sense quite different from that in which prices summarize knowledge). Thus governmentally imposed obstacles to price flexibility not only (as Sowell so well, and in such rich detail, explains) prevent prices from telling the truth – they smother the emergence of those disequilibrium-price-generated incentives upon which the system depends for its very ability to discover and announce the truth.

HAYEK AND THE MARKET DISCOVERY PROCESS

Hayek himself (especially in the earlier work in which he developed his seminal insights concerning the social significance of the circumstance of dispersed knowledge) was not as explicit as one might have wished on the role of prices in the discovery process of the market. A reader mistakenly believing that the only sense in which prices may be said to carry information is that in which equilibrium prices correctly reflect ('summarize') the true supply and demand conditions might be excused for coming away from a reading of Hayek's papers on knowledge of 1937 and of 1945 without sensing any challenge to that belief. Although a number of passages in these earlier papers of Hayek criticized the standard view among welfare economists and others (i.e. the view that saw the economic problem as that of securing an efficient allocation by society of its given scarce resources) as reflecting undue emphasis on the equilibrium state (see for example Hayek 1949a: 93, fn. 2; 188), these papers did not explicitly show how disequilibrium prices play their role in solving Hayek's problems of dispersed knowledge. Yet, as we have seen, there can be no doubt, once one has understood the co-ordination problems implied by dispersed knowledge, about the role of disequilibrium prices in this regard. That Hayek did in fact intend his formulation of the knowledge problem to include also the role of prices in providing the incentives for their own modification appears clear from his discussions of competition as a process, and particularly from his later work on competition as a discovery procedure (Hayek 1949e, 1978b).

In Hayek's 1946 lecture 'The meaning of competition' he brilliantly distinguished the *state* of perfect competition from the dynamic competitive *process*. One of the conditions required for the former is perfect knowledge; the central achievement of the latter that 'it is only through the process of competition that the facts will be discovered'. When Hayek in this paper talks of 'spreading information' (1949e: 96, 106), he is not referring to the instantaneous transmission, through equilibrium price signals, of already known information. He is referring, instead, to the 'process of the formation of opinion' (p. 106). This process of opinion formation is one built out of a series of entrepreneurial steps, made possible by competitive freedom of entrepreneurial entry, and exemplified by the entry of one 'who possesses the exclusive knowledge . . . to reduce the cost of production of a commodity by 50 percent' and thus 'reduces its price by . . . 25 percent' (p. 101).

These insights were deepened and made even more explicit in Hayek's later 'Competition as a discovery procedure'. In this paper what is emphasized is not that prices act as signals transmitting existing information – but rather that it is the competitive process which *digs out* what is in fact discovered. The competitive process relies upon market data at any particular time only in the sense that 'provisional results from the market process at each stage . . . tell individuals what to look for' (1978b: 181). The 'high-degree of coincidence of expectations' that the market achieves 'is brought about by the systematic disappointment of some kind of expectations' (p. 185). The 'generally beneficial effects of competition must include disappointing or defeating some particular expectations or intentions' (p. 180). In fact, 'competition is valuable *only* because, and so far as, its results are unpredictable and on the whole different from those which anyone has, or could have, deliberately aimed at'.

What emerges from these Hayekian insights into the *discovery* properties inherent in the competitive process is the recognition, surely, that the incentives offered by market prices *during* this competitive process are the key elements in motivating competitive-entrepreneurial entry and discovery. In this sense prices play a role in 'spreading information' quite different from their role as signals communicating *already discovered* information under equilibrium conditions.

COMMUNICATION AND DISCOVERY

Equilibrium prices permit market participants to 'read' the relevant information needed for their activities to be mutually adjusted in co-ordinated fashion. Disequilibrium prices are far less helpful in this regard; in fact a good deal of the 'information' that trusting market participants 'learn' from disequilibrium prices is quite incorrect and may be responsible for waste and frustration. As communicators, as signals, disequilibrium prices are relatively poor performers (when compared, of course, with the questionably-relevant standard set in this regard by equilibrium prices). Indeed, markets and the market system have often been criticized for the co-ordination failures that disequilibrium prices both express and help generate. What Hayek's 'Austrian' insights permit us to see is that the social function served by market prices is captured far more significantly by the concept of *discovery* than by that of communication.

In regard to discovery, market prices (especially disequilibrium prices) should be seen not so much as known signals to be deliberately consulted *in order to find out* the right thing to do, but rather as spontaneously generated flashing red lights *alerting* hitherto unwitting market participants to the possibility of pure entrepreneurial profit or the danger of loss. These discoveries, surely, constitute the crucial steps through which markets tend to achieve co-ordination, gradually replacing earlier states of widespread mutual ignorance by successively better co-ordinated states of society.

No doubt the economics profession has much to learn about the subtle manner in which this market discovery procedure works. Surely the future historian of economic thought will trace back future development in this branch of social understanding to those seminal and path-breaking papers in which Hayek taught us the crucial importance of dispersed knowledge in creating *the* economic problem which society faces.

Chapter 9

Economic planning and the knowledge problem

INTRODUCTION

It is now about forty years since Professor Hayek decisively identified the key misconception underlying mainstream welfare economics. This misconception, Hayek argued, was responsible for failure to appreciate the critique of the possibility of rational economic calculation under central planning – a critique stated most forcefully and clearly by Mises, and further developed by Hayek himself. As has been demonstrated by Professor Lavoie (1985a), the true import and significance of the Hayekian lesson was simply not grasped by subsequent welfare economists writing on the socialist calculation debate, even though Hayek's work was widely cited.

In this chapter we attempt both to restate and to extend Hayek's insight concerning the 'knowledge problem' and its implications for central economic planning, whether comprehensive in scope or otherwise. In the following paragraphs we cite Hayek's own formulation of his insight, and make certain observations concerning it. In subsequent sections of the chapter we start from a rather *different* point of departure, and in this way eventually arrive at our restatement and extension of the Hayekian position – spelling out some rather radical implications of our restatement.

According to Hayek (1949b: 77–8):

> The peculiar character of the problem of a rational economic order is determined precisely by the fact that the knowledge of the circumstances of which we must make use never exists in concentrated or integrated form but solely as the dispersed bits of incomplete and frequently contradictory knowledge which all the separate individuals possess. The economic problem of society is thus not merely a problem of how to allocate 'given' resources – if

'given' is taken to mean given to a single mind which deliberately solves the problem set by these 'data'. It is rather a problem of how to secure the best use of resources known to any of the members of society, for ends whose relative importance only these individuals know. Or, to put it briefly, it is a problem of the utilization of knowledge which is not given to anyone in its totality.

Let us call *this* knowledge problem 'Hayek's knowledge problem'. We note, at this initial stage in our discussion, that the position might be taken that Hayek's knowledge problem does *not*, at least at first glance, render immediately irrelevant the paramountcy of the social efficiency norm. It is true, as Hayek pointed out, that the dispersed character of knowledge means that the economic problem is not that of allocating 'given' resources, where 'given resources' means resources given and known to a single mind. But surely knowledge itself is a scarce resource. Thus the task of the central planner may be seen, in the light of Hayek's knowledge problem, as that of making the most effective use of the available dispersed knowledge existing in society at a given moment – with the attainment of such use constrained by the communication and search costs made necessary by the dispersed character of the available information.

It might seem, therefore, that there is nothing in Hayek's knowledge problem which places it outside the scope of economic planning. The knowledge problem, it might be argued, complicates the planning task: it introduces a newly recognized, subtle and complex resource (knowledge); it compels attention to the special characteristics of this resource (its dispersed character); and it calls for attention to a special class of costs (those required for search and communication). But Hayek's knowledge problem can still, it might seem, be subsumed under the overall economic problem, traditionally conceived in resource allocation terms. The central theme of this chapter is to deny this understanding of the implications of Hayek's knowledge problem.[1]

In this chapter I shall argue that this problem of securing the best use of dispersed knowledge, in fact, *cannot* be translated into a special case of the more general problem of securing an efficient allocation of society's resources. It will follow that societal planning, by its very character, is incapable of addressing Hayek's problem – such planning can only frustrate and hamper those spontaneous market forces that *are* capable of engaging this knowledge problem. In order to develop these arguments it will be useful to introduce a 'knowledge problem' that at first glance seems very different from Hayek's.

THE INDIVIDUAL PLAN AND THE KNOWLEDGE PROBLEM

In the course of everyday life man continually *plans*. Economists have come to formulate the individual plan as the seeking of a maximum: the planner is intent on arriving at a constrained optimum position. This is the concept of the economizing decision articulated with special precision and force by Lionel Robbins in 1932 (Robbins 1935), and widely adopted since then as the basic building block of microeconomic theory. We wish to point out that there is an inescapable potential 'knowledge problem' surrounding this concept of the individual plan.

The notion of the plan presupposes some deliberately aimed at entity – say, utility or profit – that is to be knowingly maximized. It further presupposes known resource constraints. In Robbins' terminology, both the ends and the means are presumed to be *given*. It is the presumed knowledge of these planning circumstances by the planner that permits the economist to perceive the plan as the solving of a constrained maximization problem. The validity of the plan itself, it should be noted, depends entirely on the validity of the assumption that the planner in fact accurately knows the circumstances surrounding his prospective decisions. If the planner does not know what it is that he is seeking to achieve, or does not know what resources are at his command, or what the efficacy of these resources is with respect to sought-after goals, then his plan – no matter how carefully formulated – is unlikely to result in the best possible outcome.

We can now identify the knowledge problem potentially relevant to each individual plan. *Because of inadequacies in the planner's knowledge of his true circumstances, his plan may fail to yield an attainable optimum.* Let us call *this* knowledge problem the 'basic knowledge problem'. This will distinguish it from what we have called 'Hayek's knowledge problem'. It will also indicate our intention to demonstrate that Hayek's knowledge problem can be considered a special case of what we call the 'basic knowledge problem'. To be sure, what we have called the 'basic knowledge problem' seems, at first glance, to bear little resemblance to Hayek's. Hayek's knowledge problem consists in the dispersed character of available information; our basic knowledge problem consists in an individual's simple ignorance of the circumstances relevant to his situation. Further reflection on both Hayek's knowledge problem and our basic knowledge problem, however, will reveal the important sense in which Hayek's problem is indeed a basic one. Let us first clarify a possible misunderstanding concerning the basic knowledge problem.

THE BASIC KNOWLEDGE PROBLEM AND THE ECONOMICS OF SEARCH

It might be argued that the basic knowledge problem surrounding every individual plan can be entirely escaped through the addition of new planning stages. After all, if a plan seems likely to fail because of inadequate availability of a necessary resource, this threatened failure need not be final; it may possibly be avoided by appropriate preliminary planning to obtain this resource. Instead of simply formulating a single plan directed at the immediate attainment of the final objective, it is necessary to introduce intermediate objectives to be pursued in the course of additional preliminary plans. Perhaps, then, the basic knowledge problem, too, merely calls for judicious preliminary planning.

From this perspective the basic knowledge problem would appear merely to represent an inadequacy in the available supply of an important resource, namely, knowledge. This inadequacy would then be seen to call for a *planned search* to acquire the necessary information. In principle, it might then be thought that the basic knowledge problem can be escaped, at least to the same extent that any other problem arising out of a resource shortage can be escaped. To the extent that it is worthwhile, a preliminary plan of search to overcome the shortage of necessary information may totally eliminate the basic knowledge problem. To the extent that such a costly search is held not to be worthwhile, the basic knowledge problem would seem merely to express the inescapable scarcity constraints inherent in the planner's situation. For the economist such an inescapable scarcity problem means that there is no problem at all, in the relevant sense.

To the extent that the knowledge problem is escapable, it can (and presumably will) be escaped; to the extent that it is not worthwhile escaping, there would appear to be no basic knowledge problem at all – since we defined the basic knowledge problem in terms of failure to realize an *attainable optimum*. If lack of knowledge renders a hypothetical optimum unattainable, it can generate no basic knowledge problem. And if the cost of acquiring the knowledge is prohibitive, then the 'hypothetical optimum', while indeed 'attainable', is in fact no optimum at all.

But this line of argument cannot be sustained. The basic knowledge problem potentially surrounding each individual plan is by its nature inescapable. Certainly a deficiency in knowledge may be able to be rectified by search, and the individual planner will no doubt consider, in his preliminary planning, whether such search should be undertaken or not. But the basic knowledge problem – involving possible failure to achieve an attainable optimum – remains. In fact the possibility of preliminary planning to acquire knowledge only *expands* the scope of the basic knowledge problem.

Let us consider an individual engaging in a plan seeking to achieve a valued objective. Let us call this Plan A. In formulating the specific steps that should be taken in pursuing Plan A, the individual realizes that he lacks needed pieces of information. He thereupon engages in a plan to attain these preliminary objectives, namely these missing pieces of information. Let us call this search plan Plan B. We can see Plan A as having been *expanded* (as a result of realized ignorance) to *include* the planned attainment of needed preliminary objectives, so that Plan B is 'nested' within expanded Plan A. And we can identify the later steps to be taken in the course of expanded Plan A – those steps subsequent to the attainment of the information obtained in Plan B – as Plan A'. (Plan A' consists in the steps that would have made up the originally envisaged Plan A had the planner in fact *not* lacked the needed information.) We can easily see that the basic knowledge problem is a potential hazard both for Plan B and Plan A'. Plan A which includes Plan B and Plan A', is of course subject to the vulnerabilities of both of them.

Even if Plan B is completely successful in attaining precisely the optimal amount of information capable of being searched for (and believed to be worth the costs of such search), Plan A is none the less still subject to the hazards of the basic knowledge problem. After all, although our decision maker, in originally seeking to formulate Plan A, realized he lacked specific items of information (and therefore undertook preliminary Plan B), he may have in fact *lacked far more information* than he realized. (Most important, such unrealized information may have taken the form of a firm, but totally mistaken, belief in the validity of information that is totally false.) Moreover he may be mistaken in his belief that the items of information he realizes he lacks are necessary for the implementation of Plan A. He also may be mistaken in his belief that he really lacks these items of information (in the relevant sense of lacking). The truth may be that these items are already within his grasp.

For example, he may believe that Plan A, in the course of which he must communicate with individual Z, requires information concerning Z's telephone number, information that he believes himself to lack, so that he undertakes Plan B to search for Z's telephone number. But the truth may be quite different. The truth may be that Z is in fact the wrong person to speak to altogether, or again the truth may be that Z is now in the very same room with our planner, so that no knowledge of Z's telephone number is in fact needed for Plan A. Or, it may be, our planner does not really 'lack' Z's telephone number at all; he may in fact have that telephone number clearly written and identified in the list of telephone numbers that lies next to the telephone that he uses. Given these possibilities for sheer error that surround Plan A' and/or Plan B, possibilities in which the planner is entirely unaware of the extent of his ignorance, Plan A (because it includes Plan A' and Plan B) may be far from optimal even if Plan B is wholly successful in terms of its own objectives. In addition it may be the case that Plan B overlooks more efficient available ways of achieving its own objectives (e.g. there may be less costly methods of search of which the searcher is unaware).

To sum up, the possibility of planned search for information perceived to be lacking does not eliminate the knowledge problem. First, the planned search may itself be undertaken without awareness that more efficient search techniques are easily available. Second, the information sought may in fact not justify the costs of search because the truth (of which the planner is unaware) is that the information is *not* of significance for the attainment of the planner's ultimate objectives. Third, quite apart from the information that the planner realizes he lacks and for which he may attempt to search, he may lack other information that he does *not* realize he lacks and for which he does not think of undertaking any planned research.

CENTRAL PLANNING AND THE KNOWLEDGE PROBLEM

We are now in a position to appreciate Hayek's insight into the problem of dispersed knowledge as revealing *the central planning task to be one that is deeply and inextricably bound up in the basic knowledge problem.* Let us put ourselves in the position of the central planners, earnestly and single-mindedly seeking after the most efficient possible pattern of resource allocation.

Our task as central planners is to formulate a plan for society in a manner analogous to that in which an individual plans his own course of action. We formulate our social plan with respect to specific social objectives and in the light of specific perceived arrays of available social resources.[2] This framework for the central plan is relevant (in principle and with the necessary changes having been made) both for comprehensive social planning and for central planning designed merely to supplement or modify, rather than totally replace, decentralized economic activity. The analogy between the social plan and the individual plan compels us, of course, to acknowledge the relevance of the basic knowledge problem for the social plan, in exactly the same way as we have seen it to be an inevitable and inescapable hazard for the individual plan. *Hayek's contribution permits us to recognize that the central plan may be subject to hazards (arising out of the basic knowledge problem) that might have been escaped by decentralized planning.*

That the centralized plan is inescapably subject to the hazards of the basic knowledge problem follows almost trivially from the very notion of the basic knowledge problem. Because the individual planner may not be aware of his true circumstances and may be totally unaware of his ignorance, his best formulated plans may fail to yield an attainable optimum. The central planners, too, may be unaware of their own ignorance concerning the true circumstances relevant to the social plan. Our understanding of the implications of dispersed knowledge deepens our appreciation of the seriousness of the basic knowledge problem, and reveals how the hazards of this problem *might* have been entirely escaped in the absence of the centralized plan.

Recognition of the fact of dispersed knowledge – especially as regards 'the knowledge of particular circumstances of time and place' (Hayek 1949b: 80) – immediately illuminates our understanding of the basic knowledge problem that threatens central planners. For a planning individual, the basic knowledge problem derives from the possibility that what he thinks he knows about his circumstances may differ from what he *might* have known (without additional resource expenditure) had he been more alert or aware of the true environment.

The same possibility, of course, is fully relevant for a central planner, but it is heightened by the central planner's peculiar predicament. What the central planner thinks he knows about the relevant circumstances *must necessarily take the form of what he thinks he knows about the availability of dispersed bits of knowledge that can somehow, at some cost, be mobilized in formulating and implementing the social plan.* There is little chance that the central planner can ever know where to find, or how to search for, all the items of dispersed information known somewhere in the economic system. Moreover there seems little chance that the central planner can ever be fully aware of the nature or extent of the specific gaps in his own knowledge in this regard. He may realize, in a general way, that there is information the location of which he is ignorant, but this gives him no clue where to look. The end result is that the planner is unlikely to be able to exploit all the information that is within his command. Clearly the dispersal of information is responsible for a new dimension of application for the basic knowledge problem.

Earlier we raised the possibility that Hayek's knowledge problem – despite its novelty – might be subsumed under the general economic problem, traditionally conceived in terms of achieving an efficient allocation of given resources (with available information included as an important given resource). We can now see how inappropriate it is for us to consider central planners as being able to grapple with Hayek's knowledge problem in terms of conventional planning to achieve a constrained optimum pattern of resource allocation. The unknown ignorance that is the heart of the knowledge problem created by the dispersal of information defies its being able to be squeezed into the Procrustean bed of the allocation plan. Just as the individual planner is unable to grapple deliberately with the basic knowledge problem surrounding all decision making, so too is the central planner unable to invoke planning techniques to grapple deliberately with Hayek's knowledge problem.

What renders the Hayekian knowledge problem critique of central planning so devastating is the circumstance that in a market system, with decentralized decision making, *the insoluble knowledge problem confronted by central planners tends to dissolve through the entrepreneurial-competitive discovery procedure.*

THE ENTREPRENEURIAL-COMPETITIVE DISCOVERY PROCEDURE

The Hayekian case of decentralized decision making has frequently been misunderstood. All too frequently this case is presented as arguing only that the decentralized market economy escapes the problem of dispersed knowledge because prices accurately *and economically* convey necessary information to relevant decision makers (replacing any need for them to know *all* the detailed information that is dispersed throughout the system). It must be emphasized that while this line of reasoning is certainly present in Hayek's work, it fails to do justice to the full implications of that work.

To argue that market prices convey information, and thus directly overcome the problem of dispersed knowledge, is to make a case for markets that depends upon a dubious assumption: namely, that markets are always at or close to equilibrium. It is only in equilibrium that it can be claimed that a market participant guided by market prices is automatically steered toward those actions that will co-ordinate smoothly with the actions of all the other (similarly guided) market participants. Moreover, to make the assumption that markets are close to equilibrium is essentially (quite apart from our other reasons for feeling uncomfortable concerning the realism of this assumption) *to beg* (rather than to overcome) the Hayekian problem of dispersed knowledge. After all, just as the phenomenon of dispersed knowledge offers a formidable challenge to central planners, this phenomenon offers markets a wholly analogous challenge, namely that of *achieving*, in fact, those arrays of market prices that will clear markets.

One does not 'solve' the problem of dispersed knowledge by *postulating* prices that will smoothly generate dovetailing decisions. Dispersed knowledge is precisely the reason for the very realistic possibility that market prices at a given date are *unable* to clear markets and to ensure the absence of wasted resources. The truth is that the market *does* possess weapons to combat (if not wholly to conquer) the problem of dispersed knowledge. These weapons are embodied in the workings of the price system, but *not* in the workings of a hypothetical system of equilibrium prices. The importance of prices for coping with the Hayekian knowledge problem does not lie in the accuracy of the information which equilibrium prices convey concerning the actions of others who are similarly informed. Rather, its importance lies in the ability of disequilibrium prices to offer pure profit opportunities that can attract the notice of alert, profit-seeking entrepreneurs. Where market participants have failed to co-ordinate their activites because of dispersed knowledge, this expresses itself in an array of prices that suggests to alert entrepreneurs where they may win pure profits.

We know very little about the precise way in which pure profit opportunities attract entrepreneurial attention. But there can be little doubt about the powerful magnetism which such opportunities exert. To say that pure profit opportunities attract attention is not at all to say that awareness of these opportunities is secured by deliberate, costly search on the part of entrepreneurs. Rather it is to recognize that the lure of pure profit is what permits an individual decision maker to transcend the limits of a given, perceived planning frame-work and to escape, to some extent, the basic knowledge problem that surrounds all individual decision making. Man's entrepreneurial alertness operates at all times to place his narrow planning activities within the broader framework of *human action*.[3] *At the very same time* as man is routinely calculating the optimal allocation of given resources with respect to given competing ends, he keeps an entrepreneurial ear cocked for anything that might suggest that the available resources are different from what had been assumed, or that perhaps a different array of goals might be worth striving for.

This entrepreneurial element in human action is what responds to the signals for pure profit that are generated by the errors that arise out of the dispersed knowledge available in society. It is this yeast that ferments the competitive-entrepreneurial discovery process, tending to reveal to market participants more and more of the relevant infor-mation scattered throughout the market. It is this entrepreneurial-competitive process that thus grapples with that basic knowledge problem we found inescapably to confront central planning authori-ties. To the extent that central planning displaces the entrepreneurial discovery process, whether on the society-wide scale of comprehen-sive planning or on the more modest scale of state piecemeal interven-tion in an otherwise free market, the planners are at the same time both smothering the market's ability to transcend the basic know-ledge problem and subjecting themselves helplessly to that very problem. The problem's source is Hayek's dispersed knowledge: central planning has no tools with which to engage the problem of dispersed knowledge, and its very centralization means that the market's discovery process has been impeded, if not brought to a full halt.

MARKETS, FIRMS AND CENTRAL PLANNING

At least as far back as Coase's 1937 paper on the theory of the firm, it has been recognized that each firm in a market economy is an island of local 'central planning' in a sea of spontaneously seething competi-tive market forces. Within the firm, activities are co-ordinated by central direction, not by market competition via a price mechanism. Our discussion in this chapter throws light, perhaps, on the forces governing the location of the boundaries separating the realm of freely adopted 'central planning' from that of the competitive price system.

We have seen that the replacement of market discovery (working through entrepreneurial alertness to profit opportunities) by central planning generates a new scope of potency for the basic knowledge problem arising out of the dispersal of knowledge. In a free market, therefore, any advantages that may be derived from 'central planning' (e.g. the avoidance of 'wasteful' duplication often apparently present in situations of market rivalry) are purchased at the price of an enhanced knowledge problem. We may expect firms spontaneously to tend to expand to the point where additional advantages of 'central' planning are just offset by the incremental knowledge difficulties that stem from dispersed information. On a small scale the latter difficulties may be insignificant enough to be worth absorbing in order to take advantage of explicitly co-ordinated organization. Knowledge dispersed over a small geographical organizational area may mean a Hayekian knowledge problem that, unlike that relevant to large, complex entities, is solvable through deliberate search. Beyond some point, however, the knowledge difficulties will tend to reduce the profitability of firms that are too large. Competition between firms of different sizes and scope will tend, therefore, to reveal the optimal extent of such 'central planning'.

On the other hand if central planning is *imposed* on an otherwise free market, whether in comprehensive terms or not, such planning will almost always involve the knowledge problem, and to an extent *not* likely to be justified by any advantages that centralization might otherwise afford. Governmentally enforced central planning sweeps away the market's delicate and spontaneous weapons for grappling with the knowledge problem, Such centralized planning is by its very nature, and the nature of the knowledge problem, unable to offer any substitute weapons of its own.

CONCLUSION

We should remember that the nature of the knowledge problem is such that its extent and seriousness cannot be known in advance. Part of the tragedy of proposals for industrial policy and economic planning is that their well-meaning advocates are totally unaware of the knowledge problem – the problem arising out of unawareness of one's ignorance.

Chapter 10

Knowledge problems and their solutions: some relevant distinctions

INTRODUCTION

A central role in Hayek's thought has been played by his insights into the problems posed by the phenomenon of dispersed knowledge. These insights first emerged as a result of Hayek's participation in the inter-war debate on the possibility of socialist economic calculation and were crystallized in his classic 1945 paper 'The use of knowledge in society' (1949b). Although these insights were originally born out of Hayek's economics, for the past three decades they have nourished those profound contributions to other branches of social philosophy which have come to dominate Hayek's recent work.

The classic 1945 passage in which Hayek definitively articulated his original, economic insight, reads as follows:

> The peculiar character of the problem of a rational economic order is determined . . . by the fact that the knowledge of the circumstances of which we must make use never exists in concentrated or integrated form but solely as the dispersed bits of incomplete and frequently contradictory knowledge which all the separate individuals possess. The economic problem of society is thus not merely a problem of how to allocate 'given' resources – if 'given' is taken to mean given to a single mind which deliberately solves the problem set by these 'data'. It is rather a problem of how to secure the best use of resources known to any of the members of society, for ends whose relative importance only these individuals know. Or, to put it briefly, it is a problem of the utilization of knowledge which is not given to anyone in its totality.
>
> (Hayek 1949b: 77–8)

Some thirty years later, in introducing his three-volume *Law, Legislation and Liberty*, Hayek recognized the seminal part played by these insights for his more general discussions of later years.

> The insight into the significance of our institutional ignorance in the economic sphere . . . was in fact the starting point for those ideas which in [*Law, Legislation and Liberty*] are systematically applied to a much wider field.
>
> (Hayek 1973: 13)[1]

Indeed, already in 1960, in *The Constitution of Liberty*, Hayek was applying his 1945 economic insights into a far wider field. Hayek there points out that the 'sum of the knowledge of all the individuals exists nowhere as an integrated whole. The great problem is how we can all profit from this knowledge, which exists only dispersed as the separate, partial, and sometimes conflicting beliefs of all men.' He proceeds immediately to observe: 'In other words, it is largely because civilization enables us constantly to profit from knowledge which individually we do not possess and because each individual's use of his particular knowledge may serve to assist others unknown to him in achieving their ends that men as members of civilized society can pursue their individual ends so much more successfully than they could alone.' All this leads Hayek to refer to the 'identification of the growth of civilization with the growth of knowledge' (1960: 25), pointing out that the 'more civilized we become, the more relatively ignorant must each individual be of the facts on which the working of his civilization depends. The very division of knowledge increases the necessary ignorance of the individual of most of his knowledge' (p. 26). Our discussion in this chapter explores the meaning of the problem of dispersed knowledge by probing the legitimacy of Hayek's extension of his original, narrowly economic insight to apply to civilization in general, and to its various institutions in particular.

THE EXTENSION OF HAYEK'S KNOWLEDGE PROBLEM

In his recent work Hayek has indeed concentrated on the significance of the 'knowledge problem' (as, following Lavoie (1985b: Ch. 3), we shall now call it) as extending far beyond the capacity of market processes to co-ordinate the mutual expectations which market participants hold concerning one another. Hayek has emphasized the significance of the knowledge problem for the evolution of social and cultural norms and institutions. The intricate webs of mutually sustaining expectations required for the emergence of our most valuable social institutions, Hayek argues, could never conceivably have been deliberately simulated by any centralized organization. What has nurtured the spontaneous emergence of such benign cultural norms and institutions, Hayek maintains, is the circumstance that social processes of spontaneous co-ordination have been able to evolve. It is only in this way that a social fabric consisting of innumerable threads of mutual expectations – a fabric the totality of which displays a complexity transcending the capacity of any single mind – could possibly come to be woven.

Now, it is no doubt incorrect and unfair to attribute to Hayek the categorical assertion that whatever institutions evolve spontaneously are more likely to be socially benign than any deliberately constructed institutions could possibly be. Yet various writers have noted their discomfort at feeling how close Hayek appears sometimes to be to such a view. Although Hayek points out that he 'has carefully avoided saying that evolution is identical with progress', he makes it clear that 'it was the evolution of a tradition which made civilization possible', and asserts flatly 'that spontaneous evolution is a necessary if not a sufficient condition of progress' (Hayek 1979: 168). Buchanan, in particular, has placed his finger on the theme that has become increasingly important in Hayek's recent writings:

This theme involves the extension of the principle of spontaneous order, in its *normative* implications, to the emergence of institutional structure itself. . . . There is no room left for the political economist, or for anyone else who seeks to reform social structures to *change* laws and rules, with an aim of securing increased efficiency in the large. Any attempt to design, construct, and to change institutions must, within this logical setting strictly interpreted, introduce inefficiency. Any 'constructively rational' interferences with the 'natural' processes of history are therefore to be studiously avoided. The message seems clear: relax before the slow sweep of history.

(Buchanan 1986: 75–6)[2]

Buchanan struggles to exonerate Hayek from the charge of actually supporting the full extreme position outlined in the preceding paragraph, and to resolve apparent contradictions between Hayek's more consistently anti-constructivist statements and his own attempts (such as his proposal for the denationalization of money, and his proposals for political constitutional reconstruction) at institutional reform.[3]

Yet the strong impression one gains from Hayek remains that he has profound faith in the possibility, in general, of benign institutional evolution.

In the present chapter I shall join Hayek's critics in questioning the asserted parallelism (between the achievements of free markets within a given institutional setting and the spontaneous evolution of institutions themselves) which has formed the foundation for Hayek's work in recent decades. I shall proceed by first carefully dissecting the original Hayekian knowledge problem into two distinct component problems, both of which have their counterparts in the context of the emergence of social norms and institutions. It will then become apparent that only one of these two component problems permits solution, in the context of institutional development, in a manner parallel to that in which its counterpart problem is solved in markets. The remaining component of the knowledge problem turns out, in the institutional development context, not to be solvable by the spontaneous process through which its counterpart problem in markets is solved. The purpose of our critique, it should be emphasized, is not so much to challenge the analogies which Hayek draws between market and society, as to explore some subtleties in the knowledge problem which Hayek has taught us to appreciate. That Hayek has himself not always seemed sensitive to these subtleties makes this task, of course, only all the more important.

THE KNOWLEDGE PROBLEM IN MARKET CONTEXT

Consider a single commodity market in competitive equilibrium. A market clearing price prevails. No market participant need know more than the market price to be able to carry out his plans without disappointment or regret. Each seller finds himself able to sell what he wishes to sell at the market price. Each buyer finds himself able to buy what he wishes to buy at the market price. The amount of knowledge possessed by each market participant need not be more than miniscule. No one need know the shape or position of either the demand or the supply curve. Yet the market price stimulates a series of independent decisions which permits all possible mutually gainful trades between any pair of market participants to occur. Suppose now that some catastrophe strikes the industry producing our commodity, drastically shifting its supply curve to the left. Market price will rise and buyers of the commodity will find themselves constrained to economize more than previously on the use of this product – and will be guided by the higher market price to do so, without ever learning about the catastrophe, knowing only that the market price is now higher than it had been before. Many textbook presentations of Hayek's vision of how markets solve the knowledge problem see this achievement of the equilibrium market as the paradigmatic illustration of the knowledge problem and its market solution.

What the market solution has achieved, these expositions show, is that the market is able to mobilize dispersed knowledge as if all the information were concentrated in a single mind. Although knowledge is in fact dispersed, to a degree making it inconceivable that all of it might indeed be available to a single mind, the market successfully and spontaneously yields a social result which exploits every relevant bit of knowledge.

Careful consideration of this achievement of the market in equilibrium reveals, we wish to point out, two quite different achievements. Each of these achievements, we argue, corresponds to a distinct component of Hayek's knowledge problem. Let us see how this is the case.

The market clearing price can prevail only because no market participant makes any offer to sell or to buy which is not accepted. Each market participant correctly anticipates the responses which others will make to any offer or bid he proposes. No attempted decision has been based on undue optimism; no attempted decision has thus been disappointed. Of course we can easily imagine situations in which this happy state of affairs does not occur. Market participants may mistakenly believe that others will buy even at very high prices or that others will be prepared to sell even at very low prices. Such over-optimistic mistakes are very natural: they arise because market participants may not know what the other market participants know about themselves, namely that they are not prepared to buy at the high prices (or sell at the low prices). As a result of this dispersed knowledge (people knowing only their own attitudes, not those of others), markets may easily fail to clear (since over-optimistic sellers may have held out for prices that were too high *etc.*). We shall recognize this possible failure, due to over-optimism (resulting from the dispersion of knowledge), as the first of the two knowledge problems we wish to identify. We shall refer to it as Knowledge Problem A.

A little thought will convince us, however, that Knowledge Problem A is not the only knowledge problem successfully solved in the case of the market clearing price. Over-optimism is not the only reason why the market clearing price may not be achieved throughout the market. Imagine a situation – the stylized conditions of which are postulated only to illustrate a point relevant to far more realistic and typical problems – in which a wall, or an ocean, separates one half of the market from the other (but with this separation entailing no costs of transportation for the journey from one market sector to the other). It could easily happen, in such a situation, that this separation generates two separate markets, in each of which a (different) market clearing price prevails. It should be clear that here, too (just as in the *single* market clearing price case discussed earlier), Knowledge Problem A has been successfully solved. No market participant (in the two separate 'markets') has made a buying/selling proposal, fully expecting it to be accepted, which turns out to be rejected. No one has been over-optimistic concerning the responses of others to offers made available to them.

But it should also be clear that, in this case of the two 'markets', even though in each of them the local price clears the market, errors have none the less been made. The existence of two separate prices (in these two markets) for the identical commodity indicates that those paying the higher price erroneously overlooked the possibility of buying more cheaply in the other market; those selling for the lower price erroneously overlooked the possibility of selling at a higher price in the other market. Some participants in the high-price market refrain from buying (because of the high price) and remain without the commodity, even while that commodity is available in the other market. This is matched by the circumstance that some participants in the low-price market refrain from selling (at the low price) while potential buyers willing to pay higher prices could have been found in the high-price market. Market participants have failed to grasp opportunities that *might* have been grasped – if only they had more accurate knowledge concerning what others *might* have been prepared to do. Clearly these errors (while not constituting a problem identical with Knowledge Problem A, which arose because market participants were over-optimistic) constitute a knowledge problem: market participants are (over-pessimistically) unaware of what others *might* be willing to pay (or be willing to sell for). We shall call this second problem, the problem of undue pessimism arising from dispersed knowledge, Knowledge Problem B.

THE TWO KNOWLEDGE PROBLEMS

A little thought will convince us that Knowledge Problems A and B really are distinct problems.[4] Both arise from the circumstance of dispersed information, but consist in distinctly different kinds of error. My incomplete information concerning what others would like to do may lead me over-optimistically to expect to sell at very high prices. Here my incomplete information has led me to expect behaviour on the part of others which will in fact not occur. The errors thus constituting Knowledge Problem A tend to be *self-revealing* – since they stimulate proposals which are bound to be disappointed. Knowledge Problem A, in the market context, generates a process of equilibration which appears well-nigh inevitable. As Hayek himself put it, in apparently referring to this kind of equilibration process, the relevant knowledge which a market participant 'must possess in order that equilibrium may prevail is the knowledge which he is bound to acquire in view of the position in which he originally is, and the plans which he then makes'.[5]

My incomplete information concerning what others would like to do may, on the other hand, unduly pessimistically lead me to believe it impossible to sell at quite low prices (at which others would in fact be delighted to buy), compelling me to give up the idea of selling altogether. Here incomplete information has led market participants (between whom the possibility for mutually gainful exchange exists) to overlook this possibility, to their mutual (but never sensed) misfortune. Knowledge Problem B is here responsible for failure to make a move required for Pareto optimality. This Knowledge Problem B does not result in disappointed plans; it results in failure to achieve potential gains (because they remain unperceived). Because the misfortune caused by Knowledge Problem B has been unperceived, there is (unlike in the case of Knowledge Problem A) no inevitability that the problem will ever be revealed and corrected. What market participants fail to know about each other today, they may easily continue to fail to know tomorrow.

In market clearing equilibrium, of course, *both* Knowledge Problems have come to be solved (in regard to the market under consideration). It is not only the case, in market clearing equilibrium, that each attempt to buy or to sell is successfully able to be carried out. It is also the case that no possibly mutually gainful trade between a potential buyer and seller (both of whom are participants in this market) fails to be consummated. We can easily understand how it has come about, in this equilibrium, that no one has been led over-optimistically to ask any too-high price (or to offer any too-low price). We understand, that is, that any such over-optimistic errors have *corrected themselves*: disappointments have taught market participants not to expect unrealizable responses. We understand, that is, how Knowledge Problem A has been solved.

But we are not so immediately able to understand how, in market clearing equilibrium, Knowledge Problem B, as well, has come to be solved. It is not at all so obvious how the many overlooked possibilities for mutually gainful trade – possibilities which, given initial dispersed knowledge, could hardly have failed to have been overlooked – have somehow come to be revealed. What has caused market participants to know (about each other's potential attitudes) what they did not know yesterday?

Of course, economic theory explains how Knowledge Problem B has come to be solved in market equilibrium. It turns out that this solution is in fact quite different from that which has solved Knowledge Problem A. Whereas Knowledge Problem A was self-correcting, Knowledge Problem B created *an incentive for its solution by discovery in the activity of profit-alert entrepreneurs.* Where undue pessimism caused possible Pareto-optimal moves to fail to be made, the opportunity was thereby created for the possible grasping of pure entrepreneurial profit. Potential seller X, being pessimistically ignorant of potential buyer Y's willingness to pay as much as $10 for an item, failed to offer it for sale, even though he would himself have been very pleased to sell it for as low as $3. This overlooked opportunity for a mutually gainful trade between X and Y constitutes an inviting opportunity for the winning of pure entrepreneurial profit. Anyone, say entrepreneur Z, alert to this opportunity can, without any capital resources whatsoever, offer to buy from X at, say, a price of $4 (so that X, on our assumptions, will be delighted to accept), paying this price out of the gross revenue available to him through his offering to sell to Y at a price of $9 (which, again, on our assumption, Y will gladly accept). Wherever mutual ignorance, due to dispersed knowledge, causes Pareto-indicated moves not to be made, we have before us a situation inviting the alert entrepreneur to make pure profit.

Economic theory teaches us that, in this way, there is a powerful market tendency for all pure profit opportunities to be noticed and grasped. Knowledge Problem B comes to be solved through entrepreneurial discovery of hitherto overlooked opportunities.

Thus our understanding that in market clearing equilibrium *both* Knowledge Problems have been solved – ensuring that both over-optimistic and unduly pessimistic mutual errors (that might arise out of dispersed information) are *not* being made – rests on two distinct completed processes of market learning. The process whereby Knowledge Problem A is solved is a process which, without relying on entrepreneurial, profit-motivated alertness, arises from well-nigh inevitable learning of the unrealism of over-optimistic expectations. The process whereby Knowledge Problem B is solved, is a process which must rely entirely on the discovery by entrepreneurs of available opportunities of which nobody was hitherto aware.

THE TWO KNOWLEDGE PROBLEMS IN A WIDER SETTING

As Hayek came to emphasize, the Knowledge Problem is not only a problem in the context of the market. It is a problem crucially relevant to the emergence of social institutions as well. Such institutions as the law, language, the use of money, the respect for private property, require a concurrence of mutual knowledge and expectations completely analogous to the mutual knowledge required for market equilibrium. What we wish now to point out is that the problem which the phenomenon of dispersed knowledge creates for the emergence of benign social institutions is made up (exactly as the corresponding Knowledge Problem in the market context was) of two distinct problems. Let us consider the use in society of a common unit for the measure of distance. Obviously, the common use of a single scale of measurement is an important element in social intercourse. It would be most cumbersome and most obstructive to the emergence of standardized dimensions relevant to innumerable possible situations were several different measurement systems to be in use in the same society. For the emergence of a common system of measurement we require that members of the society correctly expect others to be employing that measurement system. A system using feet and inches can prevail only when, and because, each correctly expects others to use that system. More precisely it can prevail only when and because each correctly expects others to expect that system to be universally used. And so on.

Clearly such mutually sustaining expectations may be absent – resulting in and expressing the absence of a common system of measurement. What Hayek has emphasized is that the spontaneous emergence of such institutions has occurred throughout history. Members of society have learned, without central direction, to participate in social systems of language, measurement, monetary exchange – all of which have required mutually sustaining patterns of expectations. As Hayek has taught us, much of our civilization consists of such spontaneously developed systems of mutually reinforcing anticipations.

What must, for our present purpose, be stressed is that these institutions do not necessarily require that all conceivable opportunities for Pareto-superior social institutions be grasped and exploited. The common use of the system of feet and inches for measuring length does not in the slightest degree require that it be the end result achieved by grasping all conceivable opportunities for more efficient measurement. It could be that a superior system of measurement might have emerged. The fact that it did not does not deny usefulness to the system of feet and inches. That system is based on the concurrence of expectations on the part of millions of members of society. No one of them is disappointed in his expectations that others will employ this sytem. The usefulness of the system depends entirely and solely upon the successful solution of Knowledge Problem A (ensuring that expectations not be disappointed). It does not intrinsically depend on the solution of Knowledge Problem B. Even if some superior measurement system *could* be somehow devised and put into operation (by persuading the members of the society of its merits and its imminence), failure to do so in no way affects the viability of the measurement system that has in fact been adopted.

It is so with all of the institutions we usually cite. Use of a common language does not depend on the emergence of the simplest, clearest form of interpersonal communication. It depends only on members of society having learned to expect a single vocabulary and grammar.

Spontaneous order, in the sense of the spontaneous emergence of a set of rules, such as rules of language, behaviour or law, requires only that *some* given set of rules come to be universally expected. For the existence of none of these institutions is it inherently necessary that we go beyond the solution of Problem A, the avoidance of disappointment regarding the behaviour of others.

THE SPONTANEOUS EMERGENCE OF INSTITUTIONS

We understand, therefore, Hayek's convictions concerning the possibility of spontaneously emerging benign social institutions. Such institutions can emerge, it is clear, by the same solution of Knowledge Problem A which contributes to the spontaneous emergence of market equilibrating tendencies. People do tend to learn correctly to expect what other people will do, and the emergence of such mutually sustaining expectations may constitute the establishment of stable social institutions.

But it is equally clear that the solution of Knowledge Problem B, involving the discovery of hitherto unexamined attractive opportunities for mutual gain through interaction, is *not* needed for the emergence of any single institution. What we wish to point out in the following pages is that, except in the context of the market, we have in fact no generally operative tendency at all for Knowledge Problem B ever systematically to be solved.

If this contention of ours be accepted, we will surely have established grounds for challenging any assertion that spontaneous processes are able, in general, to generate not only stable institutions expressing mutually sustaining expectations, but also tendencies, parallel to those operating in markets to solve Knowledge Problem B, towards the replacement of socially inferior institutions by superior ones. There *may* be long-run survival-of-the-fittest type tendencies (or, for that matter, other kinds of tendencies) for societies to generate more rather than less 'useful' social norms and institutions. It is our contention here that any such tendencies are entirely distinct from the tendency, within markets, for socially useful opportunities to be discovered and exploited through the solution of Knowledge Problem B.

Institutions, whether more useful to society, less useful to society, or even downright harmful to society, require only the solution to Knowledge Problem A. This solution, in the context of wider social interaction, can indeed be counted upon to be forthcoming in the same way as it is forthcoming in the market context. For this reason institutions may and do indeed emerge spontaneously, constituting classic examples of spontaneous co-ordination.

But the replacement of an inferior institution (say, a measurement system based on feet and inches) by a superior institution (say, the metric system) requires more than the solution of Knowledge Problem A: it requires also the solution of Knowledge Problem B. Our contention is that no solution of Knowledge Problem B, parallel to its solution in markets, can be counted upon, outside the market context itself. Thus a belief in the spontaneous development of better and better social institutions cannot rely on the analogy with, or uncritical extrapolation of, our insights into the processes whereby

Knowledge Problem B is solved in the attainment of Pareto-optimal outcomes in market equilibrium. Our contention requires some further elaboration.

THE SOLUTION OF KNOWLEDGE PROBLEM B: THE EXTERNALITY PROBLEM

As will be recalled, the market process includes a tendency for the solution of Knowledge Problem B resulting from the incentives provided by pure profit opportunities. Alert entrepreneurs are attracted to notice suboptimalities (constituting expressions of Knowledge Problem B) because they respond to the scent of pure profit which accompanies such suboptimalities. By grasping the profit accompanying such suboptimalities, the entrepreneur benefits the market as a whole (since he moves prices and costs closer to equality, eliminating hitherto unnoticed, unexploited opportunities for mutually gainful exchange between unalert market participants). But there was no externality. The stimulus needed to attract the entrepreneur to benefit society was provided by the prospect of pure profit for himself. Every possibility for social gain through the overcoming of Problem B implies the attraction of private gain for the alert entrepreneur who can notice the opportunity. We wish to point out that no such fortunate coincidence of private and social profit occurs in the context of the emergence of social norms and institutions.

Let us imagine a society employing a measurement system based on feet and inches. Let us postulate that use of the metric system would substantially lower transaction and other costs throughout the system. There appears no obvious way in which any private entrepreneur could be attracted to notice the superiority of the metric system – let alone any chance of it being within his power to effect its adoption. The externality of the relevant benefit to society arising from a change to the metric system appears to block the translation of this unexploited opportunity, jointly available to members of society, into concrete, privately attractive opportunities capable of alerting entrepreneurial discovery.

The metric system remains unadopted as a result of a special case of Knowledge Problem B. Individuals are not aware that use of the metric system would be an improvement. Moreover, even if some (or all) were to become so aware, they (correctly) believe others (even where they are so aware) not to be using the metric system (because *they* believe that nobody is using the system). The possibility of *all* members of society simultaneously becoming aware of the social preferability of a metric system (or, at any rate, of all members of society somehow coming correctly to expect others to expect universal use of the metric system . . .) is a possibility running head-on into conflict with the concrete-like obstacle of Knowledge Problem B. How is it possible to generate among a population who have happily been employing the common measurement system of feet and inches the realization of the imminent actual workability and superiority of the metric system, or, at least, the expectation that others will from now on use only the metric system?

Solution to Knowledge Problem B always calls for entrepreneurial imagination. The externality feature endemic to Knowledge Problem B outside the market context discourages us from having faith in any spontaneous discovery procedure that is patterned after the process of entrepreneurial discovery which drives the market process.

HAYEK, MENGER AND THE EMERGENCE OF MONEY

Hayek frequently cites Carl Menger's insight into the spontaneous emergence of socially useful institutions (Hayek 1967a: 94; 1969b: 100–1; 1955: 83; 1973: 22; 1978c: 265n). It will be instructive to observe how the most famous Mengerian example of the spontaneous emergence of such a socially benign institution, namely the spontaneous emergence of a commonly accepted medium of exchange (making possible the transition from a barter economy to the far more efficient monetary economy), in fact occurs in Menger's exposition (Menger 1981: 257–62; 1985: 151–5). We shall discover that the spontaneous social process through which the evolution of a widely used money occurs is *not* one in which Knowledge Problem B is solved *analogously to its solution in market processes of equilibration.* To understand how Knowledge Problem B is overcome in the Mengerian process through which money emerges, it may be helpful to consider a similar spontaneous social process which does not involve any knowledge problem at all.

Consider the way in which a well-trodden path through the snow may be spontaneously achieved, without any deliberate, centralized plan to create it. At first, some hardy soul who has an urgent need to get to a destination makes the difficult crossing through the high snow. It is a costly journey (in terms of getting wet) but is apparently worthwhile. The precise route taken across the snow may be quite random, or it may be dictated by the pioneer's destination as viewed from the pioneer's starting point. What is important is that the first hike across the snow lowers the costs to others of crossing the snow subsequently. The snow is somewhat less intimidating where the first crossing was made. Others (who might otherwise perhaps not have crossed the snow at all, or who might have chosen some different route across the snow) now feel it worthwhile to cross exactly where the pioneer made the first crossing. Notice (a) that the reduced cost to subsequent snow crossers is an unintended consequence of the first crossing and (b) that subsequent crossings will obviously tend to follow the path taken by the pioneer. Those who do indeed cross the snow in the footsteps of the pioneer make their own unintended contributions to the spontaneous emergence of a clear path across the snow. Each crossing treads down the snow a little more, thus further reducing the costs to others of walking across the snow. In this way, the familar, socially benign phenomenon of a new path is the unintended consequence of self-regarding behaviour.

Now the sequence of actions which led to the spontaneous creation of the path has nothing to do with the solution of any knowledge problem. It is simply the fortunate implication of the different degrees of urgency with which people need to cross the snow (and also, possibly, of the different times at which different people need to cross the snow). No creative, imaginative, entrepreneurial leap was needed – and none has occurred – for the path to be spontaneously created. The emergence of the path occurred without central planning for it to be created – not because entrepreneurs were independently inspired to produce it, but because each step in the snow unintentionally induced further steps to be taken.

We should remember, incidentally, that, just as processes may occur in which (as in the path-in-the-snow case) each step reduces costs in a way that promotes benign, spontaneously achieved results, we can easily envisage exactly opposite kinds of process. We can easily envisage, that is, processes each step of which unintentionally, *but perversely*, changes costs to others (of taking further steps). If urban concentration increases the chances of economic survival in the city compared with the surrounding villages (or at any rate if villagers believe this to be the case), then the city may spontaneously sink into congestion which becomes progressively more and more horrible and intolerable. Feuding tribes or nations may find it wise to arm themselves against possible attack; but each such step taken may enhance the danger to others, leading to a spiralling sequence of armament building, heightening the suspicions on all sides and increasing the likelihood of war. Such tragic processes are well known and well understood (if not easily controlled). Our point is that, whether benign or otherwise, these spontaneous processes proceed as they do because each step taken systematically renders it more rational for other similar steps to be taken by others. This results in the familiar snowballing effect. Menger's process of the spontaneous emergence of money proceeds in exactly this fashion.

What drives the dynamic Mengerian process through which money evolves is the gradually increasing liquidity of some particular commodity that has come to be used, not yet as money, but as a means for indirect exchange between resourceful, bartering market participants. Starting from a barter economy, alert market participants find they can improve their chances of trading what they initially possess for what they would prefer to possess if they trade the former for something which they themselves do *not* wish to acquire for final consumption use, but which they believe *is* likely to be sought after by those who possess the items which these alert market participants *do* wish to acquire. As this occurs, the 'liquidity' of this item (which they acquire even though they have no wish to consume it themselves) increases. That is, the very circumstance that *these* alert market participants are buying this item increases now the chance that *other* market participants will find that initial acquisition of this item increases *their* chances of finally obtaining the items *they* wish finally to consume. The dynamics of this process of increasing liquidity becoming attached to certain items can lead to the emergence of a degree of liquidity so complete as, in effect, to render an item no longer an ordinary commodity but rather a generally accepted medium of exchange. Let us consider carefully the sense in which Menger's process (unlike our path-in-the-snow example) does involve the solution of a knowledge problem. We shall then more carefully appreciate how Menger's process, while it very certainly does solve Knowledge Problem B, does so in a way quite different from the market process solution to Knowledge Problem B.

In an initial barter society, the inconveniences attributable to the absence of a generally accepted medium of exchange can be seen as caused by Knowledge Problem B. (Knowledge Problem A, in which participants in society entertain false expectations about what others will do, is not a problem here. Everyone correctly expects others to engage only in barter transactions. No one mistakenly expects to be able to receive 'money' in exchange for offered commodities.) What is preventing use of a monetary medium is the failure of market participants to know, not what in fact others *are* doing, but what others *might* be very willing to do (if they, in turn, knew that others would act similarly). Because the transition from a barter economy to a monetary economy involves grasping a new, universally gainful opportunity which has not yet been perceived, barter remains the prevailing mode. Even were I to understand the superior efficiency of moving to, say, a silver monetary standard, I will not try to sell anything for silver because silver is not now money (i.e. I do not expect others so to accept silver). Where in fact others, like me, do understand the advantages of moving from barter to a silver monetary standard, I am correct in my judgement that silver is not money only because each one of us (who does understand the virtues of silver money) fails to know what *might* be acceptable to others. Surely if I knew that others knew that I knew their appreciation of the virtues of silver money, et cetera *ad infinitum*, silver *would* now be accepted by all as money. Thus the knowledge problem obstructing the transition to widespread use of a silver money is Knowledge Problem B.

The transition from a barter society to a monetary economy, out-lined in the Mengerian process, has thus certainly involved the spon-taneous overcoming of Knowledge Problem B. After the transition, market participants have learned to behave in new ways which benefit them all. But these lessons have been learned in a manner that does not parallel the entrepreneurial processes which tend to overcome Knowledge Problem B in the market context. In the market context Knowledge Problem B manifests itself in market errors which reveal themselves as opportunities for entrepreneurial profit making. In the Mengerian context this was not the case. (The alertness which market participants display in the course of the Mengerian process regarding the steadily increasing liquidity of the commodity in question is never alertness to prospects of *further* increasing that liquidity; what is involved is strictly alertness to the personal efficiencies to be achieved by taking advantage of that commodity's *already increased* liquidity.) No entrepreneur could, by himself, discover opportunities for pure profit by attempting to move the barter society towards the use of money. None the less a spontaneous process which did move the society in that direction occurred in Menger's story. Our point is that it occurred in the same non-entrepreneurial fashion that marks the creation of paths in the snow.

CONCLUSION

What stimulates solutions to Knowledge Problem B in markets is the circumstance that in the market context this problem consists in unexploited opportunities for mutually gainful exchange. Such opportunities offer opportunities for private entrepreneurial gain to their discoverers. This sets in motion the familiar entrepreneurial process tending to bring separated markets into full contact with each other, eliminating price discrepancies (and opportunities for further profit).

But in the broader societal context the manner in which Knowledge Problem B stands in the way of the emergence of feasible, cost-efficient, social institutions is not such as to offer opportunities for private gain to its discoverers. There is thus no systematic discovery procedure upon which we can rely for the spontaneous emergence of superior institutional norms.

This circumstance does not prevent genuinely spontaneous processes of institutional development from occurring. Paths in the snow happen. But it does mean that we cannot use, as copybook example for such spontaneous processes, *the manner in which markets systematically tend to solve Knowledge Problem B.* To be sure, the spontaneous emergence of *any* institution indeed relies on the very same processes through which Knowledge Problem A is solved in markets. Hayek is on firm ground in seeing his insights into the market qua discovery procedure as providing the foundation for his own later work on the spontaneous emergence of cultural norms and institutions and its link with the phenomenon of division of knowledge.

On the other hand, however, it has been our aim to point out in this chapter that these earlier economic insights into the spontaneously co-ordinative properties of markets do not, in themselves, provide any reassurance concerning the benign quality of the long-run tendencies of institutional development. Such benign tendencies may well be powerful and important in some or many instances; but the spontaneous co-ordination which occurs in markets provides us with no basis for any extension of the welfare theorems relating to markets to the broader field of the theory of institutional evolution. The explanation for such benign tendencies, if indeed they exist, must be sought elsewhere.

Chapter 11

Welfare economics: a modern Austrian perspective

Among the most notable of Murray Rothbard's many contributions to the literature of modern Austrian economics is surely the major paper on utility and welfare theory that he wrote for the 1956 Mises Festschrift (Rothbard 1956). This writer can personally attest to the excitement engendered by the lucid manner in which this paper deployed Austrian insights to illuminate fundamental theoretical issues (concerning which contemporary economics was floundering) and by the characteristic erudition which Rothbard poured into that single essay. Whether or not one fully accepted Rothbard's conclusions, it was impossible not to glimpse the power of consistent Misesian thinking which that paper so excellently exemplified. The present chapter, written thirty years later, seeks to re-examine a small part of the terrain covered by Rothbard's essay. In offering a modern Austrian perspective on welfare economics we shall be emphasizing some of the same basic Austrian tenets that Rothbard so rightly insisted on thirty years ago. While our perspective may not entirely dovetail with some of Rothbard's conclusions, we venture to hope that our observations concerning welfare economics be judged to be in the same subjectivist, methodologically individualistic tradition that Rothbard's work has so valuably carried forward for so many years.

SOME OBSERVATIONS CONCERNING WELFARE ECONOMICS

Welfare economics, in its numerous incarnations, has sought to offer criteria by which it might be possible scientifically to evaluate the economic merits of specific institutions, pieces of legislation or events. Such evaluation would have to transcend the narrow economic concerns of specific individuals whose interests might be involved, and to express, somehow, a perspective flowing from the economic interests of all individuals in society. As we shall see, Austrian economists have been particularly sensitive to the difficulties that must beset such an undertaking. Indeed, many of the difficulties have been recognized again and again by the economic profession at large, and it is for these reasons, of course, that welfare economics has undergone so many attempted reconstructions 'from the ground up'.

We shall briefly survey the more important of these attempts from a perspective that seeks consistently to apply the following (related) Austrian concerns.

1 Methodological individualism: we shall refuse to recognize meaning in statements concerning the 'welfare of society' that cannot, in principle, be unambiguously translated into statements concerning the individuals in society (in a manner which does not do violence to their individuality).
2 Subjectivism: we shall not be satisfied with statements that perceive the economic well-being of society as expressible in terms (such as physical output) that are unrelated to the valuations and choices made by individuals.
3 An emphasis on process: we shall be interested in the economic well-being of society not merely in terms of its level of economic well-being (however defined) but also in regard to the ability of its institutions to stimulate and support those economic processes upon which the attainment of economic well-being depends.

WELFARE ECONOMICS – SOME HIGHLIGHTS OF ITS PAST

1. During the period of classical economics it was, of course, taken for granted that a society was economically successful strictly in so far as it succeeded in achieving increased wealth. Adam Smith's *Inquiry into the Nature and Causes of the Wealth of Nations* expressed this approach to the economics of welfare simply and typically. It was taken for granted that a given percentage increase in a nation's physical wealth (with wealth often seen as being able to be seen as consisting of bushels of 'corn') meant a similar percentage increase in the nation's well-being. From this perspective a physical measure of a nation's wealth provides an index of that nation's economic success, regardless of its distribution. A bushel of wheat is a bushel of wheat. Clearly

this notion of welfare offends the principles of methodological individualism and subjectivism; it was swept away by the marginalist (subjectivist) revolution of the late nineteenth century.

2. Marshall and Pigou sought to preserve certain central elements of the classical approach, while avoiding the trap which sees well-being as identified with (or directly proportional to) physical wealth itself. They focused attention not on goods themselves, but on the *utility* of those goods. In principle a nation's physical wealth, given its pattern of distribution, corresponded to a given level of aggregate utility. Moreover they believed this aggregate to be measurable, in principle, by the 'measuring rod of money'. They sensed no problem in conceiving of 'aggregate utility'; they thought of utility as something that could be compared and aggregated across individuals. They certainly did not see utility as associated uniquely with an individual act of choice; rather, they saw it as a kind of psychological shadow that closely followed physical wealth. (Its central advantage over wealth, as an index of well-being, was that it incorporated the refinement of diminishing marginal utility. It was no longer acceptable to consider a bushel of wheat to be identical, welfare-wise, with every bushel of wheat: the margin of consumption by the individual must be considered. But it was still considered valid to treat one dollar's worth of utility as entirely equivalent to a second dollar's worth of utility.)

This approach to welfare economics is clearly unacceptable to economists who have absorbed the Misesian (and Rothbardian) lessons concerning the true meaning of utility in economic analysis. Utility, for Austrians, is not a quantity of psychological experience; it is merely an index of preferability as expressed in acts of choice. To attempt to aggregate utility is not merely to violate the tenets of methodological individualism and subjectivism (by treating the sensations of different individuals as being able to be added up), it is to engage in an entirely meaningless exercise: economic analysis has nothing to say about sensations; it deals strictly with choices and their interpersonal implications.

3. The approach to welfare economics that has, of course, been central to economics for the past half-century is that which revolves round the notion of Pareto optimality. A change is seen as enhancing the economic well-being of society if it renders some of its members better off (in their estimation) without rendering any others worse off. This approach certainly avoids the problems of interpersonal comparisons of utility, and would thus seem to be consistent both with the

methodological individualism and with the subjectivism that Austrians insist upon. Several points, however, need to be noticed.

While the notion of Pareto optimality is indeed concerned with the individual members of society it none the less reflects a supra-individual conception of society and its well-being. After all, a Pareto-optimal move is considered to advance the well-being *of society* – considered as a whole. Otherwise it is not at all clear what is added (to the bald observation that the change is preferred by some and objected to by none) by the judgement that the move is 'good for society'. Indeed the Pareto criterion turned out to become an integral element in the development of the idea that society faces an 'economic problem' – that of allocating its resources among its competing goals in the most efficient manner. Societal inefficiency in resource allocation came to be identified with suboptimality according to the Pareto criterion.

Now this notion of society facing its economic problem in the resource allocation sense arose, as is well known, as an extension of the concept of individual economizing behaviour that was articulated so definitively by Lionel Robbins in 1932. But, as has before now been recognized, this extension is in fact an illegitimate extension, not at all faithful to the spirit of Robbins's formulation. Robbins was concerned to identify the economic problem facing the *individual*. It is the individual who has goals and who deliberately deploys his perceived resources in order to achieve his goals most efficiently, so far as is possible. To transfer this important concept of individual allocative choice to society as a whole is, at best, to engage in metaphor. Society, as such, neither possesses goals of its own nor deliberately engages in allocative choice. In so far as the idea of Pareto optimality came to reinforce the faulty and misleading notion of society's 'economic problem', it was part of an approach to the analysis of economic welfare that fell grievously short of consistent adherence to the principles of methodological individualism.

HAYEK AND THE CRITIQUE OF WELFARE ECONOMICS

It was against this mainstream notion of society and its purported allocative problem that Hayek's famous 1945 paper (Hayek 1949b) was directed. Hayek's attack might, it is true, be seen as not being *primarily* against the welfare notion that was embedded in the idea of society's economic problem. Hayek focused on the circumstances of dispersed knowledge. The relevant information that 'society' would have to possess in order to solve its economic problem is widely dispersed. Society is thus simply not in a position to address its supposed economic problem (even if, for the sake of discussion, this societal allocative task could be held to be meaningful). Hayek's critique might thus be seen as emphasizing the problems obstructing the practical solution of a nation's economic problem, rather than as a critique of the standard conception of that problem itself. But Hayek's paper constituted, none the less, a profound – if indirect – critique of the very meaningfulness of societal efficiency as developed, for example, in the Paretian context.

For once it is recognized that the relevant information *is* inevitably and definitely dispersed among many minds, it is impossible to avoid the conclusion that the notion of social efficiency is correspondingly devoid of meaning. Social efficiency must refer to the extent to which the allocation of social resources corresponds to the priorities implied in the relative urgencies of social goals. But in order for the notion of 'social resources' to be meaningful, and in order for the notion of 'relative urgencies of social goals' to be meaningful, it must, at least in principle, be possible to imagine a single mind to which the relevant arrays of social resources and social objectives are simultaneously given. Hayek's insight concerning dispersed knowledge was, in effect, to deny such a possibility. Thus dispersed knowledge turns out to be not merely a phenomenon that constitutes a practical difficulty with which would-be planners must grapple, but a phenomenon (not necessarily the only one) that robs the very concept of social efficiency of its meaningfulness, even in principle. To choose *presupposes* an integrated framework of ends and means; without such a presumed framework allocative choice is hardly a coherent notion at all (Buchanan 1964). Hayek's insight into the subjectivism of knowledge and information has thus decisively dislodged the foundations of Paretian welfare economics, at least in so far as those foundations have been held to support the concept of social choice and social efficiency. (More recent extensions by Hayek and others of this subjectivism of information to encompass also Polanyi's idea of 'tacit knowledge' – knowledge incapable of being deliberately communicated to others – have rendered these damaging implications for standard welfare economics even more destructive (Hayek 1979: 190).

CO-ORDINATION AS A HAYEKIAN WELFARE CRITERION

Several writers, pursuing the implications of these Hayekian insights, have seen the concept of 'co-ordination' as offering a normative yardstick consistent with these subjectivist and methodologically individualistic insights (Kirzner 1973: Ch. 6; O'Driscoll 1977). As discussed, the notion of social choice (and thus of the efficiency of such choice) has been fatally undermined (except at the level of metaphor). If Jones (who prefers Smith's food to his own enjoyment of a day's leisure) fails to trade with Smith (who prefers the labour of Jones over his own food), we may not be able to say that society has failed efficiently to allocate the food and labour time between Jones and Smith, but we could surely still say that Jones and Smith have failed to co-ordinate their activities and their decisions. It seems plausible and intuitively appealing to perceive co-ordination – permitting each agent to achieve his goals through the simultaneous satisfaction of the goals of the other agent – as constituting a desideratum transcending the individual goals of the respective agents. Failure to achieve co-ordination might thus be seen as a failure of the social apparatus to achieve a supra-individual result – but such a judgement relies not at all on any notions inconsistent with subjectivism or with methodological individualism

It is of course true that the fulfilment of the co-ordination norm appears to be formally equivalent to the fulfilment of the Paretian welfare criterion. Any suboptimal situation (in the Paretian sense) clearly corresponds to the failure of a pair of market participants to trade with one another on feasible, mutually attractive terms – in other words, it corresponds to a failure to achieve co-ordination. But, unlike the Paretian norm, the co-ordination norm escapes interpretation as a yardstick for social efficiency in social allocative choice. Co-ordination does not refer to the well-being achieved through its successful attainment; it refers only to the dovetailing character of the activities that make it up.

Thus Hayek's emphasis on the dispersed character of knowledge appears to provide not merely the definitive critique of standard Paretian welfare economics, but also the basis for an alternative normative yardstick, one thoroughly consistent with the tenet of methodological individualism. Scope for this new normative yardstick is provided precisely by the circumstance of dispersed knowledge. Fragmented knowledge is responsible for activities that are *not* mutually co-ordinated. The 'social' problem faced by Hayek's economic society is precisely that of overcoming the discoordination to be expected to flow out of such fragmentation.

There is a deeper issue here. If one abstracts from the fragmented character of information, if one treats all existing information as if it were known to all market participants, one is, of course, abstracting from the possibility of discoordinated activites. With the Hayekian 'economic problem' assumed to be out of the way in this fashion, it might seem that the standard (Paretian) economic problem comes back into its own, invulnerable to Hayekian strictures. The problem facing society, on such assumptions, would appear to reduce to that of achieving Paretian optimality in respect of the relevant social objectives, in the face of its limited resources. But, surely, if we assume away the dispersed character of information, the standard economic problem facing society presents no challenge at all. If we can assume that what is known to one is known to all, then (averting our gaze from the remaining quibbles which the methodological individualist might have against the concept of social efficiency) it seems difficult to imagine the possibility of any social allocation of resources that might be pronounced socially *in*efficient. Given perfect mutual knowledge it appears obvious that all possible Pareto-optimal moves *must have already been implemented.* To imagine otherwise would be to imagine that agents deliberately refrain from taking advantage of available opportunities known by them to exist. Knowledge of all such opportunities, and knowledge of all relevant transaction costs, must appear inevitably to lead to Pareto optimality (given these trans-action costs) – achieved either through market activity or through centralized organization (with the latter choice itself determined by comparison of the respective transaction costs).

So Hayek's insights concerning fragmented knowledge might appear to provide not merely a critique of standard welfare criteria, and also a substitute yardstick (in terms of the co-ordination norm) – they might appear at the same time to salvage welfare economics from the extinction to which it would be doomed by the inevitability of perpetual optimality. But the situation is not quite so simple.

HAYEK IN THE PANGLOSSIAN WORLD

The truth is that many of the observations made in the preceding sections might seem to be vulnerable to serious challenge. Such challenges, it would seem, can be launched at several distinct levels, with the challenges stemming precisely from the paralysis arising from the inevitability of perpetual optimality. On the one hand it might appear that the circumstance of fragmented knowledge does *not* salvage welfare economics from the extinction spelled by perpetual optimality. Further it might be argued that Hayek's insights in fact deepen the perplexities created by such Panglossian concerns. We shall in the present section develop these challenges. In subsequent sections we shall rebut these challenges, showing how the observations made in the preceding sections with regard to Hayekian welfare economics *can* be defended (despite the challenges developed in the present section). Moreover we shall use our discussion to point out a novel sense in which 'co-ordination' offers a normative criterion that escapes Panglossian paralysis. (It will be in the context of the latter discussion that we shall deploy the third Austrian tenet referred to at the outset of this chapter, that of maintaining a concern with *processes* rather than exclusively states of affairs.) We turn now to develop the apparent challenges to Hayekian welfare economics referred to at the outset of this section.

The difficulties that we must face up to, in considering the Hayekian thesis of dispersed knowledge and information, consist in the fact that, from a mainstream perspective, the Hayekian 'knowledge problem' might appear not to be a problem at all, in the relevant sense (see Chapter 9). To point out that knowledge is scattered in society is, it might be argued (contrary to our earlier assertions), not necessarily to note that standard welfare analysis is inapplicable – it is merely to point out that such standard welfare analysis is to be carried on in the context of a hitherto unsuspected cost, the cost of ascertaining and of communicating information. Dispersal of knowledge and information indeed introduces new costs for the acquisition of the knowledge necessary for economic choice. But surely the presence of a novel class of costs does not, in principle, render inapplicable the standard criteria for the evaluation of social efficiency.

Moreover, once it is recognized that the fragmentation of information complicates standard welfare analysis without vitiating it, it seems appropriate to point out that the Panglossian paralysis referred to earlier offers threats as serious for a 'co-ordination'-based approach to welfare analysis as for the mainstream approach. After all, any discussion of Jones and Smith 'co-ordinating' their activities must refer to a potential for co-ordination in the context of the relevant resource constraints confronting the respective parties. Surely, then, the availability and costliness of information acquisition must be counted as part of these 'relevant resource constraints'. If engineer Jones, Sr, and farmer Smith can exchange engineering services for food, with mutual gain, it may seem that only a co-ordination failure could prevent such exchange from taking place.

But it will not constitute a co-ordination failure if Jones, Jr, schoolboy, refrains from enrolling in an engineering programme on his graduation from high school if the costs of the training programme are too high. Similarly, it might appear, all co-ordination 'failures' attributable to Hayekian knowledge fragmentation turn out not to be failures at all once one properly considers the cost of searching for the information needed to bridge the dispersed knowledge gaps. If Jones, Sr, and Smith fail to engage in mutually gainful exchange as a result of knowledge dispersal, they are not, it might be contended, acting suboptimally from a social point of view; they are fully taking advantage of each other's availability in the context of their limited knowledge of each other's situation. To pronounce this state of affairs to be socially inefficient or 'uncoordinated' might seem to be succumbing to a temptation warned against in elementary economics, namely that of pronouncing welfare judgements without regard to resource scarcities. Participants in an economy can be counted upon to engage in mutually gainful exchange transactions in so far as their knowledge permits. Moreover, in so far as participants are aware of worthwhile possibilities for learning useful information that may reveal as yet unexploited opportunities for mutual gain, they can surely be counted upon to engage in such useful learning. It does seem, then, that, in a world of dispersed information as in a world of omniscience, suboptimality or states of discoordinatedness cannot be postulated to exist (if one properly includes the costs of information acquisition).

Indeed it might be contended that it is precisely Hayek's dispersed information insights that are capable of focusing needed attention on the costs of learning and of knowledge communication. Once the paralysing assumption of perfect knowledge has been dropped it becomes impossible to avoid grappling with the economics of learning and communication. Our contention thus far is that, once such economics of learning and communication has been taken into account, Panglossian perpetual optimality paralysis sets in once again. At all times agents will be engaging in the optimal mix of decisions (including decisions to learn and to communicate). No pair of decisions can be pronounced uncoordinated, given the costs of learning.

DISPERSED KNOWLEDGE, OPTIMAL IGNORANCE AND GENUINE ERROR

We shall discover, however, that these contentions are invalid. The Panglossian paralysis we have found to afflict mainstream welfare economics is *not* a threat to the Hayekian co-ordination approach. It is *not* the case, we shall see, that Hayek's fragmentation of information does nothing more than complicate matters through the introduction of a new cost. Rather, the dispersal of knowledge creates scope for a genuinely fresh approach to normative analysis. This is so because such dispersal of knowledge necessarily involves not merely new costs (of learning and communication) but also the very real possibility of what we may call *'genuine error'*.

This writer has elsewhere argued (Kirzner 1979a: Ch. 8; 1985a) that genuine error, so often exorcised from economic analysis, in fact deserves a central place in that analysis. Genuine error occurs *where a decision maker's ignorance is not attributable to the costs of search, or of learning or of communication*. In such cases the decision maker's ignorance is *utter* ignorance, i.e. it is a result of his ignorance of available, cost-worthy, avenues to needed information (which includes, of course, the possibility of his being altogether ignorant of the very existence of valuable information). At the level of the individual decision maker we may describe his activity as having been suboptimal when he subsequently discovers himself to have inexplicably overlooked available opportunities that were in fact worthwhile. He cannot 'condone' his faulty decision making on the grounds of the cost of acquiring information, since the information was in fact costlessly available to him. He can account for his failure only by acknowledging his utter ignorance of the true circumstances (i.e. his ignorance of the availability of relevant information at worthwhile low cost). Such utter ignorance cannot be explained in cost–benefit terms; it is simply a given.

Two implications of the phenomenon of utter ignorance, of genuine error, may be noticed. First, the injection into economic reasoning of the possibility of genuine error introduces a degree of 'looseness' into our understanding of economic processes that is of great importance. It is no longer true that the configuration of exogenous variables, tastes, resource availabilities and technological possibilities, unambiguously marks out the course of individual activities. This is because, while these data do mark out the optimal opportunities, we cannot be confident that such optimal opportunities will be known to the relevant decision makers – even if we make provision for deliberate processes of search and learning. We cannot be sure that available processes of search and learning are known to those who might benefit therefrom. The second implication (flowing from recognition of the phenomenon of genuine error) is that we must now recognize the possibility of corrective actions within an economy that are not to be traced to shifting cost patterns. Corrective action may be set off by the sudden ('entrepreneurial') discovery by a market participant of a hitherto unperceived opportunity for pure profit. Let us now return to examine Hayek's dispersed information.

We objected that the introduction of the need for costly search, learning and communication (forced upon us by Hayek's insight) does not really threaten the mainstream economizing view. The fragmentation of knowledge, we pointed out, merely introduced an additional cost dimension – that of mobilizing and centralizing scattered bits of information. We now see that the fragmentation of knowledge is likely to affect matters far more seriously and fundamentally. *The fragmentation of knowledge injects into the picture scope for genuine error, resulting from utter ignorance.* Pursuing once again the line of reasoning introduced earlier (and subsequently challenged in the preceding section) the circumstance of dispersed and fragmented knowledge compels us not merely to recognize a practical difficulty to be encountered in seeking to address society's allocative efficiency problem – this circumstance undermines the very meaningfulness of such a social 'economic problem'. Given the scope for genuine error we now see to be implicit in the circumstance of dispersed information, we see that this circumstance indeed erodes the meaningfulness of the concept of social allocative efficiency. Before we can even begin to contemplate what we may mean by social allocative efficiency we must somehow confront the problem of overcoming that utter ignorance which obstructs the relevancy of the efficiency concept for social policy. It is here that the norm of 'co-ordination' is to be perceived in a fresh light, rather different from that co-ordination norm discussed earlier.

CO-ORDINATION AND CO-ORDINATION

We must distinguish carefully between (a) a possible norm of co-ordination in the sense of a co-ordinated state of affairs and (b) a possible norm of co-ordination in the sense of the ability to detect and to move towards correcting situations in which activites have until now been discoordinated (see also Chapter 8). The distinction between these two possibilities corresponds to the two different meanings of the word 'co-ordination': it may refer to the activities being carried out when these activities are indeed dovetailing with one another; alternatively it may refer to the process through which initially clashing, discoordinated activities are somehow being hammered out in a manner such as to approach a more smoothly dovetailing pattern of activities. The discussion earlier in this paper implicitly referred to co-ordination only in the first of these two senses. (It is for this reason that we were able to note formal equivalency between the co-ordination norm and the norm of Pareto efficiency.) We wish now to draw attention to the possible relevance of the second co-ordination norm for a modern Austrian approach to welfare economics.

Once we have identified genuine error as a culprit responsible for a failure of a society's economic system to fulfil its functions successfully, we have placed ourselves in a position to appreciate the meaning of this second co-ordination norm. Without the phenomenon of utter ignorance, we have seen, our *first* co-ordination concept (like its Paretian counterpart) turned out to be of little normative interest. After all, we noted, given the absence of utter ignorance, all activities must be carried on in optimal fashion. Even if some activities are being carried out 'erroneously', because of incomplete information, we saw, we could hardly describe these activities as being suboptimal or 'wrong' – after all, they took advantage of every scrap of information it was judged worthwhile to lay their hands on. In this sense the world at all times is at a Pareto optimum, in a state of full co-ordination – the best of all possible worlds, given the costs of change. But injection of the possibility of genuine error arising out of simple utter ignorance introduces us to the possibility of *genuine* discoordination – and to the possibility of evaluating the institutional environment in terms of its potential to inspire genuine discovery (of opportunities previously overlooked as a result of utter ignorance). Thus a norm of co-ordination looms into centre stage in the sense of permitting us to ask what potential a society's economy possesses to inspire such pure discovery of its earlier genuine errors. Such an approach to welfare economics is made possible by our escape from the Panglossian world; that escape was, in turn, made possible by our emphasis on genuine error (arising out of utter ignorance); we have seen in this chapter that scope for genuine error is widened most considerably by the circumstance of dispersed and fragmented information identified by Hayek. It is for this reason that we see Hayek's criticisms of standard approaches to welfare analysis as opening the door, at the same time, for the possible reconstruction of normative economics along truly Austrian lines, i.e. in a manner fully consistent with (a) subjectivism, (b) methodological individualism and (c) an emphasis on dynamic processes.

Part IV

Some related issues emerging from the Austrian approach

Self-interest and the new bashing of economics: a fresh opportunity in the perennial debate?

A spate of recent attacks on the rationality assumption in economic theory is noticed. Some of these attacks are fresh and, in many ways, original, but the central ideas underlying them are not new. They appear to have been provoked by the direction in which much of mainstream economics has been moving in recent years. On the other hand, it is suggested here, certain developments in contemporary economics, associated particularly with the revival of interest in the Austrian paradigm, offer a fresh understanding of the way in which the rationality assumption, its role in economics properly understood, is able to meet these old–new attacks.

The self-interest assumption in economic theory has aroused passionate debate again and again in the history of the discipline. The passions were first ignited in reaction to classical economics, which appeared to assume not only a world of self-interested persons but one in which they were intent on nothing else except material satisfaction. For a John Ruskin all this meant that classical economists and those who could read their work with acceptance 'must have got into' an 'entirely damned state of soul' (Ruskin 1934: 14n.). As the nineteenth century advanced, the tone of the criticism of the role of *homo oeconomicus* in economics shifted from indignation to methodological outrage. Both on the Continent and in England, and very soon in the United States, critics of economics, in both its classical and neoclassical versions, denounced as irredeemably flawed those cardinal assumptions upon which economic theory seemed to rest. From Cliffe Leslie in the United Kingdom to Thorstein Veblen in the United States, historicist and institutionalist critics demanded a reformed economics that should recognize the complexity of human nature, the variety of human goals and motives, and the degree to which sociological and psychological forces are intertwined with (or even swallow up entirely) those singled out by economic theorists. An entire literature burgeoned around these controversial issues, with the same charges and rebuttals being raised again and again.

A spate of recent books – by Robert Frank (1988), Gregg and Paul Davidson (1988) and Amitai Etzioni (1988) – has once more injected these hoary issues into current debate. These volumes are not simply rehashes of the old outcries of the moralists or historicists; each of them attacks mainstream, late-twentieth-century economics in a fresh way. Yet basically the points of substance from which these attacks derive their force are, with some notable exceptions, the very same points which nourished the attacks on economics over a century ago. Although the authors display scant interest in possible intellectual predecessors, their fundamental disagreements with mainstream economics boil down to a few key, classic, objections – in fact objections that have been debated repeatedly. Although at certain places in these books reference is made to standard responses that can be anticipated to be forthcoming from the defenders of mainstream economics, these defences are dismissed as insufficiently serious.

Our purpose in these pages is not to review these books but to reflect once again on the venerable issues of which they remind us. In particular, the circumstance that these book-length critiques of standard economics have appeared at this time is itself worthy of attention. What have today's mainstream economists done to arouse once again the old passionate denunciations of their science? Or, to take a different tack, can the economics of the 1990s perhaps lay these criticisms to rest in a more definitive manner than the economics of the 1890s – or the 1930s – was able to do? We shall in fact argue that (a) some modern developments in mainstream economics may indeed have played a role in provoking these criticisms, but (b) that (not entirely coincidentally) other modern developments in economics, developments which have themselves emerged out of a separate strand of critical analysis of mainstream economics, can help show how the classic defences of economics against the kinds of criticisms raised in these new books can be appreciated, and extended, in a new way. Thus it is perhaps just possible that the complicated state of modern economics, while provoking renewals of the old critiques in ever more aggressive forms, can also point the way to deeper appreciation of the ultimate irrelevance of these critiques.

SELFISHNESS AND ECONOMICS

An only slightly unfair caricature of the ancient criticisms levelled against economics would be to portray these criticisms as understanding economics to be the theory of a society in which all individuals are strictly selfish and coldly logical, with not an iota of morality or ounce of emotion in their veins. The economic man which these criticisms perceive to be central to economic theory is unattractively intent, in the first place, only on more and more wealth, motivated exclusively by the urge to enjoy those pleasures which money can buy. His character is unredeemed by any altruistic sympathies; his drive to satisfy his appetites is unrestrained by any moral reservations. His actions are governed by steel-trap-like logic, never softened or dislodged by emotion or weakness of will. From the perspective of the critics, economic theory is able to reach firm conclusions, and in particular to ascribe benign properties to the free market economy, only by developing models populated exclusively by such economic men. The three books cited above begin with roughly this perception of mainstream economics. Each of them attacks this economics from a slightly different point of departure.

Robert Frank's critique is, in a sense, the mildest, and the least 'dangerous' for the practitioners of mainstream economics. There is no need, Professor Frank argues, for economics to assume exclusive rationality, understood as complete freedom from emotion and passion. The validity of economics is therefore not threatened by pervasive real world examples of passionate behaviour. It can be shown, by ingenious theorizing and striking hypothetical examples, that it may, in the long run, be entirely useful to permit one's decisions to be shaped by moral sympathy, by the urge for revenge, by the prick of conscience, by trust and the like, even where cooler reasoning might at first glance appear to point to different courses of action. Building on earlier work by Thomas Schelling and others, Frank shows how the practice of moral behaviour, for example, may not only be good for society, it may also be materially beneficial to the practising individuals themselves. Clearly, while all this would permit the economists' models to encompass kinds of behaviour traditionally excluded, the overall perspective attributed to economics need not be substantially altered. So far from calling for severely restricted scope for the models of economists, Professor Frank's work can in fact be construed as demonstrating the relevance of these models for rationalizing behaviour once thought to be beyond their scope. Highly original in many ways, this work can in no way be dismissed as merely rediscovering nineteenth-century criticisms of economics.

The Davidsons certainly do not come to extend the applicability of the models of the economists. They construe economics as lauding the social usefulness of exclusively self-regarding behaviour. Economics arrives at theorems demonstrating the social optimality of strictly individualistic behaviour. Not only does economics appear to frown on the civic virtues, it is seen as promoting technical efficiency for its own sake (even where such efficiency may be sought to promote genocidal goals!) and of measuring social worth only in so far as it can be captured by a market price in dollars. For the Davidsons the world explicated by economic theory is a most repulsive place; a civilized society, they argue, requires a totally different economics. The moral and scientific blindness of economists, the Davidsons feel, is not only responsible for their promotion of this repulsive, uncivilized society. This blindness prevents the economists from realizing that even the material well-being upon which they focus such exclusive attention must suffer in a world bereft of civilized values. Without trust and civic virtue markets cannot work. The cynicism concerning moral values which pervades mainstream economics is ultimately inconsistent with the prosperity which is being sought. Much of the Davidson's critique is strongly reminiscent of mid-nineteenth-century condemnations of economics, particularly those of Carlyle and Ruskin.

Professor Etzioni's attack on economics is the most ambitious. The focus of his criticism is on the validity of economic theory in explaining the phenomena of the real world, rather than on the moral (or other) desirability of a world built according to the specifications of the economists' models. For Etzioni economics is simply not good social science; its assumptions are false and its conclusions invalid. The falsity of the assumptions of the economists relates, in particular, (a) to the nature of the consumer (whom economists falsely assume to be in pursuit only of pleasure) and (b) to the decisions made by economic agents (which economists falsely believe to be made entirely rationally and without any distortion arising from passion and emotion). Although it is impossible here to do justice to the richness of Etzioni's exhaustive critical survey of modern economics, it should be pointed out that his critique is, at base, entirely similar to the late-nineteenth-century appeals for a reformed science of economics. Just like earlier critics, Etzioni is asking for an economics (he calls it 'socio-economics') which should in fact be a kind of economic sociology. In fact his objections to economics, like those of his century-old predecessors, attack the very concept of a pure science of economics. Indeed, this line of criticism has consistently maintained that economics can be rescued only by abandoning the traditional boundaries of the discipline. For explanations of social phenomena which, for analytical purposes, begin by postulating a separate field of strictly economic action are fatally flawed from their very beginning.

THE STANDARD DEFENCES AND THE STANDARD REBUTTALS

Traditionally, economists have defended themselves against attacks on the unrealisticness of economic man along one or other of two possible lines of reasoning.

One line of defence has been to argue that the rationality assumption (or the assumption of selfishness, or whichever version of the fundamental assumption of economizing activity is under attack) is never meant as *more than a useful first approximation*. The assumption is held to be roughly valid for much of human activity, so that the models of economic theory provide indispensable guidance in understanding the real world. This guidance must, admittedly, be supplemented by careful consideration of actual behaviour in specific situations; none the less it would be folly to reject out of hand the guidance of the pure economic models. The inclusion of all relevant sociological and and/or psychological features of real world situations can only obscure those powerful chains of cause and effect which arise from the significant extent to which the economist's assumptions *are* empirically relevant to those situations.[1]

The critics of economics (including, in particular, Professor Etzioni) have, in one way or another, rejected this line of defence. They have denied the empirical usefulness of the economists' assumptions. They have accused economists of ignoring, at least in their policy recommendations, their own fine-print lip-service to the limited actual relevance of their models. In fact, the critics maintain, economists have permitted their models to run away with them, so that they are simply unable to shake off their adherence to these suspect assumptions. This rebuttal has been sharpened by the contemporary work of economists such as Gary Becker, who has applied the models of economics to areas of human life (such as marriage and the family) in which (the critics believe) the economists' assumptions are, even more than usual, egregiously unrealistic. These critics are deeply offended by the economists' insistence, not merely on barring the insights of sociology from their explanations for economic phenomena, but on in fact 'imperialistically' laying claim, on behalf of their own caricature-like models of human behaviour, to territory traditionally recognized as the preserve of the other social sciences.

The second of the two traditional defences of economics has been to argue for a highly refined version of the assumption of economic man. It is argued that economics does not need, and never has needed, the cruder assumptions sometimes employed in the characterization of *homo oeconomicus*. Economic man does not need to be materialistic, or selfish; he does not even have to be efficient in any objective sense. *He merely has to pursue goals purposefully*, in the light of his own perceptions of relevant possibilities and constraints. Ever since, in 1932, Lionel Robbins built on the ideas of Philip Wicksteed in the United Kingdom and a number of Austrian economists of the 1920s and early 1930s to formulate this rarefied depiction of the economizing agent (Robbins 1935), economists have felt justified in brushing aside much of the standard criticism. As Mises (one of the Austrians on whose ideas Robbins had drawn) had explained as early as 1922, there is nothing in the economist's approach which implies absence of moral restraints. There is nothing amoral or 'uncivilized' in the economist's perspective. Truly sensitive natures, Mises pointed out, need not be dismayed by the economist's way of putting things. 'Called upon to choose between bread and honour, [such truly sensitive natures] will never be at a loss how to act. If honour cannot be eaten, eating can at least be foregone for honour' (Mises 1936).

The critics have not accepted this line of defence. As Etzioni (1988: 21) points out (with regard to the more modern version of the Wicksteed–Mises–Robbins line of defence, which treats utility as a 'strictly formal concept, as the common denominator of all human preferences'), this defence involves first the reduction of utility theory to a tautology. Second, it suppresses important substantive differences which separate human actions designed to pursue pleasure from those taken in response to moral imperatives (Etzioni 1988: 23–50). To insist on the 'mono-utilitarian' paradigm is both to offer theories empty of empirical content and relevance and to obscure significant and easily understandable differences in behaviour patterns.

Our position in what follows will be generally on the side of the defenders of economics, especially those employing the Mises–Robbins approach. But we shall argue that the full significance of this reply to the sociological and historicist critics has not yet been properly articulated. Our elaboration of the Mises–Robbins argument will require us to reject (as the critics of economics reject) the first line of defence referred to earlier. Our defence of the 'rationality' assumption – using the quotation marks in order to avoid becoming embroiled in definitional debates concerning precisely which concept of rationality undergirds economics – will emphasize the significance of this assumption, not for the theory of decision making, but for the theory of *market process*.

'RATIONALITY' AND THE MARKET PROCESS: TOWARDS A FRESH ARTICULATION

We shall maintain, somewhat dogmatically perhaps, that the core of economic theory is the theory of markets. Even the harshest of the critics of economics is unlikely to deny that at least some markets work systematically at least some of the time. The explication of the responsible systematic forces, we assert, constitutes the central idea in economic theory. For us the existence of systematic market forces means the existence of *a spontaneous process of learning*. What economic theory essentially sets out to explain, therefore, is how a spontaneous learning process can be set in motion by the interaction of exchanging individuals. To assert that markets work systematically is to assert that market participants tend spontaneously to become better informed about each other, as a result of initial market experiences based on earlier erroneous perceptions about one another's abilities, attitudes and degrees of eagerness. *The great contribution of economic science to social understanding has been to discern and explain this kind of spontaneous learning process – in all kinds of specific contexts.* There is nothing, in the economic theory which explicates this process, which depends on any specific context in which it may manifest itself. There is nothing in economic theory which confines it to individuals pursuing strictly material satisfactions or which excludes the operation of moral imperatives and restraints. Perhaps more to the point for present purposes, strictly speaking, *nothing in economic theory purports to explain how individuals, with given information, make their decisions; it relates exclusively to the spontaneously changing patterns of information in the light of which these decisions are made during the course of the market process.* Our defence of the 'rationality' assumption in economics boils down to the claim that the only essential role played by this assumption relates not to the way in which decisions are made but instead to the manner in

which hitherto overlooked opportunities for market gains come to be
perceived. All this calls for some elaboration; it represents,
admittedly, a highly unorthodox understanding of the role of the
'rationality' principle.

MICROECONOMICS AND ECONOMIC THEORY

The generally perceived role of the 'rationality' assumption in modern
economic theory – in our view a somewhat misperceived role – arises
from the way in which microeconomics is generally perceived. It is
recognized (of course correctly) that the central elements in economic
theory are those which make up microeconomics. That is, these
elements are understood analytically as proceeding from the decisions
made by individual market participants. From this sound starting
point there has developed, however, the unfortunate perception that
a central task of economic theory is *to explain the individual decision*, in
the sense of providing, in principle, a way of predicting what a given
individual consumer, resource owner or owner of a firm will decide to
do under given circumstances. For this explanation, it is generally
understood, the 'rationality' assumption provides the controlling
principle. In the modern criticism of economics it is the validity of
this controlling principle which is under attack. We believe this perception of microeconomics, and thus the criticism of economics on
the basis of perceived weaknesses in the 'rationality' assumption, to
be fundamentally imprecise.

In our view the central element in microeconomic theory is its
explication of the manner in which systematic market tendencies
arise. These tendencies arise out of the interplay of individual
decisions; it is this which makes microeconomics central to economic
theory. But the prime focus of microeconomics should, in our view,
be the process through which this interplay of individual decisions
systematically generates greater mutual awareness. The central role
of 'rationality', we shall see, concerns this process of learning. In fact,
in our view, it is not the function of economics to explain decision
making at all, in any except the most formal ('tautological') sense.
The function of microeconomics is to explain how, in the course of
the market process, decisions tend to change – spontaneously but
systematically – from patterns which are initially based on more
erroneously assumed information (concerning the attitudes of one's
fellow market participants) towards patterns which are based on more
correct information. We recognize, of course, that it is certainly

important, in developing such a microeconomics, to work out a formal framework within which to envisage decisions being made. It is, after all, only in this way that we can focus carefully and precisely on the ways in which erroneous assumptions on the part of market participants tend to be systematically replaced by more correct assumptions. But the working out of such formal frameworks never has the function of providing operational theories concerning individual decisions. The role of the 'rationality' assumption in the microeconomic theory of the individual decision ought therefore to appear totally innocuous *precisely because of* its empirical emptiness. We thus fully endorse the Mises–Robbins defence of the role of the 'rationality' assumption, which emphasizes the complete *generality* of the utility towards which individuals are assumed to be purposefully aiming. But we wish to make two relevant observations. First, we shall argue that this defence is only the beginning of the full story. Second, it should be clear from our discussion that the standard rebuttals offered against the Mises–Robbins defence, denouncing it as turning the micro-theory of the decision into a tissue of tautologies, incapable of explaining important, obvious distinctions between classes of decisions under a variety of circumstances, totally miss the mark. This is because the function of the microeconomic theory of the decision is *precisely* that of providing the tautologous framework required for the subsequent theory of the market process. The usefulness and the validity of the 'rationality' assumption must, in our view, be judged most crucially in terms of its success in explicating the market process.

SELF-INTEREST AND DISCOVERY

The learning process which drives the forces of the market is made up primarily of disappointments and discoveries. Individuals are, perhaps, initially over-optimistic in regard to what they believe others will be prepared to pay for what they wish to buy, or in regard to what they believe others will be prepared to accept for what they wish to sell. Over-optimism generates disappointments. The cold realities drive home the truth. Subsequent buying and selling plans tend to be made on the basis of more realistic assessments. Price tends toward the market clearing level, at which no one need be disappointed. So runs the stuff of market equilibration theory.

Or again, individuals may be unnecessarily pessimistic regarding the interest of others in trading. They may believe that prospective buyers are only very slightly interested, that they will not buy except at very low prices (or that prospective sellers will not sell except at very high prices). Such excessive pessimism means that market participants may be overlooking valuable opportunities for mutual gain through exchange. Such opportunities for (what amounts to) pure profit tend to stimulate discovery. As discoveries are made, prices for a given commodity, or productive service or whatever, converge; input prices and output prices converge; pure profit is squeezed out until, in equilibrium, it is entirely absent. So runs the stuff of general equilibrium theory.

These processes of learning are spontaneous, not deliberate. They are driven, not by planning for the acquisition of costly knowledge, but by the spontaneous realization (resulting from experience) of earlier error. In particular they are driven by *the alertness of individuals intent on achieving their purposes.* Persons with no interests or goals will not tend to discover the changes in external conditions that favour or threaten the realization of interests or goals. Alertness without some degree of purposefulness is simply and totally implausible. Self-interest (in the rarefied Mises–Robbins sense of purposefulness) switches on one's awareness to hitherto unnoticed disappointing conditions, or hitherto unnoticed opportunities for gain. Without the 'rationality' assumption tending to assure gradual spontaneous discovery of relevant market truths, economists would have no basis upon which to account for the systematic character of market processes.

The self-interest, the purposefulness, postulated here need in no way deny either man's moral concerns or his susceptibility to blind passions. The theory does not, recall, postulate *specific* patterns of concrete decision making; it merely asks that we recognize *some* role, in human action, for 'rationality'. *To the extent that* 'rationality' plays a role in human decisions, we are entitled to demonstrate how it may generate systematic patterns of mutual learning on the part of participating individuals. To reject the scientific demonstration of the power of such systematic learning patterns, on the grounds of occasional or frequent human 'irrationality', is to refuse to see a powerful tendency which manifests itself in regard to *all* the interests of human beings. The 'laws of supply and demand' really do explicate a host of matters; they do rely on the powerful effects of human purposefulness – without in the least obscuring the influence of moral concerns, altruistic concerns or other concerns which may be expressed *through* those purposes, and without in the least presuming the total absence of passionate and emotional obstacles to the dis-coveries which might be made by pure reason alone.

Nothing in the explication of the laws of supply and demand denies the possible existence of other laws ('non-economic' laws) relevant to human behaviour. There is nothing in economic theory which need displace other disciplines (sociology, psychology, whatever) from exploring the possibility of such other regularities. But, at the same time, the insights of economic theory cannot be grasped without perceiving the role of the 'self-interested' pursuit of possibly altruistic or other purposes in generating processes of mutual discovery.

INADEQUATE AND INEPT DEFENCES OF ECONOMICS

Those defending economics on the grounds of the approximate accuracy of specific assumptions concerning the absence of altruistic or other moral concerns, or concerning the absence of passionate and emotional elements in human action, are, from the perspective here articulated, in the last analysis doing economics a disservice. To the extent that their defence proposes that economics displace other social sciences in accounting for the specifics of human behaviour, they render valid all the criticisms of those challenging the realism of selfish, calculating and ruthlessly amoral economic man. Whatever occasional usefulness, in understanding specific social or economic phenomena, may be derived from the application of such narrowly conceived, highly specific models of human behaviour is surely out-weighed by the attendant costs. These costs include, in particular, the unfortunate expectations raised in many lay – and even professional – observers that economics, by itself, can account for and in principle predict what people will do under specific circumstances. A related cost is the diversion of attention from what economics does in fact uniquely provide: a satisfying explanation of why and how markets work.

One particularly unfortunate cost of this ineffective line of defence has been to perpetuate the myth that the normative implications of standard economic theory stand or fall with the validity of this narrowly defined *homo oeconomicus*. It is largely by pointing to the presence in real world human beings of moral impulses and of power-ful passions directly influencing decisions that critics of economics feel free to reject the insights to be learned from economics concerning the socially benign consequences of free markets. Such rejection has, of course, often been the major motive inspiring the methodological criticisms made against economics, ever since the 1870s.

But once it is recognized that it is the Mises–Robbins line of defence which accurately comprehends the role of the 'rationality' assumption, matters appear decidedly differently. The Mises–Robbins line of defence points, as discussed, to the paramountcy of the 'rationality' assumption not so much in the theory of decision making as in the theory of spontaneous learning. The 'rationality' assumption permits us to recognize that markets encourage people spontaneously to discover opportunities to gain – in terms of whatever they happen to be interested in. With the emphasis shifted from the particular decision made, to the *changing frameworks of information and perceptions within which decisions can be made* (whether under the inspiration of logic, emotion, passion or whatever), the alleged implausibility of the role of 'rationality' in economics becomes an accusation more and more difficult to take seriously. It is true that the postulation of equilibrating tendencies requires a role for deliberate purposefulness, but it by no means requires an exclusive role. The theorems showing how processes of mutual learning can develop spontaneously can be seen as relevant to all kinds of human interests, and retain validity so long as human purposefulness is at least one element in the psychological make-up of market participants. Admittedly, facile deployment of the theory of markets to account for developments in particular historical circumstances is a highly treacherous enterprise. Where moral or personal concerns complicate business decisions, it may turn out to be hazardous to attempt to identify empirically the particular 'commodities' in regard to which economics is supposed somehow to postulate the existence of spontaneous processes of learning. But the general thrust of economics surely remains sound: the market is understood as a seething ocean of interacting decisions continually tending, subject to continual buffetings of 'external changes', towards systematic mutual discovery by all pairs of individuals between whom (given *their* interests) exchange (of *something*) might be mutually beneficial. This tendency is never completed, neither is it ever suspended. It is frequently interrupted, often possibly distorted, but it never ceases to exert its influence.

SELF-INTEREST AND LATE-TWENTIETH-CENTURY ECONOMICS

It may be useful to conclude briefly with some thoughts about the timeliness of this new round of debate on the role of the 'rationality' assumption in economics. These thoughts centre on two themes: why modern economics has, at this particular time, provoked this new outburst of attacks on the 'rationality' assumption; and how the contemporary revival of the Austrian tradition (the same tradition which nurtured the Mises–Robbins defence cited earlier) has made it possible to outline a fresh (and even more effective) aspect of the classic Mises–Robbins defence of the 'rationality' assumption in economics.

That modern mainstream economics has provoked the renewed spate of attacks revolving round the 'rationality' assumption is eminently understandable. It is in our time that microeconomics has once again assumed the controlling paradigmatic role in economic theory. It has done so in a manner which has emphasized the concrete contributions which, it is claimed, the 'rationality' assumption can make to empirical social science. Modern microeconomics has proceeded to 'invade' the territories of other social sciences, placing ever more weight on the crucial character of the constrained maximization behaviour which the 'rationality' assumption sees as so central. It has turned out to be those economists (associated very often with the University of Chicago) who have been understood to be the most enthusiastic supporters of free markets (as a consequence of their economics) whose economics appears most heavily indebted to the narrowest formulations of the 'rationality' assumption. It was a George Stigler who suggested (1984) that dollars and liberty are, for relevant purposes, entirely synonymous. It was a Richard Posner (1983) whose work on law and economics seemed to make the maximization of market value the sole criterion for human happiness. In other words, modern economists have seemed to permit the narrowest of formulations of the rationality assumption to dictate social policy in what critics could easily perceive to be a highly dangerous fashion. It is not surprising that all this has stimulated sharply critical reactions.

Yet at the same time as mainstream economics has been formulated on narrower and narrower conceptions of rationality, at the same time as rationality came perilously close to being seen as virtually synonymous with universal omniscience, the revival of the Austrian tradition has enabled us to extend the classic Mises–Robbins defence with renewed vigour. Developments within the Austrian tradition have emphasized the centrality, not of states of equilibrium generated by completely rational (i.e. omniscient) market participants, but of market processes of spontaneous learning sparked by entrepreneurial alertness (Kirzner 1973, 1985a).

In these processes, self-interest is indeed a central element, but this self-interest must, as we have seen, be understood with a certain subtlety. Properly understood self-interest does not exclude altruistic motivation; it depends on purposefulness, but not on any selfishness of purpose. The point to be stressed is that it is one's *own* purposes which inspire one's actions and excite one's alertness. One's purposes may be altruistic or otherwise; one's interest in achieving one's (possibly altruistic) goals switches on one's alertness to opportunities for advancing those goals. One may appear to be acting selfishly in amassing profits in market activities; but if this drive to win profits is inspired solely by a dream of endowing a research effort to fight a dread disease that threatens mankind, we would hardly label it as selfish. It is human dreams and goals which provide the motive force for market processes. Economics depends, for its understanding of market processes, upon the alert purposefulness, the purposeful alertness, of human beings. In these processes the controlling principle is goal-motivated discovery. And it is the emphasis on these disequilibrium processes of mutual discovery which has led us to underscore the relevance of the classic Mises–Robbins insistence on the utter generality of human motives.

Chapter 13

Discovery, private property and the theory of justice in capitalist society

Critics of the capitalist system have accused it of many faults. Some of these perceived problems have been the subject of debate among economists. Economists have argued over the economic merits of a system without conscious direction under an overall plan. The *justice* of a capitalist system, too, has often been the subject of criticism and debate. But the problem of economic justice under capitalism has, in the main, in recent years been debated by philosophers rather than by economists. This is perhaps because this debate has, in principle, assumed the economics of capitalism to be well understood and agreed upon, so that judgements concerning the justice or absence of justice in the system could be made purely on philosophical and ethical grounds. In this chapter[1] I shall argue that the common understanding of the economics of capitalism which has served as the basis for the philosophical debate has in fact suffered from certain serious weaknesses. When these weaknesses are corrected, I shall maintain, hitherto overlooked key features of capitalism come into view which can be seen to have important philosophical and ethical implications – implications totally overlooked in the standard philosophical debates. In particular, I shall argue, an adequate understanding of the economics of the capitalist system reveals the crucial role played in this system by *discovery*. Once the economic role of discovery is properly understood, I shall maintain, most of the features of capitalism which have provoked the charges of injustice become visible – even without any new ethical argumentation – in a totally different light. In other words the discovery theory of justice in capitalist society offers a defence of capitalist justice not by articulating novel philosophical or ethical positions but by offering a fresh economic understanding of how the capitalist economic system actually works.

THE CHARGE OF CAPITALIST INJUSTICE

Claims that capitalism perpetrates economic injustice have traditionally taken a variety of forms. At one level, the basic institution of
capitalism, private property, has been attacked philosophically at its
very roots. In the view of these critics, there is an inherent injustice
committed whenever a nature-given resource is privately appropriated. Such appropriation is seen as the private grabbing of something
belonging naturally to all mankind. (In some variants of this attack,
even the notion of self-ownership by the individual is fundamentally
denied on these grounds.) A system in which all transactions are built
on such an unjust foundation is a system in which the consequences of
injustice are being continually extended.

A different level of attack is that directed at the inevitable
inequality of incomes under capitalism. Quite apart from accusations
that private property is an inherently unjust institution, quite apart
from charges that markets permit direct forms of unjust exploitation
(such as the exploitation of labour), this attack focuses on the inherent
immorality held to be represented by economic inequality. Even if no
individual in the system sought to act unjustly, the inevitable
inequality of incomes in a market society is, in these attacks,
denounced as an ethical monstrosity *per se* (see for example, Nielsen
1985).

But the main thrust of the widespread scepticism concerning the
justice of capitalism seems to be pointed at the phenomenon of pure
profit and its consequences. Even those prepared to recognize the
ethical acceptability of private property, even those who recognize no
overwhelming ethical imperative prescribing equality of incomes, are
frequently deeply disturbed by the apparent consequences of entrepreneurial profits. This ethical concern is fuelled by an intuition that
such profits have not been 'deserved' ('earned') by the entrepreneur,
and must in some way, therefore, have been unjustly won at the
expense of the other market participants (in particular, at the expense
of labourers).[2] The pattern of income distribution under capitalism is
seen as unjust because capitalism permits – is in fact built upon – the
pursuit of entrepreneurial profits. The circumstance of income
inequality is seen as ethically offensive primarily because this is the
inevitable and unfortunate consequence of the capture of profits. The
institution of private property comes to be condemned to the extent
that it is identified as the vehicle for the entrepreneurial pursuit of
profits.

In preparation for our own exposition of the discovery theory of economic justice, we shall here briefly review two classic defences of capitalist economic justice, those associated with the names of John Bates Clark and Robert Nozick. Each of these defences, directly or indirectly, depends on particular assumptions concerning private property rights and the role of pure profits. We shall also draw attention to certain weaknesses (relating particularly to these assumptions concerning private property and pure profit) in each of these defences, with regard to the criticisms they are confronting. We shall then be in a position to identify certain perspectives on the economics of capitalism (and highly relevant to the issue of its economic justice) shared by both the critics of capitalist justice and its classic defenders. It is by demonstrating the unfortunate narrowness of this economic understanding of capitalism that we hope, in subsequent sections of the chapter, to offer a more adequate defence of the justice of the capitalist system.

PRIVATE PROPERTY, PURE PROFIT AND THE CLASSIC DEFENCES OF CAPITALIST JUSTICE

It was the economist John Bates Clark who, at the turn of the century, offered the most explicit defence of capitalist distribution of incomes. He wrote a substantial book to demonstrate that, in static equilibrium, each participant in the productive process of the market system receives the full value of his marginal productive contribution (Clark 1899). In the words of Milton Friedman, the Clarkian ethic supporting the justice of capitalism can be expressed as: 'To each according to what he and the instruments he owns produces' (1962: 161f.).

Clark's defence consisted of showing how, in equilibrium, the price per unit of each productive service is the measure of the market value of its productive contribution at the margin. (This demonstration was, in fact, an important step in the development of the neoclassical theory of resource price.) For Clark it was axiomatic that justice can require no more than that each resource owner receive the market value of what he and his resources have produced. It was also apparent to Clark that, in a world in which production is always the outcome of jointly used resource services, the concept 'what a resource has produced' is to be measured by the marginal product of the resource (i.e. the incremental output forthcoming through adding one unit of this resource to an unchanged mix of the remaining resource inputs).

Finally, Clark was quite uncurious regarding the validity of a resource owner's title to the resources he holds. He simply accepted that a labourer is unquestionably entitled to the fruit of his labour, that a landowner has arrived at his title justly, that the owner of capital is in fact its legimate owner.

It will be seen that Clark's defence of capitalist justice simply ignored possible challenges to the very idea of private ownership. Moreover he simply ignored challenges to capitalist justice based on an axiomatic egalitarian ethic. Clearly he believed that by demonstrating the justice of the marginal productivity mode of distribution he had implicitly justified any entailed departures from an equal distribution of income. Clark's defence of capitalist justice consisted, in essence, in showing that each resource used by the capitalistic entrepreneur commands a fair price (measuring fairness by value of productive contribution). If each resource owner receives a just income, fully reflecting his productive contribution, no charge of injustice can be fairly levelled at the capitalistic entrepreneur. If part of the product is received as income by others than the labourers who have sweated to produce it, this must reflect some productive contribution made by these others and not any surplus unjustly exploited from the labourers.

The problems raised by this Clarkian defence stem from his virtually complete silence on two crucial ethical aspects of the capitalist economy: (a) the source of just title in resources and (b) the legitimacy of pure economic profit. As noticed above, Clark displays no curiosity concerning the source of resource ownership. He simply assumes that labourers own their bodies, landowners their land and capitalists their capital. There is nothing in the Clarkian defence of capitalism which justifies the incomes received, in return for resource services rendered, by those who, lacking legitimate title to these services, may somehow have appropriated them from their rightful owners (possibly society as a whole). One might fully accept Clark's defence, as far as it goes, but then assert its irrelevance on the grounds of the fundamental injustice of private title to nature-given resources (if one believed in the injustice of such title). This gap in Clark's defence has often been noted.

Clark's silence in regard to the legitimacy of pure economic profit is a little more complicated to interpret, but equally troubling for the defence of capitalist justice. Clark did not have to deal with pure profit, because he confined his demonstration to the static world of equilibrium, in which pure profit is completely absent. For Clark, profit is an ephemeral, transient phenomenon associated with dynamics, which can be safely ignored in attempting to come to grips with the permanent features of the capitalist system. What Clark accounted for was the justice of the major component of what earlier economists had called profit, namely the segment which neoclassical and subsequent economists have called, not profit, but *interest*.[3] But a critic of capitalist justice could reasonably point out that *pure* profit (as entrepreneurial profit is often called) is an obvious and prevalent feature of the capitalist economy. It cannot be dismissed as a kind of trivial, frictional phenomenon. Its presence means, presumably, that resource incomes must, to a greater or lesser extent, fall short of the full value of the relevant marginal products.

Pure profit must, precisely from the Clarkian perspective, raise serious economic and ethical questions. Such profit seems, on the face of it, unjustified both economically and ethically. There seems, on the face of it, no economic explanation for the ability of the entrepreneur to capture any difference between input prices and output prices. Competition should surely be expected to ensure the absence of such differences. Any differences which somehow exist cannot be justified as the marginal product value of any resource service. (Remember that pure profit is what is left after subtracting, from the market value of output, the market values of *all* resource services that contributed to the production of that output.) It appears totally unjustified within the Clarkian criterion for economic justice.

Robert Nozick's defence of capitalist income distribution is embodied in his entitlement theory of justice, published exactly three-quarters of a century after Clark (1974: Chs 7, 8). Nozick's point of view is that, so long as no individual in a system has violated the rights of any others, the results of that system cannot be pronounced unjust, no matter how unequal the resulting distribution of income may be. For a capitalist system to consist solely of transactions free of unjust violation of rights, we must require that all titles to property be consistent with principles of just original acquisition from nature and just transfer of title. In this way we would be able to state that all present holdings are justly held, since each of them rests on an unblemished chain of just transactions, leading back all the way in time to just original acquisition from nature. Nozick's defence of capitalist justice boils down to carefully articulated claims that the institutional foundations of the capitalist economy may indeed be consistent with the principles of just title.

For Nozick, if two just holders of title voluntarily agree to an exchange transaction, no matter what the circumstances may be which induce such agreement, the subsequent reallocation of ownership can in no way be declared unjust. If a star professional basketball player becomes a millionaire as a result of many poor but eager spectators buying tickets, out of their hard-earned meagre wages, to watch professional basketball games, there is, for Nozick, nothing unjust in the resulting inequality of income. The athlete is the beneficiary of voluntary exchange; the money he receives was freely given up in exchange for the opportunity to witness his prowess. Nor is the situation rendered more unjust, in the entitlement view, if the individual becoming a millionaire is not a professional athlete but a landlord renting out apartments (justly owned by him) to desperately poor tenants. No one has violated any rights of others; the tenants voluntarily pay the rent in order to secure dwelling space. The entitlement theory is uninterested in the motives which may have 'compelled' a tenant (or a ticket-holder) to pay for dwelling space (or tickets to basketball games). The urgency of need for a purchased item need not taint the voluntariness of the transaction, for purposes of evaluating the justice of the transfers effected. 'Whether a person's actions are voluntary depends on what it is that limits his alternatives. If facts of nature do so, the actions are voluntary. . . . Other people's actions place limits on one's available opportunities. Whether this makes one's resulting action non-voluntary depends upon whether these others had the right to act as they did' (Nozick 1974: 262). With capitalism defined to exclude the violation of the rights of others, it follows that there is nothing to flaw the voluntariness of market transactions. The resulting pattern of income distribution can therefore never be an unjust one, as long as the rules of the capitalist game are scrupulously respected.

Within the confines of its own scope, the entitlement theory is unquestionably a powerful addition to the defence arsenal on behalf of the justice of capitalism. However, we must carefully note the limitations circumscribing the scope of the theory. First, the theory presumes the possibility of just original acquisition of items from nature. No matter how impeccably all subsequent capitalist market transactions meet the criterion of voluntariness, the justice of private property title rests ultimately upon the initial private appropriation of that which is subsequently transferred in markets. There is nothing within the entitlement theory itself which provides us with a rationale for justice in original appropriation from nature. Nozick appeals to the classic ideas of John Locke on this point, but is ultimately forced by consideration of the 'Lockean proviso' to modify the original Lockean formulation (Nozick 1974: 177). Nor is Locke's principle of initial ownership (based on 'mixing one's labour' with unowned natural resources) obviously or universally convincing.[4] The entitlement theory seems to require some independent support for its initial premises. But there are additional reasons for concern with the adequacy of the entitlement theory as a defence of capitalist justice. This has to do with the sense in which market transactions can indeed be described as voluntary.

The entitlement defence of capitalism is doubtless correct in asserting that, by definition, market transactions necessarily fulfil the legal requirements for voluntariness. But it is yet possible to question the ethical significance of the voluntariness of many, if not all, market transactions. This is because the market transactions which result in the winning of pure economic profit must in retrospect be judged to have been made, in part, as a result of 'sheer error' on the part of one or other of the relevant participants. Pure profit arises when an entrepreneur is successful in selling an item at a price higher than the sum of the prices of everything necessary to deliver the item to its buyer. Such profit could hardly arise unless those from whom the entrepreneur buys have been unaware of the price to be paid by those to whom the entrepreneur sells, and unless those to whom he sells have been unaware of the sum of the prices accepted by those from whom the entrepreneur bought. Pure profit must mean that those selling at the low price are unaware of the true higher market value of that which they sell; those buying at the high price are unaware of the possibility of buying the same item elsewhere in the market at a lower cost. It follows that those trading with the profit-making entrepreneur must, in the light of subsequently revealed profits, 'regret' their trades. Those who sold for the low price would never have done so had they then known what they subsequently know; nor would those who bought at the high price have done so had *they* known then what they subsequently find out to have been the case. Whenever it turns out that an action was taken under mistaken assumptions, it may be possible to question the true voluntariness of the action. It may be argued that the agent did not 'really' wish to do that which he did do – even though at the time he did it he did it gladly. To be sure the law (and perhaps also a certain hard-boiled moral perspective) may not recognize the mistake as substantial enough (or excusable enough) to invalidate the transaction, yet the observer may be less than certain that justice in transfer, requiring as it does voluntariness in transfer, is fully satisfied in such situations. After all, it may be held, willing consent based on mistaken assumptions (even without intent by anyone to defraud) may perhaps fall short of that informed consent which permits us to describe a transaction as fully voluntary, for purposes relevant to the requirements of justice.

But, it must be pointed out, the possibility of the winning of pure profit is central to the operation of the capitalist market system. From this perspective the entitlement theory, confined as it is to a capitalism in which all transactions are, by definition, *wholly* voluntary, appears not to have grappled with the phenomenon of pure profit.

It is with respect to these limitations in regard to the classic defences of J.B. Clark and R. Nozick that we believe it useful to draw attention to what we shall call the *discovery* elements in the market system. It will be helpful, in preparation for the exposition of the discovery perspective, to identify, by way of contrast, a perspective shared both by these classic defenders of capitalist justice and by those who have sharply questioned the justice of capitalist distribution. We shall argue that this perspective overlooks a highly significant and characteristic feature of the economics of the capitalist system.

THE 'GIVEN-PIE' PERSPECTIVE

This perspective on the economics of capitalism which we wish to criticize, a perspective shared, it seems, by *all* the participants, so far, in the debates on capitalist justice, can be labelled the 'given-pie' perspective. The question that seems to be pondered, in the debates thus far, is how, in order to achieve distributive justice, a given pie is to be shared out among the claimants to it. This pie is given, in the sense that *its origin is not relevant to the justice* of its distribution.

Now, certainly it would be palpably false to assert that participants in the debate have failed to recognize possible ways in which justice may require that we recognize the productive contributions of claimants to shares in output. It has of course been recognized that those who have baked a pie may justly claim a share of it. None the less it remains true that, at least *with respect to the ingredients that went into the production of the pie*, with respect to the original productive resources of a society, it has been simply assumed that the original productive resources were already 'there'. Criteria for justice did not, it appears, depend on how these resources came to be 'there' in the first place. More specifically, no room, in these debates on distributive justice, is left for the possibility that the pattern of just distribution of output may depend on *who originated* the inputs that made its production possible. The question asked about original inputs is rather how an individual can establish just title to them now (*after* they have somehow come to be 'here'), or whether, being 'here', they somehow belong to society as a whole.

The question of who originated original inputs is, apparently, not asked because it appears to be a nonsense question. Original inputs, i.e. inputs that have not themselves been produced but exist in nature, could not have been originated by any person, because such origination would be inconsistent with their not having been produced. That which is produced, is produced out of inputs. These inputs may themselves have been produced out of other inputs. An original input, one that is itself not produced, could not have been originated – it was simply 'there'.

Thus the given-pie perspective seems, at first glance, a sound one. Sooner or later, in the analysis of justice in the ownership of produced output, we are pushed back, in principle, to consider the just ownership of original inputs. Criteria of justice may, possibly, be agreed upon with regard to the output forthcoming from original inputs – once it can be settled what justice has to say about ownership of such original resources. But in order to say something about just ownership of original resources, we must, in the given-pie perspective, remember that these original resources are – given pies. And, since pronouncements concerning the justice of produced output depend on what we say concerning just title to the original inputs, it turns out that ultimately our theories of distributive justice boil down to principles asserted about the just distribution of given pies. Whether a Rawls considering, from behind a veil of ignorance, just title to differentially superior personal qualities and talents, or a Nozick considering the validity of Lockean principles concerning initial private acquisition of nature-given land resources, our philosophers of justice agree on treating all non-produced resources as belonging to a category to which the notion of human origination is irrelevant. In what follows, we shall point out that this stance excludes the possibility of hitherto undiscovered resources entering into the economic world except as a result of luck. We shall, by contrast, argue that a most important human element in the economic process is made up of the *discovery* by individuals of hitherto unperceived resources or of other opportunities for gain (including pure profit opportunities). Let us turn to examine this notion of discovery.

THE MEANING OF DISCOVERY

One who enjoys a desirable situation is, in economic discussion, usually viewed as having reached his present happy state as a result of either of two possible kinds of circumstances. Either such a situation is seen as the deliberately achieved outcome ascribable to an earlier plan, or it is the fortunate result of a stroke of good luck. Economists discuss the first of these possibilities under the theory of *production*. The outcome produced is attributed to the deliberate deployment of inputs. In terms of the Clarkean ethic discussed earlier, just title to output arises out of the ownership of and marginal contribution made by the respective productive inputs. On the other hand, a situation the fortunate occurrence of which is ascribed to pure luck is viewed as in no way ascribable to human will and motivation. Beneficiaries of luck, from this perspective, are often seen as possessing no inherent claim, in justice, to that which good fortune has swept into their laps. We wish here to draw attention to a neglected, but extremely important, third alternative. A desired situation may be enjoyed not as the result of a deliberate plan of production, not as the result of sheer good fortune, but *as a result of perceptive discovery made by a human being*. It will be instructive to contrast an act of discovery with an act of deliberate production.

1 An act of production is the outcome of a plan; an act of discovery is spontaneous. (Deliberate search, during which known inputs are systematically deployed to comb available data for some searched-for item, is a special kind of production. The deliberate production of information, e.g. looking up the meaning of a word in a dictionary or looking up a telephone number in a telephone directory, is not discovery, in the presently discussed sense of the word).

2 An act of production can be seen as conforming to the criteria for economic efficiency: the producer employs inputs in an optimal mix; he maximizes the output of any given mix of inputs; he minimizes the cost of production of any aimed-at output result. An act of discovery contains no such expression of constrained maximization; it involves no plan, no allocation – merely the grasping of a perceived, available, objective.

3 Credit for a pure of act of production (one containing no element of discovery) accrues to the owners of the combined inputs. *All* the output is seen, along Clarkian lines, as ascribable to the productive contribution of owned inputs. Credit for a discovery accrues to the discoverer whose alertness brought the discovered item to his

notice. But this alertness is not itself in the nature of a possessed input deployed to achieve a planned result. Alertness is not *deployed*. The discoverer simply notices that which has hitherto escaped attention (including his own). Thus one does not, in the discovery context, treat 'alertness' as an ingredient to be mixed with others in order to achieve a planned result, and therefore as the bottled-up form presently taken by its future marginal contribution (as productive resources are viewed in marginal productivity theory).

4 The aimed-at result of an act of production can be seen as having *already existed*, in embryonic form, in the input bundle responsible for the outcome. The decision to produce is simply the decision to pull the switch that effortlessly converts inputs into output. The future, in a world of only production decisions, is fully inherent in the present. History is merely the inexorable, inevitable unfolding of that which is already here, in bottled-up form. But discovery is quite different. Each discovery is a genuine novelty; it does not consist of the conversion or unfolding of earlier inputs. There is nothing at all inevitable about an act of discovery; we cannot, *ex-post*, describe the outcome as having been *caused* by anything that existed in the past. Prior to the discovery, the state of the world – even taking into account the alertness of the (persons who subsequently turn out to be the) discoverers – was not such as *to ensure* the subsequent course of events, in so far as these express discoveries subsequently made. The discoverer is in fact injecting something totally new into history. History consists, in part, in a series of total surprises, wholly unpredictable.[5]

DISCOVERY AND LUCK

But if an act of discovery is not able to fit into the box labelled 'production', it is also not able to fit into that other box labelled 'luck'. It really does require a box of its own. An individual whose alertness inspires a discovery is not to be treated as merely the fortunate beneficiary of good luck. Theorists of justice tend to dismiss the justice of claims made by those who have benefited from good luck; they dismiss these claims because these fortunate claimants did nothing to bring about their present fortunate circumstances; they have therefore not 'deserved' their good fortune. It is our concern here that such dismissal not lead also to summary dismissal of claims *of an entirely different* character – those made by discoverers. An act of discovery, even though it is not an act of deliberate production, is the expression of human motivation and human alertness. That which has been discovered might *never* have been discovered but for this motivation and alertness; it is quite wrong to see the discovery as merely the product of blind chance.

To see how a discoverer may be held to 'deserve' that which he has discovered, even though he has not deliberately produced it, consider the following. If the discovery is to be dismissed as due entirely to pure luck, it follows that the earlier *failure* to have discovered (what is discovered later) must be excused as having been the result of bad luck. No one who has made a belated discovery should be able to berate himself for having done anything wrong in the past, for having made any error, since all earlier failures are to be ascribed, not to any earlier human shortcoming on his part, but simply to atrociously bad fortune. But in fact we know from our everyday experiences that truly deplorable errors – as judged subsequently by their perpetrators – do occur. That is, we know that desirable situations were entirely within our grasp, but were let go merely as a result of oversight. We blame ourselves for these past lapses, we do not simply shrug our shoulders, regretting our atrocious past luck. But if earlier failures to see what is staring us in the face are indeed seen as a series of deplorably 'stupid' errors on our part, it follows that our alert discovery of what is now staring us in the face must be ascribed to us, not to blind luck.

We must, that is, distinguish sharply between one who has produced nothing, discovered nothing – who was in fact unalertly slumbering – who wakes up to find a windfall in his lap,[6] and one who has alertly grasped an attractive opportunity that came within reach. A pure windfall may correctly be described as being wholly 'undeserved' (i.e. as not being attributable in any sense to the fortunate beneficiary), but an alertly grasped opportunity may quite plausibly, we suggest, be considered to fall into an entirely different ethical box.

It must of course be conceded that even though we emphasize the alert and motivated perception of the opportunity which constitutes the core of the act of discovery, we must also recognize that luck alone may indeed be responsible for the *very existence* of the opportunity waiting to be discovered. Certainly the discoverer of an attractive opportunity may count himself fortunate in having been at the right place at the right time. But, we wish to emphasize, to the extent that being at the right place at the right time does not in itself ensure that one will realize one's good fortune, luck cannot be pronounced as responsible for the discovery of the opportunity inherent in the situation. In fact, we suggest, it is plausible to treat the discoverer of a hitherto unperceived opportunity as its *creator*, its originator. That which is grasped by the discoverer did not, in a relevant sense, exist at all prior to its discovery.

DISCOVERY AS CREATION

To see this creative character of the discovery act, it is sufficient to notice that an unperceived opportunity, an unperceived resource, is, in an important sense, an opportunity or a resource without relevance for human history. As far as understanding the historical flow of events is concerned, nothing depends on the existence of resources of which everyone has been ignorant.

Let us recall that in an act of discovery (unlike the act of production) the outcome is not attributable to the contributions made by inputs. No inputs can guarantee a discovery. A discovered outcome is not a result already embedded, in embryonic form, in any bundle of resources. The outcome of an act of discovery is thus originated *entirely* by that act. A newly discovered island rich in natural resources has been created, for purposes of social science, in the act of its discovery. Its earlier physical existence may be significant for chains of purely physical causation; of course the island 'really did exist' even though no one knew of its existence. Its presence may well have influenced the weather, or the flow of ocean currents, whether or not any human being was aware of its existence. But as far as directly concerns human decision making and economic values – and human ethical judgements – the island entered into existence at the moment of its discovery. Its discoverer was its creator, for all purposes of direct human concern.

While the discoverer of the island may indeed consider himself lucky to have been in the position to notice the island, he may plausibly claim that even after having been placed in that lucky position the island's discovery was by no means assured. The island, not yet existing in the relevant social sense, could well have remained forever undiscovered but for the discoverer's motivated alertness. It was that alertness which brought the island, with all its resources, within the purview of human concern, human valuations and human planning for the future.

The inspired hunch which leads the discoverer to notice islands where others see only clouds, to notice opportunities for innovative products or innovative applications of technology which others fail to see, is as creative, in its own context, as the inspired vision of the sculptor who sees, in marble and chisel, not merely marble and chisel but a sublime form awaiting to be brought forth. Recognition of this creative aspect of the act of discovery seems to underlie a widely shared ethical conviction, that embodied in the notion of 'finders, keepers'.

THE FINDERS, KEEPERS ETHIC AND PRIVATE PROPERTY

It seems plausible to interpret the fairly widespread view that the first finder of an unowned object is its just owner as the moral conviction that this finder is the discoverer and thus, in the significant sense, the creator of that object. We wish to suggest that this finders, keepers ethic undergirds the widespread acceptance of the legitimacy of private property and, ultimately, of the possibility of justice under capitalism. In this section we explore the relevance of the finders, keepers ethic for the institution of private property.

Traditionally, defences of the institution of private property have relied on the observations of John Locke concerning the legitimacy of private acquisition of unowned, naturally available useful things, through the mixing of one's labour with those useful things. We have already noted (in our references to Nozick's entitlement approach) that critics have questioned the validity of the Lockean approach, and have, moreover, pointed out that a proviso circumscribing this approach enunciated by Locke himself may in practice render that approach quite irrelevant for a justification of private property in the real world. The validity of Locke's approach rests on (a) the (arbitrary?) assumption of the justice of self-ownership by individual human beings (without this assumption one could hardly talk of an individual mixing 'his labour' with nature-given objects, since the labour he mixes may be held to belong justly to society as a whole); and (b) the belief that mixing one's labour with an object does indeed confer private title to it upon the labourer; critics have challenged this belief as quite arbitrary.

The problems arising out of the Lockean proviso follow from Locke's qualification of his doctrine to make it applicable only to those situations where, even after the individual has mixed his labour with the nature-given objects, there remain plenty of these same objects for others to enjoy as well (Locke 1937). Commentators have pointed out that in the real world of economic scarcity this proviso seems to make Locke's justification of private acquisition almost entirely irrelevant. We wish to suggest that a finders, keepers approach, based on the ethical implication of seeing discovery as creative, may offer a more convincing basis for original acquisition of property from the state of nature.

The finders, keepers approach would assign just title to the one who, discovering an unowned (because undiscovered) resource, grasps it first. The justice of his title is then seen as stemming from the creative character of the pure act of discovery (rather than being derivative from the self-owned resource which the appropriator has mixed with the resources).[7] For this view on the justice of original acquisition, no Lockean proviso need be held to apply. The rationale behind the proviso has been interpreted (Nozick 1974: 177) to be that such private acquisition cannot be just if it harms others (and, unless there is plenty left over for others, private acquisition must limit the common pool available to others). But, from the perspective of a finders, keepers ethic based on the creativity of discovery, this rationale may reasonably be held not to be relevant to acts of pure discovery. An act of discovery (even if it results in private appropriation of a hitherto undiscovered *scarce* resource) does not necessarily harm others, since this resource never did exist for these others. My discovery now of a resource has not stopped you from enjoying this object now (or even in the future), since as far as you are concerned *now* (i.e. at the second prior to my discovery) this resource has not existed (and its future existence has not been anticipated). The possibility that, were I not now to have discovered this resource, you would, very likely, have discovered it a little later yourself (so that my grasping of my discovery has limited your potential future enjoyment) seems to be not really a relevant circumstance at all. The circumstance that you might, at some time in the future, have created the object which I am now in fact creating hardly means that I am harming you (by 'preventing' *you* from creating *this* object). Once I have created the object through its discovery, there is simply no way for you to create it independently; it already does exist, for human purposes. No one can, before hypothesized future discovery, in fact predict that discovery. It would, when it were to occur, have to be an act of pure origination so that, at the moment of my present discovery, the hypothetical future discovery by you is simply conjecture. To say now that you were somehow 'going' to make the discovery in the future is to rewrite history in the light of future events – events which are in no way implicit in the course of prior history. Within the finders, keepers ethic there is simply no room for any Lockean proviso.

FINDERS, KEEPERS AND THE JUSTICE OF CAPITALISM

Once we have satisfactorily grounded the notion of just original acquisition – and thus the institution of private property – in the discovery act, the road is open for a more comprehensive defence of the justice of the capitalist market system. Such a defence may be built along Nozickian entitlement lines, but with an added dimension capable of dealing with the gap we noticed in that entitlement theory. That gap was its possible weakness in regard to the justice of pure profit. Pure profit, we pointed out, may not be wholly defensible within the entitlement approach, since the pure error (involved in the transactions which make pure profit possible) may be held to invalidate the prima facie voluntariness of the relevant transactions. Our discovery perspective permits us now to perceive a new dimension in profit, a dimension obscured in the 'given-pie' perspectives which we have cricitized.

It turns out, from this discovery perspective, that the very features of pure profit which seem to raise problems within the entitlement approach are sufficient to prove profit to be *a wholly discovered* gain. The problem with pure profit, it will be recalled, was that there seemed no way of 'justifying' it in terms of productive contribution rendered (since by definition it is what remains after deducting *all* necessary costs of production, including transportation and transaction costs necessary to deliver output to its ultimate buyer). Moreover, it will be recalled, the very circumstance that pure profit is in the nature of a surplus, not strictly necessary to be paid to the primary sellers in order to persuade them to sell (that which is later resold at a profit), appears to raise serious questions concerning the informed voluntariness with which the ultimate buyers pay the higher, profitable price. (Or, alternatively, the willingness of the ultimate buyers to pay the higher price raises questions concerning the informed voluntariness with which the first sellers agreed to sell for the low price.) Our present perspective enables us to perceive that, precisely because the primary sellers have no inkling of the immediate availability of obtaining higher prices, and precisely because the ultimate buyers have no inkling of the immediate availability of what they buy at lower prices than they are paying, the gap between the low and the high prices constitutes for them an undiscovered opportunity. The entrepreneur who buys at the low price and sells at the high price is grasping a discovered opportunity. From the finders, keepers perspective he is justly entitled to this grasped gain because, in the relevant sense, he has *created* it.

Indeed, our understanding of the primary role of entrepreneurship in the market system permits us to see the entire capitalist system *as consisting essentially of acts of discovery.* From the *ex ante* perspective there is no market transaction which does not involve, to some degree, an attempt to peer ahead through the fog of uncertainty, in order to grasp opportunities which might easily escape recognition. In the ceaseless flow of dynamic competition, sellers modify their judgements on what prices they can command, buyers modify their judgements on what prices it is necessary for them to offer to pay. These bids and offers constitute attempted acts of discovery. The justice of market outcomes cannot be assessed without incorporating the extent to which gains derived from these discovery acts fit the guidelines of the finders, keepers rule.

Standard theories of capitalist justice, it emerges, appear to have treated the market as if it were, at all times, in full general equilibrium. Such a model of the market contains no scope for entrepreneurship, no scope for pure error, no scope for overlooked costlessly available opportunities – in short, no scope for discovery and for its ethical implications. Once we exorcise the 'given-pie' incubus – an incubus very much implicit in a strictly equilibrium view of the market – from discussions of market justice, the door is open for careful introduction of the possible relevance of a finders, keepers rule. The finders, keepers ethic provides a plausible basis for defending the justice of the capitalist system. Such an ethic offers a fresh basis – unencumbered by any Lockean proviso – for original private acquisition from nature. Such an ethic offers, in addition, a solid theory supporting the possible justice of pure profit. To the extent that capitalist resource incomes involve a discovery element, they, too, may be held justified, at least in part, by the finders, keepers ethic. Together these insights significantly supplement the standard defences of capitalist justice. They certainly do not declare capitalism to be free of all moral blemishes (since, in any event, strict justice is not the sole criterion for morality between human beings). They certainly do not pronounce all actions taken under historical capitalism to have been moral, or even just. They do, however, suggest that the capitalist system need not be rejected out of hand as being inherently unfair. Moral improvement may be sought within the framework of private property and free exchange, without the conviction that to participate in capitalism is to participate in an inevitably flawed human institution.

Notes

1 MARKET PROCESS THEORY: IN DEFENCE OF THE AUSTRIAN MIDDLE GROUND

1 Of course Professor Garrison is not responsible for the manner in which his idea is presented and deployed in this paper.

2 See Mises (1966: 2) for the insight that the contribution of classical economics was to show how state policies have systematic, often unintended, consequences (which ought therefore to be taken into account).

3 See Boehm (1985), for some doubts concerning the extent of this classical liberalism.

4 See this volume, Chapter 7, for an account of these developments.

5 See this volume, Chapter 3, pp. 67f, for one contemporary interpretation of the term 'Austrian economics' as 'free market economics'.

6 For earlier contributions defending the Austrian middle ground with regard to positions taken by radical subjectivists, see O'Driscoll (1978) and Garrison (1987).

7 We may add that an implication of this position urged by the critics is that Austrians also reject their traditional commitment to the viability of economic theory (as opposed to historicism). Although Austrian economics began as a sharp reaction against the German Historical School, it is now suggested that something of a reappraisal is in order (see Shackle 1972: 37f., 272f.; Lachmann 1986a: 148).

8 For criticism along similar lines see Wiseman (1990).

9 For an example of such a challenge see Wiseman (1990: 158).

10 See also Garrison (1987) with regard to Professor Lachmann's concurrence with Kregel's position.

11 For recognition of this implication of radical subjectivism, see Wiseman (1990: 155).

12 On the idea of entrepreneurial alertness see further Kirzner (1973: 2; 1979a: Ch. 10).

13 'The future is unknowable, though not unimaginable' (Lachmann 1976: 59).

14 This writer has often talked as if alertness is able to identify *existing* opportunities for future profit. Purists, in both linguistic usage and philosophical consistency, may certainly be excused for expressing unhappiness with

such loose or metaphorical use of language in regard to the non-existent future. But the economics of the situation surely depends not a whit on the validity of this use of language.

15 It must be remembered that the theory of entrepreneurial alertness does not operate by having the entrepreneur ponder the comparative merits of a list of alternative future scenarios. Instead the theory posits that, based on the entrepreneur's 'alertness', his sense of the future, his attention will tend to be grasped by the relevant profitable future scenario. Our point is that *all* relevant future alternative realities have equal potential for grasping entrepreneurial attention. The greater the degree of his alertness, the greater the likelihood that the 'future reality' which will in fact grab his attention will be that which will in fact turn out to be the case.

2 THE MEANING OF MARKET PROCESS

1 This chapter draws freely on ideas developed in earlier work by the author. See especially Kirzner (1973, 1978, 1979a, 1985a). These ideas have their roots in the writing of Ludwig von Mises and Friedrich A. Hayek.

2 For a discussion of the work of E.H. Chamberlin in this regard, see Kirzner (1973: 114).

3 For an early example of such concern see Hayek (1949c). For a more recent example see Fisher (1983).

4 For an extreme version of this point of view see Stigler (1982).

5 It should be noted that such opportunities are widely available as part of the economic environment relevant not only to pure entrepreneurs but to all market participants.

3 THE AUSTRIAN SCHOOL OF ECONOMICS

An earlier article on the Austrian School of economics was begun and substantially drafted by Professor Friedrich A. Hayek – himself a Nobel laureate in economics whose celebrated contributions are deeply rooted in the Austrian tradition. The present author gratefully acknowledges his indebtedness (in the writing of this chapter) to the characteristic scholarship and treasure-trove of facts contained in Professor Hayek's unfinished article, as well as to Professor Hayek's other numerous studies that relate to the history of the Austrian School.

4 CARL MENGER AND THE SUBJECTIVIST TRADITION IN ECONOMICS

1 A useful correction of the popular view treating Menger's contribution as simply parallel to that of Jevons and of Walras is Jaffé (1976).

2 For a critique of this aspect of Menger see Lachmann (1978).

3 To be sure, a critic might wonder why Menger could not, with equal

validity, have seen the root cause for the phenomenon of price in the physical constraints surrounding production. If a pound of beaver cannot in fact be produced without forgoing the production of deer, or of other things, may it not be maintained that it is *this* underlying reality which accounts 'essentially' for the phenomenon that beaver commands a price (in terms of other things paid for it)? After all, men will not hunt beaver unless a price is paid to make it worthwhile. Here, of course, Menger's subjectivist view of economic life is the dominant element – a philosophical, rather than an analytical, element. For Menger the real reason for the phenomenon of price lies in consumers' purposes in their pursuit of their goals, including both beaver and 'other things'. The relative difficulty of producing beaver and these other things merely marks out the channels along which consumer purposes are able to be pursued; it is seen as a background phenomenon, indeed critically important for the determination of the specific prices paid, but not itself ultimately responsible for the phenomenon of price.

4 These papers form the core of Hayek (1949a).

5 MENGER, CLASSICAL LIBERALISM AND THE AUSTRIAN SCHOOL OF ECONOMICS

1 Boehm (1985: 251), citing Menger (1884). Boehm could also have emphasized the interventionist flavour of Friedrich von Wieser's later work: see especially Wieser (1967: 408–16). See also Professor Streissler's remark that 'Wieser was by instinct at least an unabashed paternalistic interventionist, if not to say finally a fascist' (1988: 200). Recently, Carl G. Uhr has referred to Menger as a 'moderate social-minded liberal' who was 'no uncritical defender of laissez-faire' (in a book review, *HOPE* 21 (1) (Spring 1989): 152).

2 Streissler (1988: 201). See also his n.2 for further details on the Menger–Rudolph lecture-essays.

3 This Marxist perception of the Austrians as spearheading the bourgeois counterrevolutionary intellectual campaign has persisted, sometimes in bizarre fashion, into our own time. Thus Maurice Dobb has misread Schumpeter's reference to Böhm-Bawerk as 'the bourgeois Marx' (1954: 846) to mean that Schumpeter saw Böhm-Bawerk primarily as leader of the 'conscious *apologists* of the existing system' (Dobb 1973: 193). Schumpeter, of course, meant nothing of the kind by this way of describing Böhm-Bawerk. Rather he wished to draw attention to Bawerk's comprehensive, system-embracing theoretical perspective on capitalism – one which matched Marx's own view in grandeur of scope. None the less Dobb's remark confirms the point made here in the text.

4 See note 1.

5 As we shall argue, this conclusion was, to a significant degree, a justified one. It was legitimate to accept the central Mengerian message while rejecting or ignoring the fine print. Even Menger himself, in lecturing to Rudolph, felt that the importance of the central message required that the fine print be almost entirely set aside, at least for introductory purposes.

6 THE ECONOMIC CALCULATION DEBATE: LESSONS FOR AUSTRIANS

1 No claim is being made here that Professor Lavoie will accept this explanation or, indeed, that he will accept my view that no contradiction is involved.

2 See Lavoie (1985a: 26) where he maintains this despite acknowledging that there 'is always, of course, the potential danger that I have illegitimately read modern Austrian notions into the earlier Austrian contributions'.

3 For a critique of this concept (and of the way the literature has misused Lord Robbins's concept of *individual* allocation of resources), see J.M. Buchanan (1964).

7 LUDWIG VON MISES AND FRIEDRICH VON HAYEK: THE MODERN EXTENSION OF AUSTRIAN SUBJECTIVISM

1 Although a full-length analysis of the economics of Ludwig von Mises has yet to appear in print, the following works are relevant: Moss (1976), Sennholz (1978), Greaves (1978), Rothbard (1973), Andrews (1981), Ebeling (unpublished). For a comprehensive bibliography of Mises' writings see Bien (1969).

2 A number of recent works discuss the broader impact of Hayek's work in social and political science and philosophy. For detailed surveys of Hayek's economic writings see Machlup (1976) and O'Driscoll (1977).

3 See Hayek (1949c). See also Hayek (1979: 205, n.51) for a reference to a basic philosophical disagreement that Hayek perceives to separate the two.

4 Among the most important of these are Shackle (1970, 1972).

5 See Pareto (1927: 170). (I am indebted to Professor L.M. Lachmann for this reference.)

6 See Addleson (1984: 509). (The writer gratefully acknowledges his indebtedness to Mr Addleson's paper – despite the significant differences that separate it from this writer's views on several rather important points.)

7 On the relationship between Robbinsian choice and the maximization of utility, see Robbins (1935: 15n).

8 On this aspect of Misesian human action, and its advance over the economizing notion, see Kirzner (1960: 161f.).

9 See note 3.

10 The phrase is, of course, Hayek's. See Hayek (1978b).

8 PRICES, THE COMMUNICATION OF KNOWLEDGE AND THE DISCOVERY PROCESS

The author gratefully acknowledges the stimulation of and the ideas contained in a paper presented at the Austrian Economics Colloquium at

New York University by S. Ikeda: 'An essay on equilibrium prices, disequilibrium prices, and information'.

1 An important limitation in this analogy is that, for a traffic signal system to be effective, it must depend on some *extraneous* circumstance (e.g. compulsion or custom) to provide assurance that signals will in fact be obeyed by all drivers. No such extraneous circumstance is required in the case of the equilibrium price system. The very *meaning* of such a system is that the set of prices is such as spontaneously to motivate directly a completely co-ordinated set of activities.

2 Here, too, the analogy is incomplete. As will be seen in the next section of the chapter, the errors expressed in disequilibrium prices generate disappointments and regrets that may motivate those responsible for the errors *themselves* to revise, for subsequent periods, their bids and offers. For the traffic signal system we had to assume that someone in control (or some robot) responds to the consequences of imperfect timing; the signals which changed at the 'wrong' time do not improve their timing as a result of their own determination to 'learn' from past 'errors' and 'regrets'; their timing is changed by someone, or some machine, from the 'outside'.

3 For a more detailed account of such a co-ordination process see Kirzner (1963: Ch. 7).

4 See, for example, Kohler (1982: 28f.), Dolan (1983: 62), Gwartney and Stroup (1982: Ch. 3, especially pp. 56f.). (On pp. 57f. Gwartney and Stroup's book goes beyond the communication role of prices in equilibrium to draw attention to the co-ordination properties of entrepreneurial activity in the dynamic market process.)

9 ECONOMIC PLANNING AND THE KNOWLEDGE PROBLEM

1 Hayek (1979: 190) has more recently deepened our understanding of the problem of dispersed knowledge as going far beyond that of 'utilizing information about particular concrete facts which individuals already possess'. He now emphasizes the problem of using the abilities that individuals possess *to discover* relevant concrete information. This leads Hayek to point out that, because a person 'will discover what he knows or can find out only when faced with a problem where this will help', he may never be able to 'pass on all the knowledge he commands. . .'. In recent unpublished work Professor Lavoie, building on insights contained in the work of Michael Polanyi, also has emphasized the relevance of 'tacit knowledge' for the social problem of utilizing dispersed knowledge. The present chapter arrives at similar conclusions but from a somewhat different starting point.

2 We avoid here raising any of the well-known difficulties that surround (a) the notion of a hierarchy of social goals analogous to a ranking of individual objectives and (b) the related notions of social efficiency and social choice.

3 On this compare Mises (1966: 253–4).

10 KNOWLEDGE PROBLEMS AND THEIR SOLUTIONS: SOME RELEVANT DISTINCTIONS

1 In a footnote to this passage (p. 148, fn.10) Hayek cites his 1945 paper in this regard.
2 See also Gray (1982).
3 Buchanan (1986). See also Buchanan (1977) and Kirzner (1987).
4 See Kirzner (1963: Ch. 7) for an extensive discussion of the differences between these two problems, and the character of the distinct market processes of equilibration which they respectively set in motion.
5 See Hayek (1949c: 53). I am indebted to Mario Rizzo for drawing my attention to the importance of this passage.

12 SELF-INTEREST AND THE NEW BASHING OF ECONOMICS: A FRESH OPPORTUNITY IN THE PERENNIAL DEBATE?

1 Probably the most sophisticated and careful restatement of this line of defence is that of Machlup (1972).

13 DISCOVERY, PRIVATE PROPERTY AND THE THEORY OF JUSTICE IN CAPITALIST SOCIETY

1 This paper draws heavily from my recent book, *Discovery, Capitalism, and Distributive Justice* (1989), to which the reader is referred for many additional observations concerning the matters and arguments put forward somewhat dogmatically in the present paper. See especially Chapter 7 in that book for certain qualifications to the discovery approach which, for space reasons, could not be considered in this chapter.
2 The Marxist doctrine of capitalist exploitation of labour can be seen as one particular form which this category of attack has taken.
3 For some critical comments on Clark's references to pure profit, see Kirzner (1989: 50–5).
4 For some critical discussion of this point see Nozick (1974: 174f.) and Epstein (1979: 1227f.).
5 For such a view of history see especially the work of Shackle (1972: 351f.). See also Shackle (1970).
6 For present purposes we ignore the (possibly significant) element of discovery required in fact to recognize the windfall that has already been deposited in one's lap.
7 The self-ownership of the individual may be seen as a special case of the general discovery approach.

References

Addleson, M. (1984) 'Robbins's essay in retrospect: on subjectivism and an "economics of choice" ', *Rivista Internazionale Di Scienze Economiche e Commerciali* 31 (6).

Andrews, J.K. (ed.) (1981) *Homage to Mises, the First Hundred Years*, Hillsdale, MI: Hillsdale College Press.

Bernholz, P. (1971) 'Superiority of roundabout processes and positive rate of interest. A simple model of capital and growth', *Kyklos* 24 (4): 687–721.

Bernholz, P. and Faber, M. (1973) 'Technical superiority of roundabout processes and positive rate of interest. A capital model with depreciation and *n*-period horizon', *Zeitschrift für die gesamte Staatswissenschaften* 129 (1), February: 46–61.

Bien (Greaves), B. (1969) *The Works of Ludwig von Mises*, Irvington-on-Hudson, NY: Foundation for Economic Education.

Boehm, S. (1985) 'The political economy of the Austrian School', in P. Roggi (ed.) *Gli Economisti e la Political Economica*, Naples; Edizioni Scientifiche Italiene.

Böhm-Bawerk, E. von (1886) 'Grundzuge der Theorie des Wirtschaftlichen Guterwerths', *Conrad's Jahrbuch* 1–88, 477–541.

Böhm-Bawerk, E. von (1889) *Positive Theorie des Kapitales*, Innsbruck: Wagner.

Böhm-Bawerk, E. von (1891) 'The Austrian economists', *Annals of the American Academy of Political and Social Science* January: 361–84.

Böhm-Bawerk, E. von (1949) *Karl Marx and the Close of his System*, New York: Kelley, ed. P. Sweezy (originally published as *Zum Abschluss der Marxschen Systems*, 1896: trans. as *Karl Marx and the Close of his System*, 1898).

Böhm-Bawerk, E. von (1959) *Capital and Interest*, South Holland, IL: Libertarian Press (originally published as *Geschichte und Kritik der Kapitalzins Theorien*, 1884).

Bostaph, S. (1978) 'The methodological debate between Carl Menger and the German Historicists', *Atlantic Economic Journal* 6 (3), September: 3–16.

Buchanan, J.A. (1982) 'Order defined in the process of its emergence', *Literature of Liberty* 5 (4): 5.

Buchanan, J.M. (1964) 'What should economists do?', *Southern Economic Journal* 30, January: 213–22.

Buchanan, J.M. (1977) 'Law and the invisible hand', in *Freedom in Constitutional Contract*, College Station, TX: Texas A & M University Press.

Buchanan, J.M. (1982) 'The domain of subjective economics: between predictive science and moral philosophy', in I.M. Kirzner (ed.) *Method, Process, and Austrian Economics: Essays in Honor of Ludwig von Mises*, Lexington, MA: D.C. Heath.

Buchanan, J.M. (1986) 'Cultural evolution and institutional reform', in *Liberty, Market and State*, New York: New York University Press.

Buchanan, J.M. and Vanberg, V.J. (1990) 'The market as a creative process', unpublished manuscript, April.

Bukharin, N. (1972) *The Economic Theory of the Leisure Class*, New York: Monthly Review Press (first published in Russian, 1914; translated by M. Lawrence, 1927).

Clark, J.B. (1899) *The Distribution of Wealth*, New York and London: Macmillan.

Coase, R.H. (1937) 'The nature of the firm', *Economica (NS)* 4: 386–405.

Davidson, G. and Davidson, P. (1988) *Economics For a Civilized Society*, New York: W.W. Norton.

Dobb, M. (1973) *Theories of Value and Distribution since Adam Smith*, Cambridge: Cambridge University Press.

Dolan, E. (1983) *Basic Economics*, 3rd edn, London: Dryden Press.

Ebeling, R.M. 'Action analysis and economic science, the economic contributions of Ludwig von Mises', unpublished doctoral dissertation, University College, Cork.

Epstein, R.A. (1979) 'Possession as the root of title', *Georgia Law Review* 13: 1221.

Etzioni, A. (1988) *The Moral Dimension: Toward a New Economics*, New York: Free Press.

Faber, M. (1979) *Introduction to Modern Austrian Capital Theory*, Berlin: Springer.

Fisher, F.M. (1983) *Disequilibrium Foundations of Equilibrium Economics*, Cambridge and New York: Cambridge University Press.

Fisher, I. (1930) *The Theory of Interest*, New York: Macmillan.

Frank, R.H. (1988) *Passions within Reason: The Strategic Role of the Emotions*, New York: W.W. Norton.

Friedman, M. (1962) *Capitalism and Freedom*, Chicago, IL: University of Chicago Press.

Frydman, R. (1982) 'Towards an understanding of market processes: individual expectations, learning and convergence to rational expectations equilibrium', *American Economic Review* 72: 652–68.

Garrison, R.W. (1978) 'Austrian macroeconomics: a diagrammatical exposition', in L.M. Spadaro (ed.) *New Directions in Austrian Economics*, Kansas City, KS: Sheed, Andrews & McMeel.

Garrison, R.W. (1982) 'Austrian economics as the middle ground: comment on Loasby', in I.M. Kirzner (ed.) *Method, Process and Austrian Economics, Essays in Honor of Ludwig von Mises*, Lexington, MA: D.C. Heath.

Garrison, R.W. (1985) 'Time and money: the universals of macroeconomic theorizing', *Journal of Macroeconomics* 6 (2), Spring: 197–213.

Garrison, R.W. (1987) 'The kaleidic world of Ludwig Lachmann', *Critical Review* 1 (3): 77–89.

Grassl, W. and Smith, B. (eds) (1986) *Austrian Economics, Historical and Philosophical Background*, New York: New York University Press.

Gray, J. (1982) 'F.A. Hayek and the rebirth of classical liberalism', *Literature of Liberty* 5 (4): 56–9.

Greaves, P.L. Jr (1978) 'Introduction', in *Ludwig von Mises, On The Manipulation of Money and Credit*, Dobbs Ferry, NY: Free Market Books.

Gross, G. (1884) *Die Lehre von Unternehmergewinn*, Leipzig.

Grossman, S. (1976) 'On the efficiency of competitive stock markets where traders have diverse information', *Journal of Finance* 31: 573–85.

Grossman, S. and Stiglitz, J.E. (1976) 'Information and competitive price systems', *American Economic Review, Proceedings* 66: 246–53.

Grossman, S. and Stiglitz, J.E. (1980) 'On the impossibility of informationally efficient markets', *American Economic Review* 70: 393–402.

Gwartney, J.D. and Stroup, R. (1982) *Economics, Private and Public Choice*, 3rd edn, New York: Academic Press, Chapter 3.

Hausman, D.M. (1981) *Capital, Profits, and Prices*, New York: Columbia University Press.

Hayek, F.A. (1931) *Prices and Production*, London: Routledge.

Hayek, F.A. (1933) *Monetary Theory and the Trade Cycle*, London: Jonathan Cape.

Hayek, F.A. (1935) *Collectivist Economic Planning*, London: Routledge & Kegan Paul.

Hayek, F.A. (1939) *Profits, Interest and Investment: and Other Essays on the Theory of Industrial Fluctuations*, London: Routledge & Kegan Paul.

Hayek, F.A. (1949a) *Individualism and Economic Order*, London: Routledge & Kegan Paul.

Hayek, F.A. (1949b) 'The use of knowledge in society', in *Individualism and Economic Order*, London: Routledge & Kegan Paul (originally published in *American Economic Review* 35 (4) (1945): 519–30).

Hayek, F.A. (1949c) 'Economics and knowledge', in *Individualism and Economic Order*, London: Routledge & Kegan Paul (originally published in *Economica* 4, February 1937).

Hayek, F.A. (1949d) 'Socialist calculation III: the competitive "solution" ', in *Individualism and Economic Order*, London: Routledge & Kegan Paul.

Hayek, F.A. (1949e) 'The meaning of competition', in *Individualism and Economic Order*, London: Routledge & Kegan Paul.

Hayek, F.A. (1949f) 'Socialist calculation I: the nature and history of the problem', in *Individualism and Economic Order*, London: Routledge & Kegan Paul.

Hayek, F.A. (1955) *The Counter-Revolution of Science. Studies on the Abuse of Reason*, Glencoe, IL: Free Press.

Hayek, F.A. (1960) *The Constitution of Liberty*, Chicago, IL: University of Chicago Press.

Hayek, F.A. (1967a) 'Kinds of rationalism', in *Studies in Philosophy, Politics and Economics*, Chicago, IL: University of Chicago Press.

Hayek, F.A. (1967b) 'The results of human action but not of human design', in *Studies in Philosophy, Politics and Economics*, Chicago, IL: University of Chicago Press.

Hayek, F.A. (1968) 'Economic thought VI: the Austrian School', in D.L. Sills (ed.) *International Encyclopedia of the Social Sciences*, New York: Macmillan.

Hayek, F.A. (1973) *Law, Legislation and Liberty*, Vol. 1, *Rules and Order*, Chicago, IL: University of Chicago Press.

Hayek, F.A. (1978a) *New Studies in Philosophy, Politics, Economics, and the History of Ideas*, Chicago, IL: University of Chicago Press.

Hayek, F.A. (1978b) 'Competition as a discovery procedure', in *New Studies in Philosophy, Politics, Economics and the History of Ideas*, Chicago, IL: University of Chicago Press (first presented as a lecture, 1968).

Hayek, F.A. (1978c) 'Dr Bernard Mandeville', in *New Studies in Philosophy, Politics, Economics and the History of Ideas*, Chicago, IL: University of Chicago Press.

Hayek, F.A. (1979) *Law, Legislation and Liberty*, Vol. 3, *The Political Order of a Free People*, Chicago, IL: University of Chicago Press.

Hayek, F.A. (1981) 'Introduction', in C. Menger, *Principles of Economics*, New York and London: New York University Press (originally published as 'Introduction', in *Collected Works of Carl Menger*, London: London School of Economics, 1934).

Hicks, J. (1973) *Capital and Time: A Neo-Austrian Theory*, Oxford: Clarendon Press.

Hicks, J.R. and Weber, W. (1973) *Carl Menger and the Austrian School of Economics*, Oxford: Clarendon Press.

Hutchison, T.W. (1953) *A Review of Economic Doctrines, 1870–1929*, Oxford: Clarendon Press.

Jaffé, W. (1976) 'Menger, Jevons, and Walras de-homogenized', *Economic Inquiry* 14 (4): 511–24.

Jevons, W.S. (1871) *The Theory of Political Economy*, London: Macmillan.

Kauder, E. (1965) *A History of Marginal Utility Theory*, Princeton, NJ: Princeton University Press.

Kirzner, I.M. (1960) *The Economic Point of View*, Princeton, NJ: Van Nostrand.

Kirzner, I.M. (1963) *Market Theory and the Price System*, Princeton, NJ: Van Nostrand.

Kirzner, I.M. (1973) *Competition and Entrepreneurship*, Chicago, IL: University of Chicago Press.

Kirzner, I.M. (1978) *Wettbewerb und Unternehmertum*, Walter Eucken Institut, Wirtschaftswissenschaftliche und wirtschaftsrechtliche Untersuchungen 14, Tubingen: J.C.B. Mohr/P. Siebeck (translation of *Competition and Entrepreneurship*).

Kirzner, I.M. (1979a) *Perception, Opportunity and Profit*, Chicago, IL: University of Chicago Press.

Kirzner, I.M. (1979b) 'The entrepreneurial role in Menger's system', in *Perception, Opportunity and Profit*, Chicago, IL: University of Chicago Press, pp. 62–9 (originally published in *Atlantic Economic Journal*, September 1978).

Kirzner, I.M. (1981) 'Mises and the renaissance of Austrian economics', in J.K. Andrews Jr (ed.) *Homage to Mises, the First Hundred Years*, Hillsdale, MI: Hillsdale College Press.

Kirzner, I.M. (1984a) 'Prices, the communication of knowledge, and the discovery process', in K.R. Leube and A.H. Zlabinger (eds) *The Political Economy of Freedom, Essays in Honor of F.A. Hayek*, Munich: Philosophia Verlag. Reprinted here as Chapter 8.

Kirzner, I.M. (1984b) 'Economic planning and the knowledge problem', *Cato Journal* 4 (2): 407–18. Reprinted here as Chapter 9.

Kirzner, I.M. (1985a) *Discovery and the Capitalist Process*, Chicago, IL: University of Chicago Press.

Kirzner, I.M. (1985b) 'Comment on R.N. Langlois, "From the knowledge of economics to the economics of knowledge: Fritz Machlup on methodology and on the 'Knowledge Society' " ', in W.J. Samuels (ed.) *Research in the History of Economic Thought and Methodology*, Greenwich, CT: JAI Press.

Kirzner, I.M. (1987) 'Spontaneous order and the case for the free market', *Ideas on Liberty: Essays in Honor of Paul L. Poirot*, Irvington-on-Hudson, NY: Foundation for Economic Education.

Kirzner, I.M. (1989) *Discovery, Capitalism, and Distributive Justice*, Oxford: Basil Blackwell.

Knight, F.H. (1935) 'Marginal utility economics', in *The Ethics of Competition and Other Essays*, New York: Harper, Chapter v (originally published in *Encyclopedia of the Social Sciences*, 1931).

Knight, F.H. (1950) 'Introduction', in C. Menger, *Principles of Economics*, Glencoe, IL: Free Press.

Kohler, H. (1982) *Intermediate Microeconomics, Theory and Applications*, Glenview, IL: Scott, Foresman.

Komorzynski, J. von (1889) *Der Werth in der isolirten Wirthschaft*, Vienna: Manz.

Kregel, J.A. (1986) 'Conceptions of equilibrium: the logic of choice and the logic of production', in I.M. Kirzner (ed.) *Subjectivism, Intelligibility, and Economic Understanding, Essays in Honor of Ludwig M. Lachmann on his Eightieth Birthday*, New York: New York University Press.

Lachmann, L. (1973) *Macro-economic Thinking and the Market Economy*, London: Institute of Economic Affairs.

Lachmann, L.M. (1976) 'From Mises to Shackle: an essay on Austrian economics and the kaleidic society', *Journal of Economic Literature* 14 (10), March: 54–62.

Lachmann, L. (1977) 'Austrian economics in the present crisis of economic thought', in *Capital, Expectations, and the Market Process*, Kansas City, KS: Sheed, Andrews & McMeel.

Lachmann, L.M. (1978) 'Carl Menger and the incomplete revolution of subjectivism', *Atlantic Economic Journal* 6 (3), September: 57.

Lachmann, L.M. (1986a) *The Market as an Economic Process*, Oxford: Basil Blackwell.

Lachmann, L.M. (1986b) 'Austrian economics under fire: the Hayek–Sraffa duel in retrospect', in W. Grassl and B. Smith (eds) *Austrian Economics, Historical and Philosophical Background*, New York: New York University Press.

Lange, O. (1964) 'On the economic theory of socialism', in B.E. Lippincott (ed.) *On the Economic Theory of Socialism*, New York: McGraw-Hill.

Lavoie, D. (1985a) *Rivalry and Central Planning: The Socialist Calculation Debate Reconsidered*, Cambridge: Cambridge University Press.

Lavoie, D. (1985b) *National Planning: What is Left?*, Cambridge, MA: Ballinger.

Leser, N. (ed.) (1986) *Die Wiener Schule der Nationalökonomie*, Vienna: Hermann Böhlau.

Little, I.M.D. (1957) *A Critique of Welfare Economics*, 2nd edn, Oxford: Clarendon Press.

Loasby, B.J. (1982) 'Economics of dispersed and incomplete information', in I.M. Kirzner (ed.) *Method, Process and Austrian Economics, Essays in Honor of Ludwig von Mises*, Lexington, MA: D.C. Heath.

Loasby, B.J. (1989) *The Mind and Method of the Economist, A Critical Appraisal of Major Economists in the 20th Century*, Aldershot: Edward Elgar.

Locke, J. (1937) *An Essay Concerning the True Original Extent and End of Civil Government*, New York: Appleton Century Crofts, section 27.

Machlup, F. (1963) 'Statics and dynamics: kaleidoscopic words', in *Essays in Economic Semantics*, Englewood Cliffs, NJ: Prentice-Hall (originally published in *Southern Economic Journal*, October 1959).

Machlup, F. (1972) 'The universal bogey: economic man', in M. Peston and B. Corry (eds) *Essays in Honour of Lord Robbins*, London: Weidenfeld & Nicolson.

Machlup, F. (1976) 'Hayek's contribution to economics', in *Essays on Hayek*, New York: New York University Press (originally published in *Swedish Journal of Economics* 76, December 1974).

Machlup, F. (1981) 'Ludwig von Mises: the academic scholar who would not compromise', *Wirtschaftspolitischen Blätter* 4.

Machlup, F. (1982) 'Austrian economics', in D. Greenwald (ed.) *Encyclopedia of Economics*, New York: McGraw-Hill.

Mäki, U. (1990) 'Mengerian economics in realist perspective', in B. Caldwell (ed.) *Carl Menger and his Legacy in Economics*, Durham, NC: Duke University Press.

Mataja, V. (1884) *Der Unternehmergewinn*, Vienna.

Mayer, H. (1932) 'Der Erkenntniswert der Funktionellen Preistheorien', in H. Mayer (ed.) *Die Wirtschaftstheorie der Gegenwart*, Vienna.

McCulloch, J.H. (1977) 'The Austrian theory of the marginal use and of ordinal marginal utility', *Zeitschrift für Nationalökonomie* 3-4.

Menger, C. (1884) *Die Irrthümer des Historismus in der deutschen Nationalökonomie*, reprinted in *Gesammelte Werke* 3: 93.

Menger, C. (1891) 'Die Social-Theorien der classischen National-Oekonomie und die moderne Wirtschaftspolitik', reprinted in *Gesammelte Werke* 3: 245.

Menger, C. (1981) *Principles of Economics*, New York: New York University Press (originally published as *Grundsätze der Volkswirtschaftslehre*, Wien: Wilhelm Braumüller, 1871: translated and edited by J. Dingwall and B.F. Hoselitz, Glencoe, IL: Free Press, 1950).

Menger, C. (1985) *Investigations into the Method of the Social Sciences with Special Reference to Economics*, transl. F.J. Nock, New York: New York University Press (originally published as *Untersuchungen über der Methode der Socialwissenschaften und der Politischen Oekonomie insbesondere*, Leipzig: Duncker and Humblot, 1883; translation first published as *Problems of Economics and Sociology*, Urbana, IL: University of Illinois, 1963).

Menger, K. Jr (1973) 'Austrian marginalism and mathematical economics', in J.R. Hicks and W. Weber (eds) *Carl Menger and the Austrian School of Economics*, Oxford: Clarendon Press.

Meyer, R. (1887) *Das Wesen des Einkommens: Eine volkswirthschaftliche Untersuchung*, Berlin: Hertz.

Mises, L. von (1920) 'Economic calculation in the socialist commonwealth', translated in F.A. Hayek (ed.) (1935) *Collectivist Economic Planning*, London: Routledge & Kegan Paul.

Mises, L. von (1936) *Socialism: An Economic and Sociological Analysis*, London: Jonathan Cape (translation from the German of *Die Gemeinwirtschaft*, 1st edn 1922, 2nd edn 1932).

Mises, L. von (1940) *Nationalökonomie, Theorie des Handelns und Wirtschaftens*, Geneva: Editions Union.

Mises, L. von (1943) ' "Elastic expectations" and the Austrian theory of the trade cycle', *Economica* 10, August: 251–2.

Mises, L. von (1960) *Epistemological Problems of Economics*, Princeton, NJ: Van Nostrand (translation of *Grundprobleme der Nationalökonomie*, 1933).

Mises, L. von (1966) *Human Action, a Treatise on Economics*, 3rd edn, Chicago, IL: Henry Regnery (originally published as *Human Action*, New Haven, CT: Yale University Press, 1949).

Mises, L. von (1969) *The Historical Setting of the Austrian School of Economics*, New Rochelle, NY: Arlington House.

Mises, L. von (1978) *Notes and Recollections*, South Holland, IL: Libertarian Press.

Mises, L. von (1980) *Theory of Money and Credit*, Indianapolis, IN: Liberty Classics (originally published as *Theorie des Geldes und der Umlaufsmittel*, 1912: translated as *Theory of Money and Credit*, 1934; also New Haven, CT: Yale University Press, 1953).

Moss, L. (ed.) (1976) *The Economics of Ludwig von Mises, Toward a Critical Reappraisal*, Kansas City, KS: Sheed and Ward.

Mydral, G. (1954) *The Political Element in the Development of Economic Theory*, Cambridge, MA: Harvard University Press.

Nelson, R.R. (1981) 'Assessing private enterprise: an exegesis of tangled doctrine', *Bell Journal of Economics* 12 (1): 93–111.

Nielsen, K. (1985) *Equality and Liberty, A Defense of Radical Egalitarianism*; Totowa, NJ: Rowman & Allanheld.

Nozick, R. (1974) *Anarchy, State and Utopia*, New York: Basic Books.

O'Driscoll, G.P. Jr (1977) *Economics as a Coordination Problem, The Contributions of Friedrich A. Hayek*, Kansas City, KS: Sheed, Andrews & McMeel.

O'Driscoll, G.P. Jr (1978) 'Spontaneous order and the coordination of economic activities', in L.M. Spadaro (ed.) *New Directions in Austrian Economics*, Kansas City, KS: Sheed, Andrews & McMeel.

O'Driscoll, G.P. Jr and Rizzo, M.J. (1985) *The Economics of Time and Ignorance*, Oxford: Basil Blackwell.

Orosel, G.O. (1981) 'Faber's modern Austrian capital theory: a critical survey', *Zeitschrift für Nationalökonomie* 141–55.

Pareto, V. (1927) *Manual d'économie politique*, 2nd edn, Paris.

Parsons, T. (1934) 'The nature and significance of economics', *Quarterly Journal of Economics* May: 512.

Philippovich, E. von Philippsberg (1893) *Grundriss der Politischen Ökonomie*, Freiburg: Mohr.

Posner, R.A. (1983) 'Utilitarianism, economics and social theory', *The Economics of Justice*, Cambridge, MA: Harvard University Press.

Robbins, L. (1935) *An Essay on the Nature and Significance of Economic Science*, 2nd edn, London: Macmillan (1st edn 1932).

Rothbard, M.N. (1956) 'Toward a reconstruction of utility and welfare economics', in M. Sennholz (ed.) *On Freedom and Free Enterprise*, Princeton, NJ: Van Nostrand, pp. 224–62.

Rothbard, M.N. (1962) *Man, Economy, and State: A Treatise on Economic Principles*, Princeton, NJ: Van Nostrand.

Rothbard, M.N. (1973) *The Essential von Mises*, Bramble Minibooks.

Ruskin, J. (1934) *Unto This Last*, Oxford: Humphrey Milford, Oxford University Press.

Sax, E. (1887) *Grundlegung der Theoretischen Staatswirtschaft*, Vienna: Holder.

Schultz, T.W. (1975) 'The value of the ability to deal with disequilibria', *Journal of Economic Literature* 13 (3) September: 827–46.

Schumpeter, J.A. (1908) *Das Wesen und der Hauptinhalt der Theoretischen Nationalökonomie*, Leipzig: Duncker & Humblot.

Schumpeter, J.A. (1934) *The Theory of Economic Development*, Cambridge, MA: Harvard University Press (originally published as *Theorie der Wirtschaftlichen Entwicklung*, Leipzig: Duncker & Humblot, 1912).

Schumpeter, J.A. (1950) *Capitalism, Socialism and Democracy*, 3rd edn, New York: Harper & Row.

Schumpeter, J.A. (1954) *History of Economic Analysis*, New York: Oxford University Press.

Sennholz, H.F. (1978) 'Postscipt', in *Ludwig von Mises, Notes and Recollections*, South Holland, IL: Libertarian Press.

Shackle, G.L.S. (1970) *Decision, Order and Time in Human Affairs*, 2nd edn, Cambridge: Cambridge University Press (originally published 1969).

Shackle, G.L.S. (1972) *Epistemics and Economics: A Critique of Economic Doctrines*, Cambridge: Cambridge University Press.

Shackle, G.L.S. (1983) 'The bounds of unknowledge', in J. Wiseman (ed.) *Beyond Positive Economics?*, London: Macmillan.

Shackle, G.L.S. (1986) 'The origination of choice', in I.M. Kirzner (ed.) *Subjectivism, Intelligibility and Economic Understanding, Essays in Honor of Ludwig M. Lachmann on his Eightieth Birthday*, New York: New York University Press.

Souter, R.W. (1933) 'The nature and significance of economic science in recent discussion', *Quarterly Journal of Economics* 47: 377.

Sowell, T. (1980) *Knowledge and Decisions*, New York: Basic Books.

Stigler, G.J. (1959) 'The politics of political economists', *Quarterly Journal of Economics*, November.

Stigler, G.J. (1982) 'The economist as preacher', in *The Economist as Preacher and other Essays*, Chicago, IL: University of Chicago Press.

Stigler, G.J. (1984) 'Wealth, and possibly liberty', *The Intellectual and the Marketplace*, Cambridge, MA: Harvard University Press.

Streissler, E. (1969) 'Structural economic thought: on the significance of the Austrian School today', *Zeitschrift für Nationalökonomie* 29 (3–4), December: 237–66.

Streissler, E. (1972) 'To what extent was the Austrian School marginalist?', *History of Political Economy* 4 (2), Fall: 426–61.

Streissler, E. (1973) 'The Mengerian Tradition', in J.R. Hicks and W. Weber (eds) *Carl Menger and the Austrian School of Economics*, Oxford: Clarendon Press.

Streissler, E. (1986) 'Arma virumque cano. Friedrich von Wieser, the bard as economist', in N. Leser (ed.) *Die Wiener Schule der Nationalökonomie*, Vienna: Hermann Böhlau.

Streissler, E. (1988) 'The intellectual and political impact of the Austrian School of economics', *History of European Ideas* 92.

Streissler, E. (1990) 'Menger, Böhm-Bawerk, and Wieser: the origins of the Austrian School', in K. Hennings and W.J. Samuels (eds) *Neoclassical Economic Theory, 1870 to 1930*, Boston, MA: Kluwer.

Vaughn, K.I. (1976) 'Critical discussion of the four papers', in L.S. Moss (ed.) *The Economics of Ludwig von Mises: Toward a Critical Reappraisal*, Kansas City, KS: Sheed and Ward.

Walras, L. (1874) *Eléments d'économie politique pure*, Lausanne: Corbaz.

Walsh, V.C. (1970) *Introduction to Contemporary Microeconomics*, New York: McGraw-Hill.

White, L.H. (1984) *The Methodology of the Austrian School Economists*, revised edition, Auburn, AL: The Ludwig von Mises Institute of Auburn University (originally published 1977).

Wieser, F. von (1884) *Ursprung des Wirtschaftlichen Wertes*, Vienna: Hölder.

Wieser, F. von (1956) *Natural Value*, New York: Kelley (originally published as *Der Naturliche Werth*, Vienna: Holder, 1889, trans. as *Natural Value*, ed. W. Smart, London: Macmillan, 1893).

Wieser, F. von (1967) *Social Economics*, New York: Kelley (originally published as *Theorie der Gesellschaftlichen Wirtschaft*, Tubingen: J.C.B. Mohr, 1914: trans. by A.F. Hinrichs as *Social Economics*, New York: Adelphi; London: Allen & Unwin, 1927).

Wiseman, J.A. (1990) 'General equilibrium or market process: an evaluation', in A. Bosch, P. Koslowski and R. Veit (eds) *General Equilibrium or Market Process, Neoclassical and Austrian Theories of Economics*, Tubingen: J.C.B. Mohr, pp. 145–63.

Zuckerkandl, R. (1889) *Zur Theorie des Preises*, Leipzig: Stein.

Zweig, M. (1970) 'A New Left critique of economics', in D. Mermelstein (ed.) *Economics: Mainstream Readings and Radical Critiques*, New York: Random House.

Index